GAMES OF CHICKEN

GAMES OF CHICKEN

Four Decades of
U.S. Nuclear Policy

DAVID SCHWARTZMAN

PRAEGER

New York
Westport, Connecticut
London

Library of Congress Cataloging-in-Publication Data

Schwartzman, David.
  Games of chicken.

  Bibliography: p.
  Includes index.
    1. Nuclear warfare.   2. United States—Military
policy. I. Title.
U263.S378   1988   355'.0217'0973   87-29131
ISBN 0-275-92884-5 (alk. paper)

Library of Congress Catalog Card Number: 87-29131

ISBN: 0-275-92884-5

First published in 1988

Praeger Publishers, One Madison Avenue, New York, NY 10010
A division of Greenwood Press, Inc.

Printed in the United States of America

The paper used in this book complies with the
Permanent Paper Standard issued by the National
Information Standards Organization (Z39.48-1984).

10   9   8   7   6   5   4   3   2   1

For Gertie,
with love.

Contents

Tables

Acknowledgments

At the first Harvard–MIT Nuclear Defense Workshop in a hot two weeks in July 1983, I learned much from Jack Ruina, George Rathjens, Michael Nacht, Ashton Carter, Ted Greenwood, William Kaufmann, and Stephen Meyer. Robert Ducas, Jack Mendelsohn, Sidney Morgenbesser, and Arthur Singer took the trouble to read earlier drafts and offer encouraging, as well as helpful, comments. I could not ask for more devoted and loyal assistants than Anna Zapata and Joseph Consolo. Equally devoted secretaries, Karin Ray and Beverly Elliot, have put up with more nonsense from me than they should have. Dan Eades and Carol Stock have been very helpful editors. To all of these, many thanks.

GAMES OF CHICKEN

1
Two Risks,
Three Myths

TWO RISKS

The not easily forgotten, ghastly visions of destruction in the ABC television film, "The Day After," almost hid the message that a minor incident may set off a nuclear war. Nevertheless, that was the basic message. Quite deliberately, the script tried to impress viewers with that very danger by obscuring the conflict's origins and avoiding any suggestion that the Soviets had attacked or threatened West Germany. The film carefully depicted both NATO and Soviet military deployments. Evenhandedly, the news broadcasters were shown to report that NATO forces invaded East Germany, that, at the same time, Soviet forces invaded West Germany and that both sides began to fire tactical nuclear weapons. Then, on orders from the Strategic Air Command (SAC), an underground silo crew commenced launching procedures, and we saw missiles take off into a clear blue sky. At 3:38 in the afternoon a nuclear weapon aimed at a missile base in the wheat fields of Missouri exploded above Kansas City. The film thus sought to impress us with the danger that even a minor incident could set off a nuclear war. The implication was that even in a minor crisis, the United States and the Soviet Union might attempt to destroy the other side's missiles. The film underlined the risk for both sides of a preemptive attack by not specifying which side shot first. Therefore, "The Day After" denied the basic premise of U.S. national policy—that a deliberate Soviet attack for territorial or political gain is our greatest danger.

In dramatizing the danger arising from the mutual fear of a preemptive attack, the film resembles most other nuclear war scenarios.

Even advocates of a powerful nuclear defense disagree with the official line that the probability of a deliberate Soviet attack is high without a superior U.S. arsenal. These advocates do, however, regard deterrence as prudent and a superior nuclear arsenal as essential. They fail to see the inconsistency between their war scenarios and their prescription of a powerful arsenal.

It is difficult to develop a sensible policy for invoking massive destruction to achieve any political goals. The so-called experts in this weird field, including the Harvard Nuclear Study Group, are confused about the very real risks and retreat to slogans. In *Living With Nuclear Weapons*, the group described scenarios of conventional fighting escalating to nuclear war.[1] Without suggesting that the stakes were vital, the authors warned that a local conflict in Germany or Iran, in which the United States and the Soviet Union supported opposing sides, might ignite a nuclear war. Accident and happenstance were the nightmare, not a Soviet plan. The authors failed to recognize the lesson of their own scenario that the risk of a preemptive attack exceeded the risk of deliberate Soviet aggression. That the authors failed to consider the magnitudes of the two risks is apparent from their support of the Trident II program, and some members of the group also supported the MX program. These additions to the counterforce capability will deter a deliberate attack, not a preemptive attack. Worse, the policy of deterrence, which calls for a force that threatens the Soviet arsenal, raises the risk of a preemptive attack, even though it is much greater than the risk of a deliberate attack. Nevertheless, always appealing to prudence, the Harvard authors advocated strengthening our offensive capability. The confused consensus these authors represent includes even the Roman Catholic bishops who, on the same grounds of prudence, refrained from recommending unilateral nuclear disarmament even though they opposed nuclear retaliation to a nuclear attack.

The Harvard authors fell into inconsistency because they failed to assess the preemption risk (PR) and the aggression risk (AR) and to understand that measures to reduce one of these risks increase the other. Although the PR is much larger than the AR, the planned MX force will increase the PR. The MX will reduce the AR, but we should be seeking ways of reducing the PR, even at the cost of a rise in the AR. Because the attacker may gain a postholocaust advantage, the MX and other accurate multiple independently targeted reentry vehicles (MIRVs) will raise the PR. There can be no denying that more powerful nuclear weapons reduce the AR, but since the AR is small, the gain in security against deliberate aggression is not worth the price. Nuclear weapons only deter a planned attack, not a preemptive attack, in a crisis. If accurate MIRVs aggravate the danger of a preemptive attack, then the policy that requires these weapons in the name of deterrence is no longer prudent.

The causes of preemptive risk include risks other than the obvious one of the escalation of conventional war. During a crisis alert one side may misinterpret communications between enemy commands and unleash its missiles out of fear of an approaching attack. One side may feel the need to show the resolve to risk its own destruction and therefore attack enemy missiles. For example, some strategists, who view frightening the enemy into submission as the object of war, have proposed flexing muscles with one or two strikes at unpopulated, desolate areas in Siberia, which have no military value.[2] They propose such demonstration shots, even though they realize that it is a short step from such shots to a strike that destroys an isolated missile silo, and another short step leads to strikes against several silos. The argument is that the alternatives—escalating quickly to a major attack or doing nothing—entail greater risks. Muscle flexing and even the risk of a holocaust are viewed as necessary to give credibility to the nuclear threat. The urgent need to show resolve arises from the nature of the weapons. To fire weapons of massive destruction risks equally massive retaliation against the U.S. population. The threat of nuclear retaliation to deter any conventional attack, especially when vital interests are not at stake, entails a risk of retaliation, which may not be acceptable. The Soviets may undertake an aggression in the belief that the president would not order a nuclear response. The credibility of the nuclear deterrent thus is doubtful against Soviet conventional aggression. Backing up the deterrent requires demonstrating resolve by risking a nuclear exchange even in minor confrontations. The need to show resolve stems from the risk of massive reprisal, which is inherent in the weapons, not from a high probability of aggression for territorial, political, economic, or other gains. The motive for showing resolve is the same as the motive for a preemptive attack—to reinforce military power. Therefore, the PR includes the risk of triggering a war by deploying nuclear weapons or by attempting to halt their deployment, as in the Cuban missile crisis.

By contrast, the AR signifies the risk of the Soviet Union attacking with either conventional or nuclear weapons to gain important territories. Advocates of a large MX arsenal believe that the probability of such an attack is high without the arsenal. They fear that the Politburo will take great risks to gain world domination.

The distinction between the AR and the PR roughly matches the distinction between deterrence and crisis stability. The statement that the MX will reduce the AR is equivalent to the statement that the MX will deter a deliberate Soviet attack, and a high PR corresponds to high crisis instability. But the latter correspondence is only rough, for, as we have seen, the PR also embraces the risks arising from efforts to show resolve and from moves to deploy weapons.

The single word "deterrence" is much neater than the awkward phrase "reducing the AR," and when "crisis instability" is available, why bother with "PR"? I inflict these new expressions on readers because they highlight the tradeoff between the two kinds of risk. It is illuminating to say that to reduce the AR we must raise the PR, especially when we can judge which is the larger risk. The statement that a policy of deterrence raises crisis instability does not serve this purpose nearly as well. The notion of the tradeoff captures the real issue. The confrontation between hawks and doves should be on the tradeoff. Otherwise, the debaters on both sides conceal the risks they are willing to take. Hawks pretend that there is no problem of crisis instability, while the supporters of a nuclear freeze shut their eyes to the possibility of a Soviet threat. Neither side explicitly compares the two risks or recognizes the tradeoff. When the tradeoff is not recognized, the magnitudes of the two risks can be ignored, and the hawks can happily focus on their dismal eventualities of near-zero probability, regardless of the effect of proposed measures on the PR.

We are urged to acquire an MX arsenal to reduce the AR, despite the effect of such an arsenal on the PR. Back of the drive for a big MX force is the fear that a crafty Soviet leader will launch a "small" nuclear attack. Since the United States will not want to unleash a major, city-busting retaliation, it will not respond, thereby inviting a Soviet takeover. To respond "appropriately" with a limited retaliation would require a large MX force because one small attack may only begin a series of attacks of increasing destructiveness. But what is the risk of a small Soviet attack? And how will a large MX force affect the PR? Labeling the two risks calls attention to the tradeoff, making it harder to dodge the issue.

Although tradeoffs are the economist's bread and butter, even economists fail to introduce the concept into the defense debate. Instead, they have looked at strategic planning as a problem in bargaining, another of their favorite topics. The focus is not entirely misdirected: war is a form of bargaining. And the conclusion that a strong arsenal improves a side's bargaining position is no surprise. But the advocates of a strong arsenal fixate on highly improbable scenarios in which the alternatives are surrender or the destruction of the United States. Instead, they should discuss the central topic: the effect of strengthening the arsenal on the risk of nuclear war. Some advocates in positions of power have placed so high a value on a strong bargaining position in crises that they insist on the maximum possible offensive capability. No other sɭɐoᵹ are important for them.

The two risks have not been ignored entirely. Ted Koppel's guests at the panel discussion immediately following the ABC film, shown in November 1983, could hardly avoid them. William F. Buckley attacked the movie for debilitating the United States. He said, "The guy who wrote [the movie] says, 'I would like to see people starting to question the value of defending this country with a nuclear arsenal.' This is his motive, and people who have seen the film, who have sought to debilitate American defenses, have gathered around it." Clearly, for Buckley the AR was the only risk. Henry Kissinger repeated Buckley's complaint about the film's intention: "are we supposed to make policy by scaring ourselves to death . . .?" However, he did recognize the PR. He straddled the issue of the two risks. Again in our terms, while admitting that armaments raised the PR, he argued that disarmament would raise the AR: "Because if the Soviet Union gets the idea that the United States has morally disarmed itself and psychologically disarmed itself, then the precise consequences we're describing here will happen. Our problem is to avoid unilateral disarmament and at the same time to develop a policy which eliminates the danger of war." He emphasized the PR when he said, "It requires us to analyze the design of our forces and to design them in such a manner that there is a minimum incentive for first-strike by either side." General Brent Scowcroft, worried that the Soviets would underestimate U.S. resolve to retaliate and launch an attack, came down hard on the side of reducing the AR, thus for deterrence: "we must have a military posture which the Soviets, whatever they think about deterrence, whatever they think about the nature of nuclear weapons, can never imagine that resort to them makes sense."

McNamara, once the practical exponent of deterrence, had converted: "we need to stress introducing stability in the forces to avoid temptation to either side to preempt, and most of all we need to introduce steps to reduce the risk that those weapons will be used."

The concepts of AR and PR would have improved the precision of the discussion on Koppel's show. And since they are the focus of the present book, they deserve further development. Rivals for world influence, the superpowers will assist opposite sides in civil wars and in other local conflicts. Despite Gorbachev's conciliatory moves, crises will recur. The superpower leaders may insist on showing resolve, and they may be unable to restrain their troops from firing tactical nuclear weapons (TNW). We have had the good luck in past conflicts that vital interests were not at stake for at least one superpower; and at least through the sixties, the United States was the dominant nuclear power. We cannot take confidence from the past. There will be conflicts, and one of them could ignite major hostilities. A small PR per year can add up to a high total risk over 50 years. Suppose the probability of a nuclear war each year is one in 100. Over 50 years this adds up to 50 in 100. Since so much is at stake, a total probability over 50 years of 10 in a 100 is high.

We need not fear imperialist Soviet ambitions. Contrary to the basic U.S. policy premise, the withdrawal of the U.S. nuclear guarantee will not endanger Western Europe. NATO's nonnuclear forces provide adequate security against a planned conventional attack. The Soviet Union cannot be certain of conventional superiority against NATO, and, in any case, the gains from a conquest of Western Europe do not merit a long, costly war. If the Soviet Union were assured of a quick, easy victory, it might undertake an attack. But the uncertainty among U.S. military analysts about the strength on both sides warrants the conclusion that the AR is small. Further, the Soviet Union will not risk retaliation to a nuclear attack. The Soviet Union did not build up its forces to gain new territories: the AR is low. But the probability of an incident in another, more peripheral area initiating a nuclear war cannot be dismissed.

Kissinger and Scowcroft have opposed the current moves to withdraw intermediate-range and short-range missiles from Europe because they fear a Soviet conventional invasion. They plead that NATO should retain some missiles to balance Soviet conventional superiority. But the Warsaw Pact forces are not so much superior to NATO's as to make the prospect of even a conventional war attractive to the Soviets. Kissinger and Scowcroft do not recognize that the retention of missiles capable of striking Moscow will maintain the PR at a high level. They apparently prefer to reduce what many recognize now to be a low AR, despite the effect on the PR. Reagan and Gorbachev now realize that no military advantage is gained from the retention of the missiles in Europe, certainly not enough of an advantage to offset the resulting danger. The recent agreement, unlike previous talks, are on the right road. If they succeed in eliminating the intermediate- and short-range weapons from Europe, the world will be safer. It will be a truly historic achievement.

In summary, conflicts will recur, and the probability of nuclear war is high, despite the small risk of a deliberate Soviet attack on an area of vital interest to the United States (i.e., the AR is low). A powerful counterforce capability raises the PR. Any cut in the AR such a capability might provide is of secondary importance. Our present policy stems from the illusion that the AR is high and from ignoring the way weapons increases drive up the PR.

Led by hawks, the United States already has the capability to destroy many Soviet intercontinental ballistic missiles (ICBMs), even without the Trident II and the MX. But the doves may be gaining support: Originally, the air force demanded 300 MX missiles, President Carter asked for only 200, Congress forced Reagan to cut the program to 100, and more recently to about 50. The president now welcomes Soviet signals for arms reduction. But the disciples of counterforce power have not given in. Most recently they have begun campaigning for a larger MX program, and they reject the current progress in arms control negotiations initiated at Reykjavik as an aberration.

THREE MYTHS

Because a first strike may destroy most of either side's land-based missiles, much of humanity is at risk. If we knew how we got ourselves into this awful predicament and what we are doing that keeps us there, we might be able to get out of it. The danger has come mainly from the U.S. defense policy, the roots of which are in three myths: the myth of the nuclear-strategy expert, the Soviet bogey, and the economic myth. As in other policy areas, a choice must be made in this one, and these three myths have led the government into error. The danger of nuclear war has continued to increase as the advantage of first use has grown with MIRVing and greater accuracy.

The Myth of the Nuclear-strategy Expert

The voters not having chosen them for their wisdom about defense, presidents have turned to such experts as Henry Kissinger, James Schlesinger, Harold Brown, and those at the Rand Corporation. However, even the experts failed to design a coordinated set of plans with well-defined goals. Like other government policies, our defense policy is thrown up in the debris of a whirlpool of ideas, interests, fears, and ambitions. The intrinsic difficulty of developing a sensible strategy of vast destruction creates greater disarray in this field than we see in other policy areas. The confusion, together with the subject's macabre nature, has kept one administration after another in thrall to the experts, despite their weak claims to special knowledge related to the basic issues.

Indeed, the central issues fall outside the strategists' expertise. Knowing the blast radius of the SS-9 warhead does not help us decide whether or not to adopt a counterforce strategy, and a study of nuclear war strategy is equally pointless. The problem is to predict Soviet actions in crises. The strategists wrestle with this task by playing games simulating conflicts in which the contenders are abstract entities designated "Red" and "Blue." They predict the rational reactions of warring enemies to each other's moves, without any detailed reference to actual or potential disputes or even to specific enemies with histories. Based on bargaining models, the games say that powerful weapons may persuade the enemy to submit rather than fight only to lose. Since the basic unspoken premise of continuing Soviet expansionism underlies the reasoning, it is not altogether foolish. But the strategists do not examine the premise; they leave the big question to the political leaders. The experts, who prefer to handle the more tractable mathematical problems set by the theory of games, ignore the fact that they concern side issues. The important, central premise of Soviet expansionsim is simply assumed. Since the bargaining models omit the PR, the strategists have little to say about the effect of the weapons programs on the risk. They assume, as instructed, that the AR is high and that their problem is how to reduce the AR to zero. They do not realize that the solution, which calls for a powerful offensive capability, raises the PR.

Noninitiates in the strategic literature wonder why the United States acquires thousands of nuclear weapons. The theory is that deterrence is more effective if cities are not placed at risk. According to the theory, a president is more likely to respond to a Soviet conventional attack with nuclear weapons if he does not risk the destruction of U.S. cities by attacking Soviet cities. An arsenal consisting of many accurate, MIRVed missiles enables the president to retaliate by ordering the destruction of some Soviet silos. According to the theory, since the Soviet leader will share the president's reluctance to risk cities, he will respond in similar fashion. A credible threat to engage in such a war in which the silos are both weapons and targets requires a large arsenal. Therefore, effective deterrence requires a large, powerful counterforce capability. The second argument in favor of the counterforce strategy is that this strategy is preferable to the Big Bang because a larger fraction of the population will survive. The third argument regards victory as the goal. Since in a counterforce war the winning side is the one that has missiles surviving after a duel, it is advisable to have more warheads at the outset. Because missile silos provide small targets—much smaller than cities—accuracy helps, as does yield to a lesser extent. Guided by the theory, Kennedy ordered 1,000 ICBMs, McNamara developed MIRVs and greater accuracy, and Nixon deployed the MIRVs. The reasoning behind the strategy may strike one as simple, even simple-minded, but sophisticated elaboration does not add much more.

All U.S. presidents since World War II have sought to minimize the AR at the cost of a rise in the PR. The early, inaccurate, single-warhead missiles did not threaten the other side's retaliatory capability. An attacker stood to lose more missiles than did the initially equally well-armed victim. But accurate MIRVs gave the attacker victory. Having taken out the enemy's missiles, the attacker still could destroy cities. Crises became more dangerous.

Ignoring this consequence of their plans, the strategists have campaigned for the ten-warhead, accurate MX because every conflict has become part of the never-ending, great game of Chicken. In this world view the Soviets will risk war to gain world hegemony. The nightmare is that a president will shrink from ordering sea-launched ballistic missiles (SLBMs) to be fired at cities and will prefer to surrender—a nightmare because a fundamental axiom of strategic theory is that a leader who refrains from risking war will invite an enemy attack. From the beginning, nuclear strategists have repeatedly declared that only the threat of retaliation can deter an attack. However, this threat entails the risk of second, third, and subsequent strikes, all short of a war. The enemy may escalate the violence of the attacks, so unless a leader is ready to retaliate, he must surrender. The strategists fear both that a president will take a minor loss rather than face the risk of escalation and that the Soviets know this. Minor losses add up to a communist world, for the fanatical ideologues of the Left have more patience than the contented bourgeois of the West and can stand more deprivation. To give credibility to the threat of retaliation requires the MX and other weapons that can carry on a nuclear war. We cannot simply retreat in horror of the prospect. We must, as Herman Kahn said, think about the unthinkable. The case that **strong** counterforce weapons minimize the AR **cannot be denied.** But the strategists miss the effect on the PR of adding the MX. A jumpy leader, who either controls the MX or is its target, may press the button. The rarely stated central question is: Does the risk of a crisis erupting into a war exceed the risk of a deliberate Soviet attack?

In the opinion of these strategists, we need worry only about the AR, partly because the gains and losses in their theoretical games match real-world territorial gains and losses. But what greater loss can there be than a war? The games are useless. No wonder the strategists cannot specify Soviet gains worth the risk of war and must content themselves with abstract games.

The theory is that deterrence is bound to fail unless the Soviets fear defeat. The United States must build an arsenal that, after suffering an initial attack, can eliminate the remaining Soviet arsenal before being destroyed itself in a slow, protracted war in which the two sides carefully plan and execute strikes. In such a scenario, the opposing commanders initiate hostilities slowly and proceed cautiously. The president will immediately know of the strikes and losses by both sides. After the Soviets strike one or more U.S. silos, he will order retaliation. With superior power, the president can raise the stakes by striking more silos than the enemy can, or, in strategists' language, he can control the escalation. According to the scenario, the equally phlegmatic Soviet leader also will have good communication and intelligence facilities. To exercise the threat of a deliberate war, we needed to be able to win, and to win we needed many missiles—the pieces in the game—and a clever strategist leading our side. To deter, the strategy had to be credible, and credibility demanded that the enemy believe that they would lose any nuclear duel.

This vision is unrealistic. In a war the president and his Soviet counterpart must communicate with and retain control over their forces, and they must be able to assess continuously the damage inflicted and suffered. Although the political leaders need not survive, control must remain centralized on both sides. The strategy makes fantastic demands on the two countries' communication and control systems. Is it not obvious that each side will target the other's communication system and that electromagnetic pulses (EMPs) will destroy electronic equipment, power lines, and telephone wires that the enemy does not deliberately damage? The central control of missile silos and nuclear-powered ballistic-missile submarines (SSBNs) will be short lived. The central commands themselves will be early targets, and it is doubtful that they can survive.

The theory underlying counterforce strategy is that the Soviets will anticipate this sequence of events in their deliberations. A superior U.S. counterforce capability will persuade them that victory is out of reach and therefore will deter an attack. They will be less ready to refrain from going ahead with an attack, especially a conventional one against a region in which U.S. interests are less than vital, than if the only recourse available to the United States is the Big Bang.

But the Soviets may regard this scenario as highly unrealistic. They may believe that a controlled, protracted nuclear war, in which both sides have up-to-the-minute information on how many and which missiles have been struck, is impossible. If Soviet leaders deny the possibility of a controlled nuclear war, then the threat of nuclear retaliation may not deter them from undertaking a conventional attack if they do have strong imperial ambitions.

Further, the short-sighted strategy is one sided. If credibility requires a superior arsenal for one superpower, then it also requires it for the other. What is more, even superiority is not enough, for credibility demands the ability to completely destroy the enemy's retaliatory capability. We cannot retaliate against a conventional attack with nuclear weapons unless we are resigned to accepting the deaths of millions of our own people. The superiority required to take out the entire Soviet arsenal, including the SLBMs, is beyond reach. In a crisis involving no vital stakes, an administration is unlikely to take this risk. It is hard to conceive of any political goals that merit such a risk. Not even if all the Middle East were at stake would it be worth such a risk. Nevertheless, the counterforce strategy remains the heart of our defense policy.

What is worse, the strategists have focused only on the AR. They have failed to consider the effect on the PR of implementing the strategy. Powerful counterforce arsenals on both sides encourage preemptive action in crises—they heighten the danger of crises. The strategists failed to evaluate the probability of nuclear war arising from all sources, including preemptive action in crises along with deliberate Soviet aggression. They failed to evaluate the probability in crises of preemptive action induced by errors of communication and of intelligence. Nor did they consider the probability of crises that were not instigated by Soviet actions, but in which the two superpowers would find themselves supporting opposing sides. Had they done so, they might have rejected the counterforce strategy as too dangerous and adopted one that did not raise the PR.

Of course, the experts do not deserve all the blame. Administrations have chosen the path of game strategy, which in a simple-minded way utilizes the ancient and familiar language of war—with its victors, strength, attack, offense, defense, courage, and an aggressor. The strategists have refrained from addressing the critical issues that concern the AR–PR tradeoff and instead have attempted to solve the secondary problems of how to win in bargaining. And one reason the public approves of the dreadful weapons is that they are appropriate for the dreadful enemy.

The Soviet Bogey

Conveniently, Stalin and his Red army hordes were a frightening threat. The communist calls for world revolution reinforced the fears of the military threat, and to gloss over Stalin's oppression of Poland, his near victory in Greece, and the Berlin crisis was to repeat Munich.

Undersecretary of State Dean Acheson wanted to keep Greece within the West's alliance and out of the communist net, but without a Soviet attack looming, the stingy Congress would refuse the necessary funds. Truman's political prospects were not too bright, but the Greek crisis might revive them. Ultimately, George F. Kennan supplied a neat, justifying theory of the Soviet danger that warned against the inherent tendency of totalitarian dictatorships to attack their neighbors. So the Soviet bogey was born. Joe McCarthy's anticommunist campaign, the spy cases, and the following brutal suppression of Czech and Hungarian democracy nourished the infant. The bogey survived even after Stalin died, the division of Europe hardened, Nixon promoted détente, and U.S. administrations arrived at a more realistic appraisal of Soviet military capabilities. Reagan's policy would collapse without the bogey.

The bogey thrived through the Kennedy and Johnson years. By attacking Eisenhower for allowing the "missile gap," Kennedy rode the bogey to victory in 1960; and to protect the United States against an attack before the Soviets had more than a miniscule ICBM arsenal, he quickly ordered the deployment of 1,000 Minuteman missiles. In the late sixties and early seventies skepticism grew, but Nixon kept the faith. Amazing Nixon could do the twist of adhering to the bogey and promoting détente. Negotiating arms limitations with Brezhnev did not stop Nixon from deploying the MIRVed and more accurate Minuteman IIIs. Unable to continue peddling the old bogey, Kissinger shifted to the subtle psychological theory that the appearance of power swayed nations, and now they counted missiles before joining a camp. The psychopolitical theory also prescribed a large arsenal for the crises expected in the Middle East and elsewhere. In such games of Chicken, the more powerful arsenal would win.

Carter followed Nixon down the same road, but the appeal now was for the much more powerful MX. And Brzezinski followed Kissinger's lead. While ridiculing the idea of victory in nuclear war, he strenuously advocated the biggest possible missile. World influence was all that mattered. To impress other countries we needed a missile that could destroy the Soviet missiles. Brzezinski also followed Kissinger in anticipating crises and games of Chicken in which the winner would have the superior arsenal. The nation could not afford not to have a strong bargaining hand. Defense Secretary Brown hedged his bets; he thought we needed the MX both to fight a war properly and as a way to win influence.

These ideas were of no interest to Reagan, who reasserted the earlier simplicities. The tales of Eastern Europe, Africa, Cuba, and Vietnam were retold, and now there was the agony of Afghanistan as well.

The Economic Myth

One would think that an administration would choose a nuclear defense only out of desperation; that a president would ask the public to give up some goods before adopting so dangerous a policy. Yet it was the economy of the nuclear defense policy that persuaded both Truman and Eisenhower to adopt it. Both presidents ruled out what they thought would be a good conventional defense of Western Europe because it was too expensive. Frugal Eisenhower substituted strategic bombers for ground forces. He was so obsessed with the evils of high taxes and deficits that he accepted the nuclear defense policy.

U.S. and Western European policymakers, who continue to resist higher taxes, follow the same policy. NATO begs for funds, but despite the protests against the Pershing IIs and the ground-launched cruise missiles (GLCMs), the Western European governments still refuse to maintain what they deem to be an adequate nonnuclear defense.

THE CREDIBILITY OF THE NUCLEAR DETERRENT

Kennedy and his successors feared that when the Kremlin leaders plotted late in the night they would laugh at a U.S. threat to risk its own survival for Angola or even for Western Europe. The deterrent was too powerful. Unless the Soviets were certain the missiles would fly, they would roll their tanks to the English Channel. The dilemma was agonizing. Weapons that we dared not launch gave little security.

According to the strategists, only a mad leader had credibility. Perhaps suspecting the ineffectuality of a sober threat, Dulles fired up his threat of disaster for any misstep by shouting condemnations of evil, ungodly totalitarians. Subliminally, the Soviets heard a crazed American brandishing the bomb. Dulles's special package of damnation and hellfire gave Massive Retaliation some credibility.

Urbane Kennedy had to revert to secular, patriotic banalities. But the cost of apparent sanity was greater risk. Kennedy wholeheartedly endorsed the paradoxical doctrine of the nuclear strategists that a higher risk was the price of greater security. Moscow would risk aggression; the nuclear threat was incredible, particularly against a conventional attack. The only way to deter Moscow was to prove our readiness for extraordinary risks by actually taking such risks. To demonstrate national resolve, Kennedy led us forthwith into the Berlin and Cuban confrontations, which nearly became catastrophes; the Vietnam morass; and the Bay of Pigs embarrassment. Ringing clichés from Sorensen's pen were not enough. We had to give evidence by action that we meant to use the weapons in a showdown. We had to show the communists that they could not conquer friendly countries without danger. This street-gang logic dictated sending troops into wars in strange countries. We also had to acquire more weapons. Unless we could win a nuclear war, the Soviets would not take us seriously. To deter, we had to play Chicken. The clever, bright members of the administration understood that to avoid a nuclear war we had to come close to getting into one.

Kennedy gladly followed the lead of the Rand strategists who ruminated on the Santa Monica beach about macabre games. With little effort they won Kennedy and McNamara over to the new strategy—Flexible Response. A calculated, deliberate war strategy replaced Massive Retaliation, which insanely called on the Strategic Air Command (SAC) to blow everything up at once. Kennedy's successors have kept the same strategy.

The strategy demanded a much larger arsenal than Massive Retaliation's quick holocaust. To win a war in which missiles were both weapons and targets, the U.S. arsenal had to be far larger than the enemy's. To be effective, a deterrent had to be credible, but it could not be credible as long as the enemy could retaliate and destroy a city. The deterrent had to be able to take out every last Soviet missile and then have some left over to threaten Soviet cities. A president would not dare unleash any missiles if he risked the destruction of some U.S. cities. Moreover, with the then inaccurate missiles, the SAC had to expect to lose three or four to take out one of the enemy's. An adequate arsenal had to be enormous. To deter a march into Western Europe, we had to convince the Soviets of our ability to wipe out their arsenal. Santa Monica's message was that deterrence required credibility and therefore great superiority. Kennedy and McNamara bought it all, including MIRVs and better accuracy.

AN ANALYSIS OF PAST POLICY

Box 1.1 wraps up what I have said. Basic to the defense policy has been the Soviet bogey (premise 1); the AR is great. A Soviet conquest of Western Europe would shift the balance of power to Stalin's heirs (premise 2). The defense policy's guiding motive has been to deter an invasion (premise 3). Nuclear weapons are less expensive than a strong army (premise 4). Since the Soviets may doubt that a president will retaliate with nuclear weapons to an invasion of Western Europe (premise 5), the United States has had to preserve credibility by showing a national resolve to protect its allies (premise 6). For the same purpose, the United States also has had to threaten Soviet missile silos, not Soviet cities (premise 7). This strategy has had the additional advantage of putting fewer people at risk of being killed (premise 8). Finally, the Soviets might believe that the United States would not carry out its threat unless its arsenal could destroy theirs. Credibility has demanded a superior counterforce capability (premise 9).

This elaborate, dubious argument has been the rationale for our defense policy, which I have broken down into only three items for simplicity. Presidents Truman and Eisenhower built a nuclear arsenal and reduced the conventional forces (policy 1). To show resolve, President Kennedy defended South Vietnam (policy 2), and he pursued the counterforce strategy by building a superior nuclear arsenal (policy 3). His successors have adhered to this policy.

We live with the consequences of a continuing nuclear arms race (consequence 1), the deployment of MIRVed and accurate missiles (consequence 2), a high PR in a crisis (consequence 3), and we have had to bear the costs of defending governments against revolutions (consequence 4).

A NEW POLICY

Churchill's much-quoted, apparently profound statement that "safety is the sturdy child of terror," which has justified the continued arms race, is false. Even minor crises that might otherwise be settled without danger turn into deadly games of Chicken when evenly matched forces terrify the rivals. Churchill's disciples apparently

Box 1.1
An Analysis of U.S. Defense Policy

The Premises

1. The aggressive and expansionist Soviet Union seeks dominion over Western Europe. The aggression risk is high.
2. By conquering Western Europe, the Soviets will shift the global balance of power and win world hegemony.
3. The major goal of defense policy is to deter a Soviet invasion of Western Europe and to reduce the aggression risk.
4. A strong conventional defense of Western Europe is more expensive than an effective nuclear deterrent.
5. A nuclear deterrent may be incredible and therefore ineffective.
6. Credibility requires resistance to communist aggression wherever it occurs.
7. A counterforce strategy is more credible than a counter-city strategy.
8. Executing a counterforce strategy will kill fewer people than executing a countercity strategy.
9. Credibility requires a superior counterforce capability.

The Policy

1. Adopt a nuclear defense policy.
2. Resist communist aggression throughout the world.
3. Plan a counterforce strategy.
4. Strive for a superior counterforce capability.

The Consequences

1. A nuclear arms race.
2. MIRVed and accurate weapons.
3. An incentive to use the missiles first in a crisis: a high preemption risk.
4. Intervention in wars against Soviet-supported local groups.

think that Chicken is safe, but nothing is more dangerous than two well-armed nuclear powers in a crisis. One-sided preponderance is much safer. Then neither side will be terrified and jumpy. The United States and the Soviet Union are not about to embrace each other in friendship; leaders will take risks to show national resolve, but neither side can gain a preponderance of power. The intensity of the game of Chicken rises with the number of warheads per missile and with greater accuracy.

For Churchill's admirers, who believe in the bogey, the AR is the only risk. If they are correct, then Churchill's statement is true. In that case, a matching U.S. nuclear arsenal would keep the peace. But since equality with MIRVed ICBMs ensures "victory" to the attacker, crises are dangerous. Of course, with overwhelming superiority the United States could get its way without great risk, but such superiority is now an unattainable wish.

Finding reassurance in the long superpower peace is another way of hiding our heads in the sand. Should drivers who race their cars on interstate highways be reassured by their continued survival? The long peace only signifies, if anything, a small probability of war *per year*; the sum of the annual probabilities over the entire period may have been high. As we saw earlier, a small risk of nuclear war per year can easily add up to a high risk over a period that most of us find short enough to care about. We have not been wise, only lucky. Finally, we were secure over much of the period because the United States could eliminate most of the Soviet arsenal in a first strike.

The problem for policy is the choice between the goals of reducing the AR and reducing the PR. Since Soviet expansionism is a myth, the AR is small. We need not incur a high PR. Moreover, a Soviet attack against Western Europe, the Middle East, or other regions can be deterred at much less risk. We can maintain adequate deterrence by retaining an invulnerable nuclear retaliatory capability and some conventional forces. Preemption is the great danger; we should call off the race.

Administrations having incorrectly assessed the risks, the arms control negotiations have caused more harm than good. To minimize the PR, the cuts should have come in the number of warheads, not in the number of launchers. As long as neither side deploys many more launchers than the other, the number does not matter. Indeed, many single-warhead launchers on both sides will increase security. The higher the launcher/warhead ratio, the smaller is the gain from, and therefore the incentive to execute, a first strike. Nor should we readily give up cruise missiles in exchange for being allowed to deploy MIRVed ICBMs. Cruise missiles are useful only for retaliation and therefore deter a first strike.

Administrations have made the wrong concessions because they have sought to reduce the AR. We have been willing to trade cruise missiles for MIRVed, accurate missiles, which can strike many enemy missiles in silos at one time and quickly; cruise missiles are too slow. For a limited period we made the mistake of exchanging some of the range of cruise missiles for a reduction in the number of launchers. The Soviets share our interest in reducing the PR, and only when this goal guides arms control negotiations will they yield greater safety.

The negotiations exacerbate the danger because larger arsenals gain more concessions. The United States should offer a new approach emphasizing the common interest in reducing the PR. It should propose that the two nations agree to reduce the PR by redesigning their arsenals. This is not a hopeless dream. The Soviets have proposed that SLBMs be prohibited from closely approaching either country's capital. The recent agreement will result in the removal of one great source of danger—the Pershing IIs. The Soviets have not rejected the build-down proposal, which has the same purpose.

Unless both sides adopt the goal of minimizing the PR, we should abandon negotiations and proceed unilaterally to reduce the PR by not deploying the MX or the Trident II. The latter will have the advantage of invulnerability, but its high accuracy will raise the PR by threatening the Soviet forces. In addition, we should replace the Poseidons, as they are retired, with SLBMs that are no more accurate. These actions should encourage the Soviets to follow suit. Since they, too, fear preemption, they may shift toward a stabilizing arsenal, with or without negotiations. The success of the negotiations concerning intermediate-range weapons suggests that Gorbachev recognizes that the PR is high and is anxious to reduce the danger.

2
Truman's Choice

THE SOVIET BOGEY

The nuclear defense policy emerged from a fog of fear, economics, interest-group pressures, political ambitions, and immediate short-run goals, not from an integrated plan based on long-run goals and priorities. Truman did not conceive a grand military strategy dessigned to gain security over the coming years. But in the great defense swirl, economics and bogey were especially important. With the atom bomb, he did not have to raise taxes to defend Western Europe against the Soviet bogey, which itself was fabricated for immediate purposes. Unfortunately, the short-term goals gave birth to a long-lived bogey and a permanent and dangerous nuclear defense policy.

Momentous though the choice was, it did not come after careful deliberation. The immediate issue setting Truman off on the course was aid to Greece. To win this aid, Acheson had to invent an ominous military threat. The conventional route was open, but the bogey was unconvincing without a vast Red army; and with high taxes an anathema, an expensive defense program was a forlorn hope. Cheap atom bombs were a godsend. No element of the circular reasoning could be dropped. Western Europe had to be endangered by the vast hordes, the new weapons made the bogey affordable, and the bogey justified reliance on these weapons. Moreover, political gains could be reaped from the bogey.

Truman's personality was another element. Roosevelt had been less inclined to make precipitate decisions. Shortly before Roosevelt died, Churchill proposed a joint protest against Moscow's continued refusal to admit noncommunists to the Polish government. Roosevelt replied that they should "minimize the general Soviet problem as much as possible because these problems . . . seem to arise every day and most of them straighten out. . . . We must be firm, however."[1] Truman, on the other hand, was ready to confront Stalin on the Polish issue, and he decided to dramatize the problems in Eastern Europe. Moreover, neither Stalin nor anyone else was going to push him around.

Yalta and Eastern Europe

Immediately on his accession, Truman faced the problem of the Polish government. To prevent a hostile Poland from opening the gates to invading Germans, Stalin denied the right-wing London government-in-exile more than token representation in the new government. The fear of Germans was not confined to an excitable, paranoid recluse; Roosevelt and Churchill had shared it. At the Quebec Conference in 1944 the Western leaders had decided to raze German industry after the war, and they cancelled the order only because agriculture could not support a large population. Moreover, the Poles would long remember their oppression by the Russians. No friends of communism, the Western capitalist regimes could be expected to include Poland and other Eastern European countries in an anti-Soviet alliance. The prospect of again being ringed by enemies drove Moscow to seek control of Eastern Europe. George F. Kennan's call for an anti-Soviet alliance, including border countries, reinforced the fears.

Roosevelt fudged the issue at Yalta by inserting an elastically worded democratic guarantee in the agreements. Admiral William D. Leahy later told a Truman cabinet meeting that the Americans at the conference were not so naive as to expect Stalin to allow free elections in Eastern Europe.[2] Roosevelt only attempted to conciliate the American citizens who were former countrymen of the Poles, Hungarians, Czechs, Romanians, Bulgarians, and Yugoslavs. In his report to the American people, Roosevelt deceptively hid the capitulation by applauding Stalin's guarantee.

Knowledge of the guarantee's worthlessness did not inhibit Truman from belligerently reminding Molotov of Stalin's promises to the Poles. He boasted to former Ambassador Joseph E. Davies that he had given the Soviet foreign minister the "one-two, right to the jaw."[3]

This belligerence was Truman's way of proving his worth. Any successor would have been apprehensive on entering the Great Roosevelt's office, and chance had been unusually important in Truman's accession. Roosevelt had had no high regard for his running mate. Truman had won a reputation for honesty by investigating graft in war contracts, he was likeable, he had no important enemies, and the Democratic bosses accepted him. Roosevelt had wanted to rid himself of Henry Wallace, and Truman would do. No one could say that Truman was a distinguished statesman. Nor did Truman gain self-esteem by earning his Senate seat with meritorious political service. Tom Pendergast, Missouri's Democratic boss, earlier had appointed Truman to an inconspicuous political post, and he happened to find him again at his door out of work after other, more prominent Missourians had refused the nomination. Truman got the nomination and won the election.[4]

Truman set himself high standards of decisiveness and toughness. He ordered the atom bomb to be dropped, he spoke sharply to Molotov, he fired General McArthur, and the plaque on his desk read, "The buck stops here." When he reported the news of Hiroshima to the other passengers and seamen on the *Augusta* on his way back from Potsdam, he said that he had never been happier about any announcement he had made.[5]

Long irritated by Roosevelt's aristocratically dilatory, indirect manner, Acheson and Churchill enjoyed Truman's snappy decisiveness. But Truman's eulogists had little praise for the soundness of his decisions. Moreover, for one who had studied history, he showed remarkable naiveté at Potsdam. Truman hoped to persuade Uncle Joe, who reminded him of decent, well-meaning Pendergast, with his personal assurances of the United States' good intentions. Over dinner Truman told Stalin that the United States only wanted a lasting peace, and he was disappointed when Stalin refused to budge.[6] Swayed by the immediate, amiable sociability of the occasion, the president did not seek a hard analysis of Stalin's motives for insisting on control of Eastern Europe.

Decades-long consistency does not validate or prove the inevitability of a policy. Truman's choices were largely due to personal weaknesses, immediate circumstances, and short-run goals. No inexorable economic and political forces led to the nuclear defense policy. The consistency of the policy since Truman may be due more to interested parties repeating false arguments and the persuasive power of precedent for bureaucrats avoiding trouble than to its validity. The rivalry of the superpowers may have been inevitable, but not the nuclear defense policy. The task here is to explicate the origins only of this policy, not of the U.S. foreign and defense policy as a whole.

Truman did not get much help from his Cabinet. Secretary of State James F. Byrnes was too eager for an agreement. Commerce Secretary Wallace showed too much sympathy for the communists by proposing that the United States move toward socialism. Elder Republican statesman Henry Stimson urged moderation because the Soviets defined democracy in their own way. Truman preferred the apparently more realistic counsel of hard-liners Acheson, Forrestal, Leahy, and Harriman.

Kennan, Forrestal, and Churchill: Salesmen of the Bogey

In February 1946 Truman's desperately wanted quick Soviet guide arrived in George F. Kennan's famous "long telegram," the importance of which cannot be overestimated. To survive, the bogey needed the lifeblood of Kennan's plausible, simple theory, which the latter-day foreign policy thinkers, Kissinger and Nitze, have kept repeating. A year and a half later Kennan wrote what instantly became a famous article in *Foreign Affairs*, repeating what he had said in the telegram. To remain anonymous, he signed the article "X." The attempt failed, and the article has become known as the "X" article.

Kennan could not abide Byrnes's casual attitude. Old politician Byrnes trusted his perceptions about people and his well-honed negotiating skills more than the experts' economic and political analyses. Kennan believed that the Soviets knew that Byrnes yearned for an agreement, and those chess buffs would easily outfox Byrnes simply by waiting. They knew that after they installed their own police, one or two noncommunist ministers made little difference.[7] Kennan also was enraged by Byrnes's coverup of Stalin's brutality. He was fed up with diplomats who ignored the realities and who, exhausted by the long, tedious conferences, mistook Soviet hospitality and alcoholic frivolity for friendship and good will. After one such meeting, in a fit of anger, Kennan wrote out a set of negotiating rules, the main ones being to assume no mutual interests with the Soviets and to regard good-will gestures as useless.[8] But Kennan did not recommend any specific policies. He failed to recognize that Byrnes understood the sources of Soviet power and was not needlessly caving in.

When the State Department asked Kennan to explain the Soviet refusal to join the World Bank and the International Monetary Fund, he seized the opportunity to teach his superiors some truths about the Soviets. According to Kennan, since Soviet foreign policy was the inevitable expression of a postrevolutionary state, a traditional, detailed diplomatic history, which was appropriate for analyzing the routine struggles between well-established governments, would be useless. A true analysis had to trace fundamental social causes.

These dicta ruled out the possibility of a diplomatically arranged *modus vivendi*. To expect to settle issues with an expansionist, dictatorial regime was foolish. Diplomats could move boundaries and settle other small, specific matters, but not the fundamental and enduring conflicts with the Soviet Union. This was an expansionist, totalitarian state striving to maintain its cruel oppression. Needing enemies abroad to give him the excuse for attacking domestic opponents as agents of foreign capitalist governments, Stalin threatened neighboring countries. Kennan concluded that the Soviets had to be contained to stop them from winning world domination.[9] The Marxists, who traced the origins of the U.S.-Soviet conflict to the fundamental contradictions of the capitalist system, rejected the possibility of a settlement by negotiations. What was more, the capitalists would never abandon their class interests. Ironically, Kennan was blind to how much this line of thought resembled his own theory ascribing Soviet foreign policy to the fundamental problems of a totalitarian dictatorship.

Kennan carefully avoided risking a forthright forecast of an attack. Cautiously vague, he said only that at points along the periphery of their power the Soviets would apply "pressure." Nevertheless, Washington recognized the implicit warning of a military threat. Armies, not political ideas, could be and had to be "contained."

To help repair the damage, columnist Walter Lippmann wrote several essays, later collected in a small book. Contrary to Kennan, he said that Hitler had brought the Soviets into Eastern Europe. Expecting the Red army to advance as far as the Elbe, Roosevelt and Churchill were forced to agree to the takeover. Lippmann went further and said that the Soviets were keeping their armies in place to prevent a future invasion. Finally he warned that supporting anti-Soviet regimes on the fringe of that country would risk war.[10]

Stately language gave Kennan's readers a false impression of scholarship, deliberation, and fairness. A balanced analysis of Soviet foreign policy would not have neglected the West's hostility. In addition, Kennan overestimated the importance of the Marxist doctrine of the inevitability of capitalist-socialist wars to overburdened, practical statesmen who had to run a huge country, whose army was exhausted, and whose resources were depleted. The Soviet leaders were ready to support revolutions fought by others, but not costly wars. Kennan later renounced these hasty, unconsidered arguments, but other writers have taken them over.

Kennan's image of evil, ruthless, and imperialist leaders appealed enormously to policymakers hungry for a coherent theory to account for Soviet behavior, and he conveniently avoided troubling details and specific policy recommendations. He thus legitimatized and fed the communist phobia, which justified the nuclear defense policy. Novelty became orthodoxy too quickly for Kennan's recantation to gain much notice.

In 1957 Kennan reversed himself completely. We have to move ahead to the period covered in Chapter 3. In a series of BBC lectures he called for a neutralized West Germany. Instead of a Soviet military threat, the great danger now lay in the deployment of tactical nuclear weapons (TNW) along the East-West border. Not only might they set off a nuclear war, but they would make negotiations on arms control and European security much more difficult. Europe's political problems could no longer be solved without an agreement on nuclear weapons. Kennan urged West Germany not only to withdraw from NATO but also to abstain from establishing strong military forces. So complete was his reversal that Kennan now was advancing the Soviet proposals. Khrushchev had offered to take his troops out of Eastern Europe, including East Germany, in exchange for the withdrawal of the West's forces from West Germany. The Soviets might even have accepted the unification of a disarmed Germany. As Kennan soon recognized, however, the opportunity for such a solution had passed.[11]

Returning to 1946, to give Kennan an opportunity to continue his proselytizing, Navy Secretary James Forrestal appointed him to the National War College. Forrestal distributed hundreds of copies of the telegram to army and navy officers. One of the first to be enthralled by the grand struggle, Forrestal's crusade had begun earlier. Perhaps Roosevelt's most conservative appointee, he had been president of Dillon, Read, and Company, investment bankers, before coming to Washington. General Omar Bradley agreed with Truman's biographer, Robert Donovan, that the navy secretary was a "tense, introspective, hard-driving man."[12]

Forrestal was ready for a showdown on Poland as early as April 1945. He warned the Cabinet that the Soviets were carrying out their territorial ambitions in Bulgaria, Romania, Turkey, Greece, and Poland.[13] But he was surrounded by such ostriches as Stimson, Leahy, and Secretary of State George Marshall. Forrestal repeated his dire predictions to Harry Hopkins and Ambassador Lord Halifax at a British embassy dinner party. According to his diary, "the real problem was whether or not Russian policy called for a continuation of the Third International's objectives, namely world revolution and the application of the political principles of the dialectical materialists for the entire world." Forrestal went on to say,

it was not inconceivable that the real reactionaries in world politics would be those who now call themselves revolutionaries, because the dynamics of their philosophy all tended toward the concentration of power in the state, with the inevitable result of exploitation of the common man by the masses, or rather, by those, who in such a system apply power over the masses—such as Hitler, Mussolini, Stalin and Hirohito.[14]

In March 1947, as soon as he heard that the British wanted to withdraw from Greece, Forrestal intensified his campaign. At lunch, Treasury Secretary John Snyder heard that world leadership was at stake, as did Marshall, Harriman, and other members of the administration and Congress the next day. On the third day, after Clark Clifford, the president's counsel, had listened to him, Forrestal recorded the following:

We are going to prepare a memorandum for the President which will endeavor to bring into sharper focus the central problem—which is: Which of the two systems currently offered the world is to survive, and what practical steps need to be taken to implement any policies that the government may establish.[15]

Churchill sounded the same alarm. Unable to outbid the Labour party's economic appeal, he tried to impress the voters by exploiting his fame in the United States. Prime Minister Clement Attlee's demand for a share in the bomb had been getting nowhere. Seeking to outdo Attlee in his "iron curtain" speech in March 1946 at Fulton, Missouri, Churchill proposed an alliance based on the bomb. But without a military threat, he had no excuse to ask for either a share in the atom bomb or an alliance. He therefore raised the bogey. Americans could hardly ignore the one who in the thirties had warned the world of Hitler's threat. Nevertheless, Churchill had no more success than Attlee. Perhaps the "iron curtain" phrase caught all the attention, obscuring Churchill's request. He had not travelled to Fulton to flay Soviet brutality, but the colorful phrase obscured the call for an alliance. At the same time the world did hear the message about the bogey.

Acheson and the Greek Crisis

In 1947 the Truman Doctrine speech inaugurated the Cold War, and the Marshall Plan was initiated. Early in the year Stalin's speech summoning greater effort in a new five-year production plan had chilled Soviet-U.S. relations. Applying the prod of the foreign devil, Stalin repeated the hackneyed dogma about capitalist-imperialist hostility and war's inevitability. Familiar though the dogma was, the break with wartime friendship alarmed many Washingtonians, including Justice William Douglas, who said that the speech declared World War III.[16] The Soviets upset the Americans even more by driving the noncommunists out of the Eastern European governments.

About the same time, the Greek crisis began to blaze. The British government decided to withdraw from Greece, and, in Secretary George Marshall's absence late in February, so informed Undersecretary Acheson, who had been worried that Greece was to be the next Soviet victim. Agreeing to Acheson's proposal to help Greece, Truman called several congressional leaders to a meeting with himself, Marshall, and Acheson.[17] Marshall, for whom Western Europe's economic collapse was a much worse prospect, was not ready to say that humanity's fate hung on Greek independence. He felt that the current crisis was not worth inciting a frenzy or disrupting relations with the Soviet Union.

Disappointed,[18] Acheson took over and really laid it on:

My distinguished chief, most unusually and unhappily, flubbed his opening statement. I whispered to him a request to speak. This was my crisis. For a week I had nurtured it. These congressmen had no conception of what challenged them; it was my task to bring it home. . . .

No time was left for measured appraisal. In the past eighteen months, I said, Soviet pressure on the Straits, on Iran, and on northern Greece had brought the Balkans to the point where a highly possible Soviet breakthrough might open three continents to Soviet penetration. Like apples in a barrel infected by one rotten one, the corruption of Greece would infect Iran and all to the east. It would also carry infection to Africa through Asia Minor and Egypt, and to Europe through Italy and France, already threatened by the strongest domestic Communist parties in Western Europe. The Soviet Union was playing one of the greatest gambles in history at minimal cost. Even one or two offered immense gains. We and we alone were in a position to break up the play.[19]

As Acheson gleefully reported, Senator Arthur Vandenberg responded enthusiastically: "Mr. President, if you will say that to Congress and to the country, I will support you and I believe that most of its members will do the same."[20]

Acheson's memoirs do not reveal any great concern about a Greek collapse; the statement was intended only to win congressional support. He argued neither for recognizing the Soviet threat nor for blaming the Soviet Union for inciting the Greek rebellion. The memoirs were more passionate about the Marshall Plan. Acheson's strong effort in behalf of Greece was an attempt to retain allies, in accord with the traditional balance-of-power policy.

A rousing presidential address might rally the support of the anti-tax and isolationist Republicans, who controlled both houses.[21] Events had been piling up: Roosevelt had given in at Yalta, the communists had seized Eastern Europe, and China was lost. The time was ripe for an alarmist speech.

Nor did Truman see a military threat looming. He sent a draft copy of the speech to Marshall in Europe. According to Charles E. Bohlen, then Marshall's assistant, the secretary, appalled, cabled the White House that the speech contained "too much flamboyant anti-Communism." Truman's reply referred only to the scare needed to gain the Senate's approval of aid to Greece, not to any military threat.[22]

On March 12, Truman somberly declared before Congress that nations no longer could put off the choice between democracy and rule by terror, and he warned of the threat to national security. Enunciating the Truman Doctrine, the speech committed the United States to support free peoples resisting armed minorities or outside pressures. Congress gave Truman a standing ovation and later agreed to give Greece $350 million in aid and Turkey $50 million.[23]

The Czech Coup, the Berlin Blockade, and Korea

Enthusiasm for the Marshall Plan and for rearmament having waned by early 1948, the Czech coup gave the administration the opportunity again to scare the public. In February, after President Edward Benes appointed him prime minister, communist leader Klement Gottwald ordered nationalist opponents arrested and killed, and he probably also had Foreign Minister Jan Masaryk assassinated. The administration was not surprised. In the fall of 1947 Marshall had reported that with the communists' support dwindling in Western Europe, the Soviets no longer thought that appealing to voters there merited taking risks even with the semblance of democracy in Czechoslovakia. According to Marshall, the coup did not signal any military action; the motivation was purely political.[24]

Not only was Truman anxious to rally support for appropriations for defense and Marshall aid, but there were political considerations.

Clark Clifford advised Truman that a scare would garner more votes for him in November. Therefore, the president ignored Marshall's counsel against exacerbating the crisis and lashed out against the Soviet Union for destroying democracy in Eastern Europe. More significantly, he warned of Soviet plans to seize control of Western Europe.[25]

Not one to miss an opportunity, Forrestal was all for a preventive war. Trying to match him, Air Force Secretary Stuart Symington urged an ultimatum under the threat of a nuclear attack to force Soviet withdrawal from Eastern Europe. Others scrambled to get on the bandwagon. Drawing a parallel between Stalin's and Hitler's prewar seizures, Byrnes proposed universal military training, selective service, and support for the Marshall Plan. The frenzy caught even Walter Lippmann, who pressed for the declaration of a national emergency, mobilization, and the renewal of the draft.[26] Congress fell in line and appropriated funds for the Marshall Plan, reinstated the draft, and doubled the air force budget.

Next came the Berlin blockade. Worried about German reemergence, the Soviets had proposed a demilitarized, unified country. The administration recognized the blockade to be only a desperate attempt to stop the formation of an independent state, but it again warned against a Soviet attack. That the blockade did not portend an attack is clear from the sequence of events. In February 1948 the British, French, and U.S. governments started to pave the way for a West German state by deciding to combine their occupation zones and to revalue the mark. The old marks were no longer to be of any use to the Soviets for collecting reparations, and the prospect of an anti-Soviet alliance including Germany reawakened old fears.

In response, the Soviets announced that after April 1 guards would inspect the belongings of Americans on the way to Berlin and that military freight trains, but not other supply trains, would have to be cleared. General Clay wanted authority to resist train boardings by force, but Washington ordered that the guards were to fire only when fired upon. The Soviets finessed a confrontation by blocking the trains with traffic, whereupon Clay initiated a small airlift.[27] Early in June the Western allies issued a new currency in the zones, the Soviets responded with a new currency in East Berlin, and the Western powers countered with their own in West Berlin. As the crisis worsened, the Soviets blocked all surface traffic to West Berlin, including civilian supply trains. Truman then expanded the airlift.[28]

The Soviets feared the prospect of an independent, strong West Germany, preferring a demilitarized, weak federation of self-governing states. Stalin hoped that the costs of a continued airlift would force U.S. concessions. But Truman and Acheson eagerly awaited German troops joining NATO. Neither side could compromise. What was to become West Germany either did or did not gain the right to raise an army and enter an alliance. To win Congress over, Truman and Acheson had to paint a black picture. They raised an alarm that the crisis marked the beginning of a Soviet drive to conquer Western Europe. On the other hand, Kennan and Bohlen disagreed. Essentially their interpretation of Soviet motives agrees with my own.[29]

The Korean War began in June 1950. Although the administration accused Moscow, the war's origins were local. South Korea's dictator, Syngman Rhee, had been harsh toward dissidents, and this behavior provoked calls for unification with North Korea. Afraid of defeat, Rhee postponed the election scheduled for May to November 1950. Secretary of State Acheson protested. Rhee canceled the postponement and then lost the election. Expecting popular support in South Korea, the North Koreans prepared an invasion. Another precipating incident was Acheson's earlier statement placing South Korea beyond the U.S. defense perimeter.

Later in 1950 General MacArthur's offensive provoked the entry into the war of large Chinese forces, which turned back the U.S. troops. Many in Washington believed that the Chinese entry and the war itself were parts of a plot by the Soviets, who also were alleged to be behind Ho Chi Minh's revolution in Indochina, the uprising in Malaya, and the Huk attacks in the Philippines. Formosa was next on the list, and the China lobby warned against possible uprisings in Indonesia and Japan.

Many Americans, who saw themselves as the reluctant and hopeless guardians of liberty, lost patience with the complex issues; Truman himself took a simple view of the conflicts, calling only for courageous and determined resistance to evil.

Soviet Strength

Major support for the fear of the Soviet military threat over the years has come from official estimates of overwhelming Soviet strength. The defense policy needed an image of vast strength that the West could not match without a powerful nuclear arsenal. The exaggerated reports of Soviet strength began almost immediately after the war. Unable to give up the key illusion of a massive Red army posed for attack, Truman simply disregarded contradictory intelligence.

In June 1946 the Joint Chiefs of Staff (JCS) fed the bogey with staggering estimates of the Red army's strength, which they set at 208 divisions, including 66 in Eastern Europe. The chiefs predicted that the total forces would remain at 4.5 million, including 3.2 million in ground forces.[30] As early as 1947 the Joint War Plans Committee (JWPC) of the JCS was forecasting an attack on Western Europe by 67 divisions, most of which were already in Eastern Europe.[31]

Eisenhower, then army chief of staff, was an outspoken skeptic. On June 11, 1946, at a JCS meeting with the president, he angrily denied that the Soviets had the needed logistical support. After the meeting, his staff found no evidence that the Soviets were accumulating supplies.[32]

But the JCS persisted. Reports of a large Soviet demobilization brought the aggregate estimate down only to 4 million. The figure for the ground forces fell more—to 2.5 million. The fresh estimate of a total of 175 divisions now included 31 in eastern Europe. Although the occupying divisions now appeared to be less than half the original number, the JCS warned against a highly mobile armored force aimed at the heart of Western Europe.[33] They also worried about the Eastern European countries' 75 divisions.[34] A formidable force was preparing an invasion.[35]

Accordingly, the JCS expected that the United States' ten understrength divisions, most of which were at home,[36] plus Western Europe's 15 also understrength divisions[37] would be crushed in a war. Granted, a U.S. division had 50 percent more strength than a Red army division, but the Soviets still appeared to have more than the 3:1 advantage deemed necessary for a successful breakthrough by Captain B. H. Liddell Hart. Moreover, because they could choose their point of attack, the Soviets did not need this advantage *overall* to break through the West's thin defense line.

Stalin may have expected revolts in Eastern Europe, and he may have feared Western intervention. In any case, he did not advertise how far Soviet demobilization had progressed from the wartime peak of 11.3 million. Unfortunately, however, the source for the JCS estimates was Soviet official reports, which did not announce that many so-called divisions were only mailing addresses and that most were far below full strength. The JCS had to wait until 1960 for Khrushchev to reveal that by 1949 the total strength had dropped to 2.9 million.[38] The revision was probably correct. Eleven years later Khrushchev could gain little from a lie.

The JCS rang a false alarm. Only one-third of the Soviet divisions were at full strength, and only 30 divisions were occupying Eastern

Europe. The West could easily match the invasion force. Soviet attack forces would not have exceeded 700,000 or 800,000, and the combined armies of Britain, France, Belgium, Norway, Holland, and Denmark plus the U.S. forces in Europe added up to approximately 800,000.[39] What was more, the Soviets had to expect partisan attacks from behind.

As Eisenhower argued, the JCS ignored the poor Soviet logistics. The potential invaders were behaving strangely. Not only had they not repaired the roads, rails, and bridges in Eastern Europe, but they were tearing up remaining rails and shipping them home for scrap. The Soviets even sent their forces home, withdrawing nearly all their troops from Czechoslovakia. In 1946 Soviet strength there was no more than 5,000, and by 1948 the number was down to a mere 500.[40] The West feared a blitzkrieg, despite the fact that the Soviets could not make a rapid advance with their horse-drawn transportation equipment. The Red army reserves continued to rely on horses as late as 1955.[41] A blitzkrieg needed good communications systems for quickly maneuvering forces and directing their fire, but the Soviet systems were out of date. Moreover, their small divisions did not have enough men to supply ammunition in a rapid advance or enough replacements for casualties.[42] In addition, after years of extremely harsh conditions amid hostile populations. the sharp edge and aggressiveness needed for a blitzkrieg were gone. Morale was bad, tens of thousands had deserted, and even in the homeland the troops had poor discipline.[43] The Soviets had fought the Germans courageously, but a blitzkrieg demanded more than courage.

Handicapped by their own experience, the chiefs could not see any purpose for the high Red army strength other than a planned invasion. But, unlike other armies, the Red army was a police force and a pool of conscript labor as well as a regular army. It collected machinery and rails, repaired destroyed buildings and roads, and deactivated land mines. Male labor in short supply, the troops even worked collective farms.[44] The Red army applied the iron boot in Lithuania, Latvia, Estonia, Belorussia, and the Ukraine, as well as in Eastern Europe. Nationalists in the Baltic region and the Ukraine had joined the Germans, and to move hostile masses to Siberia took many troops.

Poor intelligence was not to blame; the JCS did receive correct information. In November 1945 a Joint Intelligence Staff (JIS) report judged that the Soviets could not make up their manpower losses and setbacks to industry in less than 15 years, to build a strategic air force would take 5 to 10 years, to develop a modern navy 15 to 20 years, and 10 years to rebuild the transportation system. The JIS said that Moscow would not risk a major war for at least 15 years.[45] Drawing on a message by Marshal Zhukov to Molotov, in 1946 the Central Intelligence Agency (CIA) judged that the United States had nothing to fear. The Red army was weak, the Soviets' internal security fragile, and they were not preparing for war.[46] The administration heard the same, obviously true, report from other sources. Late in 1945 Charles Bohlen said that the Soviets could not both prepare for a war and rebuild their economy. A naval intelligence source reported that economic exhaustion would preclude serious rearmament for another 15 years. According to the same source, the takeover of Eastern Europe was the Soviet equivalent to the Monroe Doctrine, not a threat to the West. In 1947 General Bernard Montgomery wrote to Eisenhower that the Soviets would need 15 to 20 years to prepare for a major war.[47] In February 1946 even the JCS agreed that the intelligence reports did not warrant large additions to the defense budget.

But anti-Sovietism was too strong, and in 1950 the CIA turned around. Suddenly, and without any noticeable prior buildup, the Soviets had mighty forces. Their relative strength now was at a maximum and would be so only until 1954. The potential enemy now could carry out vast, simultaneous operations in Europe, the Middle East, the Far East, and North America. They were ready to attack Western Europe, including Italy; to bomb Britain; to conduct campaigns in the Far and Middle East, including Greece and Turkey; to carry out a sea and air offensive against allied sea communications; and to attack by air Canada and the United States.[48] The White House would have laughed, had it not been the report that it had wanted since 1947.

The basic premises of the nuclear armament program were made up out of whole cloth. The Soviets neither had the strength to overrun Western Europe nor did they plan an invasion, as the administration knew.

THE ECONOMIC MYTH

Not only was the great Soviet strength a fiction, but the economic case for the nuclear defense decision was incomplete. The logic behind the argument that the United States could buy deterrence at a low price with the new technology would lead a dress manufacturer to replace cotton with paper. I will assume for now that because the AR was high we needed a good deterrent.

Contrary to the administration's reasoning, we could afford a strong conventional defense. Consider the Korean War expenditures. The U.S. strength in Western Europe never exceeded 400,000—far less than the two million added to all the forces during the Korean War.[49] Defense expenditures went up from 4.7 percent of the GNP in 1950 to as much as 12.8 percent in 1952. The marginal tax rate for the average family climbed from 24 percent in 1950 to a high of 29 percent in 1952. We could have bought a conventional defense program for Western Europe without raising the rate half as much. Economics was not to blame for the nuclear defense program.

Incidentally, in recent years, even before Reagan's tax cuts in 1981, the burden has been lower. In that year the average family paid about the same marginal tax rate, excluding social security taxes, as in 1950. Including the social security tax, the marginal tax rate was a little higher than the rate of 29 percent paid in 1952. Not only had real incomes doubled, but we were buying much higher old-age pensions and unemployment insurance benefits. Measuring the tax burden without allowing for increases in benefits makes no sense. We may argue about the value of the benefits, but calculating the tax burden as simply the ratio of taxes to income places a zero value on government services. If consumers reasoned in this way, they would never have bought indoor plumbing. In any case, we could pay for a conventional defense in 1950, and more so now.

Coming back to 1950, no respectable economist would dare say that the United States could afford no more than say 25 percent of the GNP for housing, nor that there is an economic limit to defense expenditures. As for any other service, an economist would compare the value of the additional service purchased—in this case defense— with the value of the private and public goods sacrificed. Not knowing how to assess gains in national security, economists make nonsensical statements about what the United States can afford. They are merely throwing up their hands, for the difficulty does not validate the assertions.

The specter of inflation was raised. On this ground, Edwin Nourse, the chairman of the Council of Economic Advisers (CEA), opposed bigger defense expenditures.[50] However, neither the amount nor the purpose was at fault, but the manner of payment was. Printing money or selling Treasury bills to the Fed produces inflation. If the Fed bought bonds issued by corporations to pay for new plants, prices would shoot up no less rapidly. Tax-financed defense expenditures were no danger. Perhaps Nourse went along with Truman because he was not a convert to Keynesianism, and an increase in the painful income tax was forbidden. Raising new funds with a general sales tax would have made the cost of conventional defense more tolerable. This tax falls heavily on the poor, but better some inequity than nuclear weapons. The tax consequences should not have decided the choice of weapons.

Truman stubbornly resisted raising defense expenditures. In October 1948 he rejected a defense budget of $15 billion, proposing to cut it to $5 billion or $7 billion.[51] Budget Director James Webb agreed that tax rates were too high, and, worse, that the economy risked a deficit.[52] His successor, Frank Pace, more appropriately said that current domestic programs had a stronger claim to the national resources than new defense programs. He neglected to say that when the administration refused to raise taxes it implicitly ranked private expenditures for cars, air conditioning, and radios ahead of new defense spending. The opposition to higher taxes in Congress was even more adamant. Senator Byrd foresaw national bankruptcy, while Senator Taft predicted socialism, and Senator McLellan proposed cutting all departmental budgets by 10 percent.[53]

Because they, too, feared high taxes, the JCS joined the chorus. Chairman General Omar Bradley echoed the warning about national bankruptcy.[54] Many years later Bradley had changed his mind. His autobiography said that the administration was careless about the costs of the containment policy. Truman wanted to block communism's worldwide march without spending more money. Looking back, Bradley said that although we could not contain the Soviets without larger conventional forces, by 1948 our forces had shrunk to a mere 1.6 million. Nevertheless, he, Eisenhower, and other leaders went along. Bradley said at the time, "It is the general feeling here, in which I concur, that a sound national economy is just as important as a large military establishment in our current situation." With hindsight, Bradley was wiser:

From this distance, I must say that this decision was a mistake, perhaps the greatest of Truman's presidency. My support of his decision—my belief that significantly higher defense spending would probably wreck the economy—was likewise a mistake, perhaps the greatest mistake I made in my postwar years in Washington. From childhood I had been tight-fisted. I had lived through the terrible Depression of the 1930s. I was a dedicated fiscal conservative. I sincerely believed in those economists who were advising Truman to sharply limit defense spending.[55]

Defense Secretary Louis Johnson concurred, saying that economic ruin was the greatest danger of all.[56]

The prospect of national bankruptcy did not stop the JCS from asking for an increase in strength to 2 million in fiscal 1949 and for a supplement of $9 billion to the defense budget of $10 billion. But Truman was more than a match for them, and he was much stricter than Congress. Congress appropriated $13.8 billion, but Truman would not spend all of it. Nor did he permit the strength of the forces to be raised above 1.5 million.[57]

Aware of the needs of the containment policy, the State Department backed the services' request. Kennan's successor as head of policy planning, Paul H. Nitze, warned in NSC-68 that a nuclear stockpile would not deter the Soviets after they acquired their own, but this caution was lost on the administration. Secretary Marshall completely rejected the use of nuclear weapons. He was so opposed to it that he advocated large ground forces, despite the fact that the United States would have to resort to a draft. He proposed a system of universal military training. At his request, the State Department prepared a $35 billion budget for a conscript army.[58] Marshall was widely respected, but his views gained no support. Universal military training and higher taxes were politically intolerable.

Dismissing the economic argument, NSC-68 said that the nation could afford four times as much as was being spent. Without explaining the ceiling, Nitze placed it at 20 percent of the GNP. He also tried to push through a large defense budget with the argument that deficits did not break any economic law. Keynes's disciple, CEA Chairman Leon Keyserling, was espousing deficits as a stimulus to economic activity. The country could get a good conventional defense for free and stimulate growth in the bargain.

If there was an economic ceiling, it suddenly vanished with the Korean War. The defense budget for fiscal 1951 shot up to $17 billion, and China's entry into the war released additional funds. The manpower goal for fiscal 1952 was 3.5 million, and the output of aircraft was to rise five-fold.[59] Miraculously, no deficit was needed. It was all paid for by higher personal and corporate income tax rates. By fiscal 1953, defense expenditures had climbed to the astronomical level of $50.4 billion.[60] What was even more wonderful was that the United States now could also send troops to Europe. In 1951 the Seventh Army gained four divisions, and by 1952 the forces in Europe were four times as large as in 1950.[61]

NITZE AND NSC-68: THE DEFENSE POLICY DOCTRINE

I have already mentioned that Nitze got the job of writing the formal defense policy document. In January 1950, after ordering the

Defense Department to develop the hydrogen bomb, Truman asked Acheson and Johnson for an evaluation of the Soviets' nuclear defense program. Nitze, the chairman of the committee, drafted NSC-68. It is noteworthy that he still accepts its basic principles. After graduating from Harvard in 1929, this fixture in defense policy-making joined Dillon, Read and Company, where he met Forrestal, and in 1940 he came to Washington as his aide. In 1949 Acheson, now secretary of state, appointed Nitze to replace Kennan as director of policy planning. Nitze reported later that, because he expected the Soviets to match the U.S. capability, Acheson was not keen to shift to nuclear weapons. He also reported that Kennan dealt with the issue of future defense policy by recommending greater diplomatic skill.[62] Nitze's own view was that since the Western Europeans were not about to strain themselves to match Soviet conventional forces, the United States should try to maintain its nuclear superiority.[63]

NSC-68 rewarmed much of the now old "X" article: the Soviet leaders were evil slave masters, who sought to dominate the world, and the Red menace had no foreseeable end.[64] However, unlike the X article, the report tried to estimate Soviet strength. The estimate was poor, but doubts about Soviet strength did not shake the now strongly entrenched bogey. NSC-68 estimated that the Soviet Union spent a huge 14 percent of the GNP on defense, compared to the modest 6 or 7 percent spent by the United States. NSC-68 would have gained less attention if it had referred to the poor quality of the basic data and to the detail that the United States' GNP was three times as large as the Soviet Union's.

Then the report indulged in the long leap of predicting an impressive arsenal of 200 atomic bombs by 1954. The document also warned against a Soviet hydrogen bomb. Nitze and his associates concluded that the United States had to rapidly build its arsenal. In short, without one, the AR was high.

The Soviets had no capability, but this did not stop NSC-68 from advocating a huge arsenal. Worse, Nitze's prescription for safety called for an accelerating arms race the moment the Soviets began to acquire their own weapons. According to Nitze, an adequate arsenal could survive an attack and then inflict unacceptable damage on the enemy. The arsenal had to have a second-strike capability to assure deterrence. So was born the doctrine of deterrence, which has been equated with prudence ever since. However, this second-strike capability depended on Soviet strength. The U.S. arsenal would have to grow with that strength to pass Nitze's test. Indeed, an arsenal would have to be some large multiple of the Soviet arsenal.

If the Soviets dared to match our strength, it was the formula for an accelerating race.

Moscow having no capability, the report referred only to the potential arsenal, to which there was no limit. Assuming that U.S. bombers would not take off until after a Soviet attack, the needed capability was much larger than any assumed Soviet arsenal. The argument justified a continuing rapid buildup over the indefinite future. To this day, Nitze continues to advance a similar argument, comparing rates of growth of the arsenals, not levels. Viewed in this way, the winner of the race is the one who is catching up or increasing its lead, not the one who is ahead. The report gave no attention to the Soviet leaders' fear that a speedup might signal the intention to launch an attack. They were unlikely to share our view of ourselves as a peace-loving nation, innocent of any imperialist goals and tolerant of their political and economic system. Of course, the report failed to consider the possibility of a fearful, perhaps competitive, Soviet reaction to the rapid accumulation of nuclear weapons by the United States because it explicitly assumed the bogey. Nitze simply inferred that the Soviets would acquire a large capability as soon as they could, whether or not the United States did. Much hung on the bogey.

The first nuclear experts, who also took a high AR for granted, made deterrence the cornerstone of their proposed strategy. That the United States required an effective deterrent, which meant a survivable second-strike capability, appeared to be mere common sense. The likelihood of the strategy defeating itself by encouraging a rapid and dangerous Soviet buildup was ignored.

THE COMMITMENT TO A NUCLEAR STRATEGY

The commitment to a nuclear strategy did not await NSC-68. One might ask why the Defense Department could not have prepared for a conventional as well as a nuclear war. It is difficult to choose, purchase, and assemble weapons for two kinds of war. In training, soldiers must handle actual weapons. The JCS must plan the coordinated activities of hundreds of thousands of people according to the strategy. When the fighting begins, troops will be helpless unless they have weapons and supplies already at hand, and they must know what to do with them. The JCS may plan for two kinds of war on paper, but they are unlikely to prepare equipment and train soldiers for entirely different sets of conditions. Further, the outbreak of war is no time for new decisions; when a war begins, plans will be carried out. The momentous choice of a nuclear strategy meant that in a major war the United States would use nuclear weapons.

Nevertheless, no overall plan directed the growth of the atomic stockpile. It grew mechanically with the demands by the air force, as it located new targets, and with the fall in the cost of bombs. The theory of deterrence was an excuse; it had little influence. The bombs were accumulated in a manner more appropriate to ordinary goods than to such great destructive capability.

Following the new strategy, an attack on the Soviet Union was planned as early as 1947. Afraid of not having any choice, Truman asked the JCS for a conventional strategy. However, with the Berlin crisis worsening, in July 1948 Forrestal ordered the chiefs to switch back to preparing a nuclear strategy. Announcing the new policy, Forrestal made the since familiar case, based on two propositions: First, the seizure of Western Europe's industry and skilled manpower would give the Soviets overwhelming power. Second, a nuclear defense system was inexpensive.

Accordingly, in 1949 when the United States and its allies established NATO, they adopted a nuclear defense policy. Since no additional large U.S. contingents were to come to Europe, NATO would have to rely on nuclear weapons.[65] The Soviets exploded an atom bomb immediately after the Senate ratification of the NATO treaty, whereupon Truman ordered the development of the hydrogen bomb.

Having only a few bombs and bombers, the SAC planned to limit its strikes to cities. In 1945 the arsenal had only two bombs; in 1946, nine; in 1947, 13; and in 1948, 50.[66] In 1948 the SAC had only 30 aircraft capable of carrying the bomb, not all of which could be sent up at one time, and to assemble a bomb weighing five tons and lift it into an aircraft was no small feat.[67] In addition, since the maps were old and the aircraft had to reach their targets under cover of dark, attacks on small targets would waste many bombs.[68]

In 1947, without offering a strategy, the air force began to demand a larger arsenal. Requests for bombs and bombers followed the location of airfields, generating plants, and other traditional targets. McNamara's estimate of the requirements for deterrence still was far in the future. The air force merely designated traditional military targets and sought the weapons to destroy them. The arsenal quickly exceeded the requirements of deterrence.

The fall in the cost of bombs as technology advanced also encouraged expansion; the policymakers behaved much like business people. Early in 1948 the Atomic Energy Commission (AEC) demonstrated that the levitation technique of production reduced the amount and thus the cost of fissionable material per bomb.[69] The Defense Department increased production, and new targets were easily found. The JCS now could plan to use them for such traditional military purposes as retarding advancing armies and striking at troop concentrations and supply facilities.[70] Between 1948 and 1950 the number of strategic bombers increased from 60 to 250.[71]

This is not to say that Truman made no decisions. Late in 1949 and again at the beginning of the Korean War Truman ordered a boost in production. To supply more fissionable materials, plutonium production reactors and U_{235} gaseous diffusion plants were built. By 1952, when the first hydrogen bomb was exploded, atomic weapons could be produced in large numbers.[72] As a result, by fiscal 1954 the air force took as much as 40 percent of the defense budget, displacing the other services.[73] All this time the Soviet arsenal still was small.

ARMS CONTROL

Although the administration did not hope for international weapons control, not to show some effort would have offended many people. Therefore, in spring 1946 the administration played a charade of making plans. At the airport before taking off for London, Secretary Byrnes informed Acheson by telephone of his appointment as chairman of the committee to develop a position for meetings at the United Nations Atomic Energy Commission. Much later Acheson observed that a serious effort would have begun with preliminary discussions with the Soviets. A public position at the outset blocked later concessions and thus negotiations.[74] The administration only made a show because it would not surrender its nuclear weapons. A serious effort was inconsistent with the policy. The administration could not point to the Red army threatening Western Europe, keep taxes down, and give up nuclear weapons.

The committee itself was unwilling to recommend serious negotiations, which would have required major concessions. The Acheson-Lilienthal Report, as it was called, demanded nothing less than that the Soviets abstain from developing nuclear technology while the control system was being set up. On the other hand, the United States was to continue producing more bombs. The committee did not even propose a deadline for the United States to stop production. Organizing and establishing the control system promised to take a long time. The new international authority would take control only after a worldwide survey of highly concentrated uranium and thorium deposits was made, and in the interval the United States would have the right to decide when to stop production.[75] The Soviets could hardly swallow this one-sided agreement.

The chief negotiator, Bernard M. Baruch, has been blamed for killing the negotiations. Truman appointed the well-known, popular, elder stock speculator turned statesman, who was known to be a tough bargainer. Lilienthal was bitterly disappointed: "When I read this news last night, I was quite sick. . . . We need a man who is young, vigorous, not vain, and who the Russians would feel isn't out simply to put them in a hole, not really caring about international cooperation. Baruch has none of these qualifications."[76] Lilienthal later blamed the failure on Baruch's intransigeant opposition to the Soviet power in the UN Security Council to veto the decisions of the Atomic Development Authority.[77] In Lilienthal's view, the veto issue could be ignored. Whenever the Soviets began testing a weapon, the United States would resume building the arsenal. However, the real barrier was the U.S. refusal to surrender its monopoly, expressed by the Acheson-Lilienthal Report. Truman fully concurred, for, as he said, "We should not under any circumstances throw away our gun."[78]

The Soviets proposed the immediate destruction of all atomic weapons, but this common sense position had no hope. The U.S. objection concerning the lack of safeguards was a sham, since Washington would have known of any Soviet violations. As has been mentioned, Acheson revealed much later that the administration opposed arms control, and the unreasonable conditions set out in the Acheson-Lilienthal Report reflected this opposition.

NATO AND EUROPE

The Western Europeans, who refused to pay for conventional forces, cannot escape some of the responsibility. The now powerful Social Democrats still dreamed of the elimination of poverty and of good housing and good health care for all. But an expensive defense program added to the social programs would impose a politically impossible tax burden. Even in prosperity, the Western Europeans refused to bear the costs. The worthy social programs had top priority, and why cancel good education and health programs when the United States gave them the bomb as a gift? Moreover, that choices had to be made was not always apparent because advocates proposed the social programs as demands by the working class on the capitalists: They claimed to represent workers' interests. They did not present the programs as claims on resources that should have priority over those of defense. However, with public expenditures exceeding 30 percent of the GNP and an already highly progressive personal income tax schedule, additions to defense expenditures became politically difficult.

Their memories of depression and unemployment still vivid, the British elected a Labour government. Even the Conservatives would not have reneged on the war government's promises of social programs. The country could not pay for both these programs and an adequate conventional defense. Most of the industrial plant had remained intact, but six years was a long time to go without maintenance. In addition, the foreign investments that used to pay for imported food and raw materials had been liquidated during the war.[79]

Nevertheless, the new government rushed to provide free medical service, initiated old age pensions, and insured workers against unemployment. Trouble did not come immediately. A remarkably rapid recovery raised the national income back to the prewar level by 1946. However, an economic crisis set in after output recovered. Despite the Marshall Plan, which in 1948 helped raise exports by 25 percent, the government had to contend with inflation. Voluntary wage and dividend restraints did not cure the balance of payments problems brought on by the U.S. recession and the fall in British exports.[80] The government devalued the pound and cut defense and other expenditures,[81] but in 1950 inflation continued.[82] To avoid raising taxes, the government made further cuts in defense and other expenditures.[83]

Not about to abandon their mission, the socialists grasped the bomb. Those who fought against large defense expenditures did not deny the Soviet threat. Thus left-winger Aneurin Bevan argued that the bomb freed Britain from the need to maintain large ground forces. Outraged over cuts in public housing and social service programs, he resigned from the cabinet.[84]

The devastated continent recovered more slowly than Britain. A year after the war industrial output in France, Belgium, and West Germany was only one-fifth or less of the prewar level, and food still was short in 1947. With the United States paying for new industrial equipment, recovery picked up, and in 1948 Western Europe produced more than before the war. After 1948 West German growth began to run ahead; industrial output increased by 126 percent between 1948 and 1952. Although less startling, the growth elsewhere was substantial: in France it was 27 percent, in Holland 36 percent, in Belgium 13 percent.

As in Britain, the bomb solved the defense problem. In 1950 Defense Secretary Johnson and JCS Chairman General Omar Bradley told the Western European governments that they needed only small ground forces.[85] Little was spent on defense even after NATO's birth.

In 1950 fears inspired by the Korean War provoked extravagant pledges. The French promised no fewer than 15 additional divisions within three years. The British committed themselves to place five divisions in West Germany by the end of 1951. Not to be outdone, Belgium promised a rise of 50 percent in defense expenditures.[86] However, the Korean War did not spread, and domestic priorities were reasserted. Again, the leaders fell back on the atom bomb. Back in office in 1951 in the midst of an economic crisis, Churchill said that the U.S. atomic weapons made NATO's economically impossible goals unnecessary.[87] Accordingly, in 1952, ahead of Dulles, the British government urged the United States to adopt a strategy of Massive Retaliation.[88]

Thus, in 1955 NATO failed to meet its objective of fielding 36 divisions. The French provided only 9 of the promised 24 divisions, and only 3 were in Germany. The Indochinese War accounted for only 10 of the missing 15 divisions.[89] The UK did not supply any ground forces, limiting its contribution to air and sea power.[90] Even when the allies made pledges, they reserved the right not to strain their economies, or, in other words, to go on increasing other expenditures.

The former allies did not enthusiastically welcome the recent enemy into NATO, and they feared damaging relations with the Soviet Union. Nevertheless, in 1952 economic considerations won out and West Germany gained admission. NATO announced the very generous Lisbon goal of 96 divisions, of which 50 were to be active and 34 were to be located on the central front. West Germany agreed to provide 12 divisions.[91]

The promises notwithstanding, in 1953 the British cut their defense expenditures. The French Assembly rejected the government's proposed 15 percent tax increase for defense. The resulting new government reduced the planned NATO contribution from 15 to 12 divisions.

The movement toward atomic weapons accelerated. Recognizing the realities, in December 1954 the NATO Council agreed to use nuclear weapons even at the start of hostilities. The new plans set a goal of 30 active divisions, far below the Lisbon goal.[92]

Thus, the Western Europeans accepted the risk of nuclear war. They preferred this risk to giving up social programs or paying higher taxes. No economic problem forced the nuclear posture. It was simply a choice.

3
The Economics of
Eisenhower

THE ECONOMIC MYTH AGAIN

Too sophisticated to take seriously either the Soviet bogey or the associated ideological issues, Eisenhower avoided a dangerous confrontation over Berlin. But his aloofness from these issues allowed John Foster Dulles to make dogmatic pronouncements and, on at least one crucial occasion, to take the lead. A more continuously involved president might have insisted on negotiating with Stalin's successors. Despite his own optimism, Eisenhower allowed suspicious Dulles to block any serious effort.

Eisenhower said that a small nuclear arsenal was adequate. Not only was he not blinded by the bogey, but he was skeptical about the realism of the counterforce strategy that justified the accumulation of nuclear weapons. He resisted the pressure to accelerate the nuclear buildup in the Sputnik panic over the "missile gap." Nevertheless, the arsenal continued to grow rapidly. Eisenhower's aloofness was partly to blame, but, more important, he relied on nuclear weapons to keep a tight lid on defense expenditures.

Eisenhower insisted on his economic and budgetary views. Defense costs came down sharply after the Korean War ended, and incomes were rising. Nevertheless, Eisenhower worried about the high cost of conventional forces. To save money, he replaced expensive army and navy manpower with cheap nuclear weapons. High taxes upset Eisenhower more than the danger of nuclear confrontations.

But Eisenhower's personal views were not the only reason. He probably would have faced strong popular opposition to a tax increase. The baby boom was in full swing, and families were buying suburban homes, cars, and other appurtenances of the good life. In addition, even Eisenhower could not block the beginnings of the Great Society. The new public revenues generated by economic growth could not carry both much higher defense expenditures and the new social expenditures. Keynesian economics had had its moment, and deficits again were anathema.

Eisenhower complained bitterly that the Democrats were saddling the country with an expensive civil service.[1] He distrusted the Congress that disregarded the danger of inflation,[2] and he paraphrased CEA Chairman Arthur F. Burns:

huge federal spending, even when covered completely by tax revenues, can in itself provoke inflation. [Burns] cited as causative factors: government officials tend to be less efficient shoppers than private buyers; government prices are often computed by the 'cost plus' method; government contracts are subject to special labor provisions; government spending, especially for defense, is unlikely to contribute to the improvement of industrial capacity and productivity as much as the same amount of private spending would.[3]

So obsessed was Eisenhower with costs that in his autobiography he objected to missiles only on the grounds of their expense.[4] At the time of writing his memoirs, he evidently forgot that he relied on nuclear weapons as the cheaper alternative.

Although Dulles usually gets the blame for the policy of Massive Retaliation, Eisenhower's parsimony deserves the major share. Only the economic argument made any sense. Why else threaten nuclear retaliation against Soviet conventional aggression? But the economic argument was weak, particularly in prosperity and when the administration was in no great budgetary squeeze. As we will see, the army showed the weakness of the economic argument.

Congressional profligacy, government inefficiency, and the risk of inflation did not excuse a dangerous defense policy. Nuclear weapons were no cure for government inefficiency. Efforts to raise money painlessly caused inflation, defense spending did not. A president who was less obstinate about economizing and more worried about the nuclear danger would have approved of higher defense budgets. It was a matter of priorities.

THE SOVIET BOGEY AND THE DEFENSE POLICY

Dulles and Massive Retaliation

Eisenhower's frugality was important, but the image of an evil, tyrannical Soviet regime relentlessly seeking world domination also was essential. However tolerant of the Soviets Eisenhower himself was, the incredible policy of Massive Retaliation needed the bogey. Dulles's rage and suspicion did the necessary dirty work.

This extremism was odd in so experienced a foreign policy professional as Dulles. As a young man he was a member of President Wilson's delegation to the Paris Peace Conference in 1919, as a partner in the law firm of Sullivan and Cromwell in the twenties he represented clients with international interests, and in the late thirties he lectured on foreign affairs for the Federal Council of Churches. To appease hostile Republicans, Truman added Dulles to the delegation for a meeting of the Council of Foreign Ministers. Truman's victory in 1948 delayed Dulles's becoming secretary of state. Eisenhower might have preferred a less ideological secretary, but to pass Dulles over would have enraged the virulently anticommunist Taft faction.

We have the benefit of Dulles's writings. His *Life* articles resembled Kennan's "long telegram," which appeared only a few weeks earlier. The future secretary wrote that Stalin challenged other regimes and so deliberately created a foreign threat to justify his oppressive rule. To preserve his control at home, Stalin provoked foreign troubles. He was ready to pounce on Greece, Iran, Turkey, and Kurdistan, and he instigated the colonial uprisings. Expressing great moral fervor, Dulles decried the godlessness, the tyranny, the cruelty of the dictatorship in the Soviet Union and in Eastern Europe and summoned the nation to a crusade. The appeal justified accelerating rearmament and the nuclear threat.[5] In 1952, again lashing out against the evil tyranny, Dulles also advanced economic arguments for Massive Retaliation, blaming Truman's large defense expenditures for high taxes. Further, he now advocated a more aggressive policy. No longer content to deter an attack, Dulles called on the United States to liberate the peoples of Eastern Europe. He suggested that the Voice of America incite a mass escape from that region.[6]

By contrast, Eisenhower saw only that Massive Retaliation would save money. Indeed, his skeptical letter to General Lucius Clay anticipated the counterforce strategists' criticism that no nation would expect nuclear retaliation against minor aggressions. He also said that revolutions, which the policy could not stop, were the main threat.[7] But, for Eisenhower, the economic argument was enough.

The New Soviet Regime: A Missed Opportunity

The succession struggle may not have ended when, in March 1953, Malenkov and Khrushchev called for a close to the Cold War. Probably seeking popular support with a promise of more goods, their message emphasized the economic gains from massive cuts in defense expenditures.[8] Since plenty could not be had without better relations, the appeal probably was genuine.

Struck by the economic appeal, Eisenhower instructed Emmet John Hughes to draft a sympathetic reply. However, he was reluctant to battle Dulles, according to whose theory the worldwide communist tide would continue to rise.[9] But, instead of urging a continued Cold War, Dulles more deftly said that the appeal showed that the pressures were having the desired effect and should be continued. He also warned that Marxist writings advocated deceptive tactics in the war against capitalism.[10]

Disappointed at Dulles's hostility to suggesting a Korean settlement, the president said,

All right, then. If Mr. Dulles and all his sophisticated advisers really mean that they can *not* talk peace seriously, then I am in the wrong pew. For if it's *war* we should be talking about, I *know* the people to give me advice on that—and they are not in the State Department. Now either we cut out all this fooling around and make a serious bid for peace—or we forget the whole thing.[11] [Emphasis in original.]

To block a rapprochement, Dulles proposed a long list of demands that the Soviets would refuse to or could not meet. These included free elections in a united Korea, the end of communist revolts in Malaya and Indochina, an arms control agreement providing for site inspections by a UN agency, a freely elected government of a united Germany, and free elections in Eastern Europe. Eisenhower agreed to the proposed insertions. Churchill's comment on a copy of the draft was that it was a mistake to assume that nothing could be settled until everything was. A settlement of the Korean War and an Austrian treaty would have been important gains.[12]

Thus, Eisenhower missed the opportunity for an early détente.

The Nuclear Threat in the Far East

Eisenhower did not want to prolong the Korean War, or to send troops to Formosa or to Indochina. He could not resist brandishing the nuclear threat against enemies who had no deterrent.

Eisenhower was frustrated by the fruitless talks with the Chinese. In February 1953 General Mark Clark, then the U.S. commander, reported that the Chinese were massing forces in the Kaesong area for an offensive. To force the Chinese to relent, Eisenhower threatened an atomic strike.[13] As he reported in his memoirs,

The lack of progress in the long-stalemated talks—they were then recessed—and the nearly stalemated war both demanded, in my opinion, definite measures on our part to put an end to these intolerable conditions. One possibility was to let the Communist authorities understand that, in the absence of satisfactory progress, we intended to move decisively without inhibition in our use of weapons, and would no longer be responsible for confining hostilities to the Korean Peninsula. We would not be limited by any world-wide gentleman's agreement. In India and in the Formosa Straits area, and at the truce negotiations at Panmunjon, we dropped the word, discreetly, of our intentions. We felt quite sure it would reach Soviet and Chinese Communist ears.[14]

In 1954 Eisenhower encouraged Admiral Radford to meet the French to plan an atomic attack against the Vietminh around Dien Bien Phu. Although Eisenhower later told the French that he had not agreed to such an attack,[15] he had contemplated one.

Nuclear weapons again were brandished against Beijing in the Quemoy crisis in 1955. In March Dulles said that the United States was prepared to use tactical nuclear weapons.[16] At a news conference a few days later Eisenhower confirmed the threat. He said, "In any combat where these things can be used on strictly military targets and for strictly military purposes, I see no reason why they shouldn't be used just exactly as you would use a bullet or anything else."[17]

In these instances he threatened or considered the use of atomic weapons against enemies who were not similarly armed.

The 1958 Berlin Crisis

In the 1958 Berlin crisis Eisenhower faced a potential enemy who could retaliate. Unable to deploy strong conventional forces and reluctant to risk a nuclear war, he had little bargaining power.

On November 10, 1958, Khrushchev set a six-month deadline for the end of the city's occupation and for West Berlin to become a demilitarized "free city." All foreign forces were to leave, and the Western allies would have to negotiate access to the city with the German Democratic Republic (GDR). Not ready to recognize the GDR, the United States refused to undertake such negotiations. Soviet troops began to harass U.S. Army truck convoys. Eisenhower replied that he would discuss only free-city status for all of Berlin.[18]

Forced to rely on the nuclear threat or give in, Eisenhower first did one and then the other. Early in the confrontation Eisenhower considered the use of nuclear weapons. He told his advisers, "In this gamble, we are not going to be betting white chips, building up the pot gradually and fearfully. Khrushchev should know that when we decide to act, our whole stack will be in the pot."[19]

Throughout the crisis Eisenhower refused to plan a serious conventional defense. He ordered the preparation of only a small probe to test Soviet intentions.[20] In January 1959 he rejected the JCS's advice to respond to an expected Soviet closing of the Autobahn by attacking with a single division. Such a force would be more than a mere show and too small to be effective. Accordingly, he announced a reduction of 50,000 in the strength of the armed services.[21] At the same time he signaled a nuclear threat by announcing an increase in the budget for ICBMs.[22] He then warned Moscow that the United States might respond with nuclear weapons to either a blockade or a full-scale conventional attack.[23] He added that the United States did not have to fear retaliation.[24]

On the other hand, he refused to take other actions because they were dangerous. As Khrushchev's May 27 deadline approached, Eisenhower rejected Acheson's call for a full mobilization because it would be provocative, and, over a long period, would turn the country into a garrison state. He also rejected the dangerous proposal of an airborne alert.[25] Thus, although Eisenhower was willing to say that the United States might retaliate to Soviet actions with nuclear weapons, he refused to play Chicken by ordering a full mobilization or by an airborne alert, which would alarm the Soviets. Eisenhower judged the available conventional forces to provide an ineffective deterrent and he was unwilling to risk provocative actions.

Overwhelming though it was, U.S. nuclear superiority did not guarantee a first strike, and, faced by the risk of retaliation, Eisenhower surrendered. The Western powers agreed to limit their troops in Berlin to 11,000 and to permit the GDR to control access to the city. But reacting hysterically to the news of the U-2 spy plane incident, Khrushchev refused to accept the concessions and terminated negotiations. He put off their resumption until a new president was in office.

In this crisis the risk of even a small Soviet second strike was enough to cancel the deterrent against a conventional attack. Yet Kennedy was again to brandish the nuclear threat. Nor did the evident ineffectuality of great nuclear superiority stop Kennedy's massive ICBM buildup and the development of the continuing policy based on the counterforce strategy.

THE DEFENSE POLICY AND THE BUDGETS

Although Eisenhower's parsimony failed to prevent the near doubling of social expenditures over his two terms, he did hold the growth of constant-dollar total federal expenditures down to 4 percent.[26] Unfortunately, he kept the lid on by substituting nuclear weapons for manpower. Let us make no mistake. No economic crisis drove Eisenhower to rely on nuclear weapons. With revenues growing, larger conventional forces were not beyond our means. To focus on the effect of the economic myth, I assume a real Soviet threat. Since what were "adequate" conventional forces increased with the Soviet forces, the attempt is not completely successful.

After the Pentagon's warning of the imminent threat, Truman had budgeted large defense expenditures for 1954. However, because he believed that the country could not permanently bear so heavy a load, Eisenhower cut the total budget of $78.6 billion by as much as $10 billion, with most of the reduction coming from defense. Deferring to the president, the JCS requested a small increase in fiscal 1955—from $41.5 billion to only $42 billion.[27] However, worried by the inflation rate of 4.5 percent, as well as by the prospect of a permanent large tax load, Eisenhower insisted on a large cut. He cautioned the Cabinet, "We cannot defend the nation in a way which will exhaust our economy." The atom bombs gave him the opportunity to economize, for, as he said, "instead of conventional forces, we must be prepared to use atomic weapons in all forms." Regarding manpower, he said, "I have directed a cutting back this year—and more next year—so as to allow us to concentrate on those things which can deter the Russians." To prevent a panic, he also said that the Soviets were not seeking a general war.[28] Eisenhower knew that there was waste—that each chief exaggerated his own service's needs.[29] Nevertheless, the savings resulted chiefly from the shift to nuclear weapons. Eisenhower cut the army's budget from $12.9 billion to $8.8 billion and the navy's from $11.2 billion to $9.7 billion. He allowed a small rise in the SAC's budget from $15.6 billion to $16.4 billion.[30]

The army would do anything to save its budget, even deny the bogey. Nuclear weapons were the threat, and it was the bogey that made them appear to be essential. Accordingly, Chief of Staff General Matthew B. Ridgway argued that since Western Europe was safe from invasion, nuclear weapons were useless. According to Ridgway, we needed a large army to fight small, limited conflicts in many different places. Replying only to the argument concerning small conflicts, Eisenhower said, "I just don't believe you can buy one hundred percent security in every little corner of the world where someone else wants to start trouble."[31]

The economic argument was central. He might scoff at the bogey, but Eisenhower would not risk a weak defense against even an improbable attack on Western Europe. The nuclear weapons made no sense unless they saved money in providing this defense. The army denied the economic case. General James M. Gavin argued that nuclear warfare demanded more, not less, manpower. The policy unreasonably assumed that, faced with U.S. nuclear weapons, the Soviets would refrain from also deploying them. Nuclear weapons on both sides transformed warfare. More complicated logistics, higher casualties, and deeper battle lines would raise the army's manpower requirements.[32] Moreover, lacking large reserves, the army could not use the TNW. An offensive army needed large troop concentrations to smash through the defense's large reserves. If NATO lacked reserves, the Soviets could disperse their troops to avoid exposing them to nuclear attack. Thus, without the reserves, the TNW would lack targets. In short, not to build up strength meant defeat.[33] Eisenhower was ignoring the end of the U.S. nuclear monopoly.

Going even further, Ridgway's successor, General Maxwell B. Taylor, said that once Moscow had a strategic capability, only conventional forces could deter a conventional aggression. Taylor also warned Eisenhower that the policy would force the United States into dangerous nuclear Chicken games. The United States could threaten only nuclear retaliation against even small conventional attacks, and a nuclear-armed enemy might trigger a holocaust by risking a conventional attack.[34]

Eisenhower ignored the risk of setting off a strategic attack. He replied only that the TNW were no more dangerous than big blockbusters.[35] The Soviets did not fear the few U.S. divisions in Europe,[36] and only the nuclear threat deterred the communists from breaking the Korean armistice. Modern warfare had no use for the kind of forces he led across the English Channel in 1944; two small atomic bombs could have wiped out the beachhead.

The discussion was confused. Some of the issues would have been clarified by adopting the concepts defined in the present book. The army argued that the AR was small and that, in any case, reducing it required stronger conventional forces. The army also argued that reliance on nuclear weapons raised the PR. Eisenhower argued that only nuclear weapons would reduce the AR. In the debate he made no comment on the probability of a Soviet attack, but we have other evidence that he thought that it was small. Use of the concepts of AR and PR would have forced Eisenhower explicitly to compare the AR and the PR and to have recognized that reliance on nuclear weapons would raise the PR. Eisenhower ignored the PR completely, avoiding any direct reply to the army's assertions.

He had no problem with the air force, the policy's beneficiary, and, winning the navy's support, he gained a majority in the JCS. According to Taylor, Chairman Admiral Arthur Radford argued that the nation no longer could afford to fight a conventional war.[37]

The debate over, the army was reduced from 1,481,000 at the end of calendar 1953 to 1,164,000 at midyear 1955. Eisenhower withdrew two divisions from Korea. The navy was cut from 740,600 to 688,900. The air force gained, increasing its strength from 115 wings to 120 wings and then to 137 wings by the end of fiscal 1957.[38]

Not only did Eisenhower shift to nuclear weapons, but he deployed them in potential trouble spots. In December 1954 Eisenhower ordered 36 percent of the hydrogen bombs and 42 percent of the atomic bombs placed overseas. He would not heed Defense Secretary Wilson's objection that the transfers to Europe, the Middle East, and the Far East might frighten the Soviets. Eisenhower refused to give up the capability of launching a retaliatory attack almost instantly.[39]

Eisenhower went ahead with the promised cut in personal income taxes. Corporations did not get off so easily. To balance the budget, he kept corporate income taxes at their wartime rates and he postponed the promised cut in excise taxes.

The services' troubles continued. Nondefense spending, which had held steady at about $15.5 billion, rose sharply after 1956. Over the next five years expenditures for housing, education, highways, and other domestic programs spurted by as much as 50 percent. In addition, during 1957 higher prices of military goods raised defense spending above the budgeted rate of $37 billion to $40.2 billion, and the Defense Department predicted continuing inflation.[40] Eisenhower managed to keep defense spending down by cutting the strength of the services by 200,000, the navy by 79 ships, and even the air force from 137 to 117 wings.[41]

Thus, "the New Look," as it was called, abandoned relying on a conventional defense of Western Europe. The JCS now refused to prepare for both conventional and nuclear wars. It requested authority to supply the ground forces with nuclear weapons as part of their regular equipment.[42]

Dulles's public case neatly tied the bogey to the economic argument in one package by stressing the great Soviet conventional superiority. The fiction that the West's resources were too limited for it to match Soviet conventional strength remained a pillar of the defense policy. Dulles announced that the United States would economize by specializing in air and sea forces and leave it to the allies to supply ground forces. He said that the nuclear weapons would enable the West to defend itself. The TNW and air power would make up for the reduction in the conventional forces. At the same time, Dulles attempted to reassure Western Europeans that small nuclear weapons would not damage civilian centers.[43]

The plans called for raising the PR. The United States intended to launch its bombers before an actual invasion. Since the bombers were to take off as soon as threatening troop movements began, any confrontation entailed much more danger.[44] Traditionally, nations bargained with troop movements, but the risks now were much greater. Indeed, preemption became part of the strategy. The SAC's first task in a war was to prevent a Soviet nuclear strike. Although recallable, slow aircraft were to carry the bombs. Chicken was dangerous even then. In the event of war, the SAC was to send out several hundred bombers to strike several hundred Soviet targets.[45]

THE ARMS BUILDUP AND THE STRATEGY

The rapid growth of the arsenal over Eisenhower's continued objections had five causes. The first was the choice of a nuclear defense. Alone, this decision did not produce a large arsenal. Eisenhower himself believed that deterrence required a much smaller arsenal. Second, it was difficult to design a good strategy for deterrence when the enemy could retaliate. The resulting confusion prevented the adoption of an overall strategy. There was no clear policy with the objective of deterrence to stand in the way of the air force adding to the arsenal. Third, the air force could justify a large number of senior commissions by acquiring more bombers. Fourth, the Rand Corporation's strategy prescribed a large arsenal. Fifth, the bombs and bombers were cheap, or, more correctly, thought to be so. Once the bombs and bombers were acquired, they remained in stock, and, since the SAC did not require a large manpower pool, the operating cost was small.

By the end of Eisenhower's second term, the delivery vehicles included 538 B-52s; 1,291 B-47s; 12 Atlas ICBMs; 90 IRBMs; and one Polaris submarine armed with 16 missiles. The bombers were to be refueled in flight by 1,094 tankers. Between 1958 and 1960 the number of TNW rose from 6,000 to 18,000. In addition, Eisenhower authorized the deployment of 650 additional ICBMs and 13 additional Polaris submarines.[46]

Massive Retaliation required only a few bombs, but the credibility problem created confusion. It made the administration more vulnerable to the air force's appeal to traditional military objectives. In the traditional view, bombs of any kind were intended to destroy airfields, supply depots, army bases, dams, and plants for manufacturing ammunition, tanks, and so forth. A large number of targets needed many bombs and bombers.

Rand's counterforce strategy provided a more systematic rationale for the overall strategy that the air force had to present from time to time. An estimate of the number of weapons required to destroy a list of targets appealed little to supporters of deterrence. Rand prescribed a capability that would destroy Soviet forces after surviving an attack. This prescription could be met only with many weapons.

Rand's case consisted largely of an attack on the credibility of Massive Retaliation. The more credible alternative was the threat of a series of limited nuclear strikes against potentially many targets. The strategy contemplated a series of strikes by both sides. A large arsenal would deter an attack by persuading the Soviets that they would suffer defeat in a sequence of exchanges. In a war, the U.S. arsenal had to outlast the other if it was to deter an initial attack. It had to be the victor in a war, and the victor was the side that had the superior arsenal. Credibility demanded superiority.

Despite its systematic rationale, the flaws in the counterforce strategy were as serious as in Massive Retaliation. A credible deterrent required more than marginal superiority. No U.S. president would dare retaliate with nuclear weapons to a conventional attack if even a few Soviet bombers would survive to destroy U.S. cities. Although it was clear that such superiority would be short lived, this was the theory of U.S. strategy. Surprisingly, the theory gained support despite the incredibility of the threat of limited nuclear strikes in retaliation to conventional aggression. The reason it gained support was the even greater incredibility of the threat of the Big Bang. Even more surprising, the theory ignored the Soviet reaction. To the degree that its implementation induced the Soviets to strive for such a substantial retaliatory capability it was self-defeating.

Eisenhower thought that the strategy was absurd. Skeptical about the ability of commanders to remain cool after a nuclear exchange and to limit strikes, he expected one major cataclysmic exchange against cities. If Massive Retaliation failed to deter the Soviets and a nuclear war did begin, then the policy failed. Detailed war plans were useless. Accordingly, in 1956 Eisenhower judged that to deter an attack the arsenal needed only the existing bomber fleet plus 150 missiles.[47]

Thus the credibility issue came to the fore in the fifties. Implicit in Rand's case was the premise of a high AR. To reduce the AR was the sole objective, and the credibility of the deterrent was the major problem. To reduce the AR required a credible deterrent, which Massive Retaliation failed to provide. The threat of a series of limited strikes was more credible. Eisenhower refused to accept Rand's strategy because he disagreed about the credibility of the threat of limited strikes. He rejected the possibility of limited nuclear warfare.

Out of desperation, other policymakers, who were more disturbed by the bogey than was Eisenhower, advocated a preventive war. There was no security when a nuclear-armed enemy had hegemonic ambitions. Although no political goals merited vast destruction, the bogey and the prospect of a deterrent-canceling Soviet capability left no alternative. The preventionists rejected planning for preemption, which would occur only when both sides had the incentive to attack first. Preparing for preemptive action did not assure security. The Net Evaluation Subcommittee of the NSC dismissed the continental defense program as hopeless. The program would not prevent or even seriously deter an attack on the United States.[48] A preventive war was the only solution. The NSC's SOLARIUM Steering Committee, headed by General James Doolittle, also was distressed by the imminent threat. It urged warning the enemy that unless it agreed to terms within two years, the United States would initiate a war.[49] A study by the chiefs' Advance Study Group also saw a preventive war as the only solution to the Soviet threat.[50] Both groups expected the Soviets quickly to build the capability of attacking the United States. The U.S. program to build a certain second-strike capability would threaten the Soviets' security, and they would react by developing ICBMs. Not wild-eyed communist-haters, the preventionists merely developed the implications of the bogey and of deterrence. However, they exaggerated the Soviet capability. The Soviets had no missiles as yet, and their aircraft were incapable of carrying atom bombs long distances.

More cautious policymakers supported a policy of preparing for preemption. But the practical difference was small, since preemption also required a first-strike capability. The preventionists only urged the acquisition of the required arsenal, not an immediate attack. The preemptionists, too, feared a Soviet conventional attack, which the United States could not deter without a first-strike capability. In 1955 the air force's Weapons Systems Evaluation Group (WSEG) said that the United States needed the capability in a first strike of eliminating the enemy's second-strike capability. If the enemy could retaliate, then the president could not credibly threaten a nuclear response to a conventional attack. The WSEG did not doubt the credibility of the deterrent against a conventional or nuclear attack on the United States itself or perhaps even against a nuclear attack on Western Europe. But the deterrent was less credible against a conventional attack on that region, particularly after U.S. policy-makers expressed such doubts. A U.S. first-strike capability was essential to preserve freedom,[51] to prevent a conventional threat from giving the Soviets domination over Western Europe and, with it, the world. Even such a capability was inadequate, for, according to the WSEG, the United States also had to be able to prevent a conventional attack from succeeding. Unless their industrial and government centers were destroyed, Soviet field forces would receive adequate fuel and lubricants to continue fighting for four to six months. The SAC therefore had to be able to strike many targets simultaneously.

Others, including the Technical Capabilities Panel (TCP), which was headed by James S. Killian, Jr., president of the Massachusetts Institute of Technology and adviser to the president, urged a first-strike capability without calling for plans for preemption.[52] Although this was 1955, before the Soviets had any strategic capability, the members of the TCP worried about the vulnerability of bombers to a surprise attack.

One of the cooler heads, Eisenhower opposed both undertaking a preventive war and a large arsenal. However, inconsistently, he supported preparing for a preemptive attack. Eisenhower's confusion reflected the difficulty of devising a sensible nuclear defense policy.

The imminence of the Polaris and Minuteman missiles in 1958 turned the debate to the still current issue of the choice between counterforce capability and survivability.[53] The strategists knew even before they were deployed that the more accurate ICBMs would be superior to SLBMs as counterforce weapons, but the latter would have greater survivability. Representing the navy's side of the debate, Admiral Arleigh Burke said that the ICBMs' counterforce capability would be useless. After a Soviet attack the ICBMs would strike empty silos, they were sitting ducks, and they would miss some Soviet silos. By contrast, invulnerable Polaris missiles would force the Soviets to negotiate in a crisis, and they could destroy cities as effectively as ICBMs could. The navy, which labeled its strategy "finite deterrence," even specified that 45 submarines would be enough to deter a Soviet attack.[54]

One of the advantages of interservice rivalry was that weaknesses in a defense policy were exposed. The navy pointed out that the air force's counterforce strategy entailed a high PR. The AR-PR issue became central as far back as 1958 without becoming explicit. The air force argued in response that the SLBMs were not a good deterrent because the threat of an attack on cities would not prevent a first strike by the Soviets, armed with their own deterrent. Raising the problem of credibility, the air force argued that the threat of ICBM exchanges was far more credible than the threat of destroying enemy cities. To prevent a Soviet attack, the deterrent had to be absolutely certain; a president must not hesitate to retaliate. The premises were: (1) Unless retaliation was certain, Moscow would attack. (2) A president would not attack cities if Moscow could retaliate. (3) The Soviets would know this. (4) A president would retaliate against a conventional attack with a limited nuclear attack. (5) The Soviets would retaliate in a similarly limited fashion. (6) Expansionist Moscow would invade Western Europe if retaliation was uncertain. In short, an attack was imminent unless the Soviets faced a certain, nuclear deterrent.

The elaborate air force premises were false. The Soviets were not mad enough to take even a small risk of nuclear retaliation. What was more, the air force ignored the effect of the ICBMs' preemptive capability, which it hailed,[55] on the PR. A preemptive capability on both sides might turn any crisis into a mutual disaster.

Denying the value of the SLBMs' survivability for deterrence, the air force said that after a Soviet first strike the sea-based weapons could not strike remaining enemy missiles. However, even the ICBMs could not assure such a capability, since many would have to survive a first strike. To retaliate by destroying still-loaded Soviet silos, the SAC would have to have enough missiles to strike many that were empty. This argument implied that an effective deterrent required such superiority that it would threaten a first strike. Overwhelming superiority would solve all problems.

Its unattainability did not stop strategists from pushing the goal and administrations from being captivated. The air force overlooked the technical command-and-control problems of carrying on a protracted, limited war. To admit them would have destroyed the credibility of the ICBMs as a deterrent. The air force also emphasized that city avoidance would minimize the number of fatalities. A 1960 Rand study estimated that fewer deaths would result from a counterforce than from a countercity strategy.[56] Again, the air force did not evaluate the command-and-control problems.

Although Eisenhower was skeptical about the realism of the limited-war prescription and judged a small arsenal to be adequate, he agreed to a preemptive strategy. The inconsistency encouraged the air force to ignore his request for a shorter target list. A committee instructed to cut the list did virtually nothing. The committee eliminated only the duplication in the separate lists of the different SAC commands. Three hundred out of 2,400 targets were found to be duplicated, and Eisenhower approved of the trimmed list, which he still thought to be excessive. However, in December 1960, when it was too late for further changes, he discovered that he had been hornswoggled. The final list, the Single Integrated Operational Plan (SIOP), included many additional targets.[57] The air force built a large arsenal because Eisenhower did not succeed in defining a coherent defense policy.

THE SOVIET BOGEY, EXPERTS, AND POLITICIANS

The Gaither Report

In November 1957, resisting demands for higher defense spending aroused by the panic over Sputnik, Eisenhower said, "We face not a temporary emergency . . . but a long-term responsibility." Further, the effort "to combat and defeat the Soviets must be designed for indefinite use and endurance. Hasty and extraordinary effort under the impetus of sudden fear . . . cannot provide for an adequate answer to the threat." Also, that "about two-thirds of the supplementary funds are more to stabilize public opinion than to meet any real need."[58]

The Gaither Committee, commissioned much earlier, added to the hysteria with the warning of a Soviet missile attack within two years. The rumor of a Soviet technological lead, which the committee spread, fed the myth of the missile gap.

Headed by H. Rowan Gaither, Rand's chairman of the board, the committee also included Robert C. Sprague, an industrialist; James A. Perkins of the Carnegie Corporation; William C. Foster, a former deputy secretary of defense; Robert C. Prim of the Bell Telephone Laboratories; James P. Baxter III, president of Williams College; and Robert D. Calkins, chairman of the Brookings Institution. MIT physics professor Jerome B. Wiesner directed the staff. The advisers included Edwin P. Oliver of Rand; nuclear physicist Ernest O. Lawrence of the Radiation Laboratory of the University of California; Robert Lovett, a Truman defense secretary; Columbia University physicist I. I. Rabi; and Rand nuclear strategist Andrew W. Marshall, as well as Killian.[59]

At the committee's invitation, Paul Nitze and Albert Wohlstetter of Rand acted as special advisers; Nitze co-authored the report.[60] On Wohlstetter's advice, the committee undertook a broad investigation, going beyond the original assignment calling for an examination of the civil defense system.[61] Wohlstetter argued that the SAC's vulnerability to attack was the greatest danger.[62]

Catering to the committee's cautious members, the report began with a double-negative assertion about the Soviet threat: "We have found no evidence in Russian foreign and military policy since 1945 to refute the conclusion that USSR intentions are expansionist, and that her great efforts to build military power go beyond any concepts of Soviet defense."[63]

The major conclusion that a Soviet missile threat was imminent was inferred from three dubious propositions that concerned the relative defense expenditures of the two countries, not the Soviet ability to manufacture missiles. The logic tying overall defense expenditures to the manufacturing ability is difficult to follow. In any case, the three propositions were as follows: (1) Soviet defense expenditures equaled those of the United States. (2) The Soviet Union spent a larger share of its GNP on defense than did the United States. (3) The Soviet GNP was growing faster than that of the United States. These comparisons were no more than assertions, and the call for a vast nuclear buildup surely deserved much more support. The report could not logically conclude that within two years (by 1959) the Soviets would achieve "a significant ICBM delivery capability with megaton warheads."[64] The committee did not have the necessary reports of observations of ICBM flight tests. It is hard to believe that the report's purpose was a close examination of the state of defenses and not to alarm what the committee considered to be a lethargic administration.

The committee (or the report's co-author, Nitze) was unnecessarily alarmed by the Soviet GNP's rate of growth, which was 1.5 times as large as that of the United States. A backward economy was likely to grow rapidly, the easiest growth opportunities would be exploited first, and the U.S. GNP was three times as large as the Soviet Union's. Moreover, the report assigned to "defense expenditures" investment in heavy industry, including plants manufacturing metals, machinery, and chemicals. Some of the capacity could be converted to the production of tanks, artillery, and so forth, but, in any case, the investment in heavy industry was unrelated to missile capability. Nevertheless, according to the report,

This growing Russian economic strength is concentrated on the armed forces and on investment in heavy industry, which this year account for the equivalent of roughly $40 billion and $17 billion respectively, in 1955 dollars. Adding these two figures, we get an allocation of $57 billion per annum, which is roughly equal to the combined figure for these two items in our country's current effort. If the USSR continues to expand its military expenditures throughout the next decade, as it has during the 1950s, and ours remains constant, its annual military expenditures may be double ours, even allowing for a gradual improvement of the low living standards of the Russian peoples.[65]

The alarmism also is seen in the following statements:

By 1959, the USSR may be able to launch an attack with ICBMs carrying megaton warheads, against which the SAC will be almost completely vulnerable under present programs.[66]

U.S. has an inadequate retaliatory capability if SAC bases are surprised at a time of lessened world tension, i.e., a time when SAC is not in a state of combat readiness. Prompt and aggressive implementation of the SAC "alert" concept would cure this defect.[67]

USSR has capability to make a destructive attack on the US.[68]

The committee, under Wohlstetter's influence, emphasized the SAC's vulnerability.[69] The report did not mention the counterforce strategy, but at a meeting of the NSC a committee spokesman vigorously advocated providing for a large retaliatory capability after a massive Soviet attack.[70]

The members despaired of the complacency of the president, who continued to reassure the nation.[71] Gaither informed Eisenhower that three committee members advocated an immediate war to prevent a surprise Soviet attack that would destroy three-quarters of the B-52s. According to Eisenhower's biographer, Stephen E. Ambrose, Gaither warned that unless the nuclear defenses were expanded rapidly, the end of Western civilization was at hand. As always, Eisenhower returned to his theme of excessive defense spending.[72]

Kennedy, Rockefeller, and Kissinger

It no longer was demagogic for Senator John F. Kennedy to warn against the "missile gap." Accusing Eisenhower of allowing a "gap," in August 1958, he said that the deterrent ratio "would in all likelihood be weighted very heavily against us," and he warned that to gain world domination the Soviets might launch a surprise attack on the United States. Alternatively, the Soviets might gain their objectives with:

sputnik diplomacy, limited brushfire wars, indirect nonovert aggression, intimidation and subversion, internal revolution, increased prestige or influence, and
the vicious blackmail of our allies. The periphery of the free world will slowly be
nibbled away. The balance of power will gradually shift against us.[73]

Early in 1960 Kennedy again attacked Eisenhower for allowing
the United States to be second in missiles and in space,[74] and for
neglecting the defenses while the Soviets threatened to conquer
Eurasia.[75] In the Senate, Kennedy demanded missiles and forces
ready to intervene in limited wars anywhere in the world.[76]

Another ambitious politician, Nelson Rockefeller, also seized on
the missile gap. He hired Henry Kissinger, the author of *Nuclear
Weapons and Foreign Policy*,[77] which said that the rival nuclear
stockpiles had created a "balance of terror." This message lacked the
needed hair-raising quality. But nothing was certain in this macabre
field, and Wohlstetter's recent article entitled "The Delicate Balance
of Terror" showed the way to a more alarming message.[78] Following
Wohlstetter, Kissinger wrote in the Rockefeller Brothers Fund Report
that if only one side applied a new scientific advance, the balance
might be overthrown. Therefore, Kissinger urged, "In a dynamic
situation, we must continually strive to improve our technological
position lest an accumulation of advantages by an aggressor ultimately confront us with overwhelming strength."[79]

Pointing to the alleged Soviet missile lead, Kissinger echoed Wohlstetter's warning that the U.S. air bases were vulnerable, and he supported the goal of a second-strike capability, which required a large
arsenal. The arsenal had to be able to survive an all-out enemy attack
and then inflict unacceptable damage on well-defended enemy territory. He called for a large ICBM force, reducing the SAC alert, and
speeding up the missile defense system. Moreover, to enable the
president to stand firm in a crisis, the deterrent needed a massive
civil defense program.[80] In addition, nuclear superiority was essential
to protect Third World countries against Soviet-supported conventional attacks. Kissinger anticipated recurrent Third World crises,
which would become nuclear Chicken games. The United States
needed superiority to win such games. Otherwise, Soviet nuclear
superiority would deter a U.S. conventional defense. Later, in the
Nixon administration, when détente made the bogey less ominous,
Kissinger relied heavily on this part of the case for enhancing the
arsenal. At this time, however, the bogey still thrived. Neither side
had any ICBMs, and the office seekers needed a dragon.

WESTERN EUROPEAN DEFENSE

Social Versus Defense Spending

The fifties were a festive decade for Western Europe. Output grew by one-half, and the resulting automatic gains in public revenues paid for most of the costs of the new social programs. However, expenditures grew so rapidly that governments did impose new taxes. Another consequence of the rise of the welfare state was the abandonment of conventional defenses and reliance on nuclear weapons. Defense and social programs together were expensive, and the social programs came first. Fearful of the bogey, the leaders could not abandon defense completely, and they grasped the free good of nuclear weapons.

The UK, West German, and Italian governments supplied free health services, while the French, Belgian, and Scandinavian governments paid 75 to 90 percent of the costs.[81] By 1960 physicians were twice as numerous in Western Europe as in the late twenties, and the number of dentists grew even more.[82] Expenditures for family allowances and old age pensions grew to several times the 1930 level. Higher education was supplied free or at nominal charges, and the UK paid students living-cost stipends. In the 1950s the number of dwellings in Western Europe doubled, even after the war-destroyed housing was replaced.[83]

In the mid-fifties total public expenditures varied among the countries between 25 percent and 34 percent of gross domestic product (GDP), compared to 26 percent in the United States. In 1955 tax receipts in Germany, Italy, the UK, and France amounted to approximately 30 percent of the GDP, compared to 24 percent for the United States. The expenditures were too high to be covered by income taxes, and the governments had to impose regressive value-added taxes. Even the poor had to pay for the new programs.

The welfare state's byproduct was a nuclear arsenal. The national income had to be allocated between private expenditures, public social programs, and defense, and the governments chose to cut defense expenditures by adopting a nuclear defense policy. Had the governments spent less on defense because they rejected the Soviet bogey, little could be said. But the governments did not reject it. They decided that higher taxes were impossible and that the social programs merited nuclear weapons and the associated risks. Together, the bogey and the welfare state conceived the nuclear defense policy.

NATO

The governments periodically pledged and then ignored their commitments to NATO. In February 1952 at Lisbon they agreed to raise 96 divisions, and as soon as their representatives reached home they tore up the agreements. Even before the meeting ended, Churchill announced that the British would be unable to meet their share.[84] The French Assembly defeated Premier Edgar Fauré's proposed tax increase, and the new government postponed the deadline for reaching the Lisbon goal.[85]

As a result, the Western Europeans insisted on a nuclear guarantee. The fiscal crises were deceptive, for the poor could have been cared for by special programs, and middle-class people could have paid for their own higher education and medical services. Taxing the rich to pay for education may have been justifiable, but higher education for all was not worth the risk of nuclear war. The fiscal problems were no more than problems of choice, nothing fundamental. Private consumption was growing, not declining, but the governments refused to spend more on conventional forces.

To gain low-cost security the Western Europeans demanded certain nuclear retaliation to a conventional invasion. The military rationale assumed that the AR was high and was the only risk, which the nuclear guarantee would reduce. Conventional forces would only delay a Soviet advance, and the U.S. troops in Europe were merely the trip wire for the U.S. strategic weapons.

The Western Europeans realized that at the critical moment the trip wire might fail; the United States might not commit suicide. The TNW were deployed to shore up the strategic threat. A lower rung in the ladder of escalation of destruction was expected to enhance credibility. The Soviets would not dare raise the risk of a strategic attack by forcing NATO to cross the nuclear threshold. The more graduated the progression to a strategic attack was, the more effective was the ultimate deterrent. Supporters of deployment close to the border wanted a high risk of nuclear destruction in any confrontation because it would deter the Soviets more than the threat of a conventional war that they were likely to win. Locating the TNW where they would be captured in a conventional war would add to the risk of nuclear war. In our language, the TNW were a means of exchanging some of the high AR for some increase in PR.

However, the PR increased more than even the hawks may have realized. By distributing warheads to the combat units during a crisis, NATO would heighten it; the Soviets would make similar preparations.

After the Red army made preemptive attacks on command units, NATO could not maintain control over the surviving troops under pressure to return the nuclear fire. The TNW would provide the spark for igniting a crisis into war.

Dulles assured the Western Europeans that the TNW would destroy only the intended targets. But this hope was shattered by NATO's Carte Blanche exercise, which produced an estimate of 5 million deaths in West Germany from tactical nuclear warfare. Bitterly blaming other governments for not meeting their commitments, Chancellor Adenauer advocated a conventional defense.[86]

Nevertheless, the TNW were deployed. In October 1954 NATO Commander General Alfred Gruenther announced that the alliance would meet a conventional attack with TNW, and, as thousands were deployed, NATO's manpower goal was reduced to 30 divisions.[87]

Although the issue was especially difficult for British socialists, it was the Labour government that in 1947 had initiated the development of the British atom bomb, which in 1952 culminated in the explosion of a bomb. Labour party members were revolted by Stalin's purges and suppressive police, and past battles with communists in the trade unions had made Foreign Secretary Ernest Bevin distrustful of them. Moreover, the empire had left the British with a large military burden.[88] To save money for social programs the Labour government developed a nuclear defense program. We saw earlier that fiscal pressures induced Churchill in 1952 not to honor the commitment to NATO, and similar problems in 1957 led the government to plan cuts in the forces of as much as 45 percent by 1962.[89]

In addition, the British distrusted the U.S. umbrella, and they hoped to continue their role as a great power. Britain had been one of the Big Three in World War II, and even Labour was reluctant to accede to the new reality. However, by 1957 many members of the Labour party had begun to doubt the usefulness of nuclear weapons against a conventional attack.[90] But the British could not have both large armed forces and social programs, and, in the end, Labour went along with the nuclear defense policy.

Also horrified by Stalin's brutality in Poland and Czechoslovakia and fearful of the Red army, the French socialists supported a strong defense policy. But they were unwilling to exchange social programs for a traditional defense program.

The French developed an atom bomb, which they exploded in February 1960. They, too, wanted to be ranked a great power, and they, too, lacked faith in U.S. protection. De Gaulle did not expect a country that was not immediately threatened to risk its own destruction.

Nevertheless, the chief reason for developing an atom bomb was again economic. France refused to contribute more to NATO's forces.[91]

Nuclear devastation was a more imminent threat to West Germany. Adenauer called for stronger conventional forces for NATO, but, pointing to the U.S. New Look and Britain's and France's NATO records, he refused to allow West Germany to be saddled with the burden. West Germany reduced the strength of its forces from 500,000 to 350,000.[92]

NATO Commander General Lauris Norstad doubted that in a crisis the members would allow the forces to bring on Armageddon. He expected them to raise questions about the Soviets' true intentions and to describe any attack as local. To provide a test of Soviet intentions, Norstad proposed that NATO not commence any retaliatory action before Soviet forces actually invaded Western Europe, despite threatening prior troop movements. Initially, NATO troops would fire only conventional weapons; the TNW would come into action after a continued Soviet advance. However, the troops were not to wait until they were being routed. NATO acquired thousands of TNW so that it would not be forced to rely on conventional weapons until much of West Germany was overrun. Whether NATO would wait several hours or several days no one knew.

Realizing that the fears took away some of the deterrent's credibility, Norstad hoped that a planned pause would limit the problem. By facilitating the transition to strategic warfare, the planned pause would add to the credibility of the ultimate deterrent and therefore to the entire sequence. The deterrence of an attack would be more effective because the Soviets would have more reason to expect that each step would be followed by the next one. The Soviets would know that the gradual escalation would make it easier for the president to order the ICBMs to be fired.

The approval was not unanimous. Some Western Europeans feared that nothing less than the threat of an immediate massive attack on their cities would stop the Soviets. Indeed, the plan for a pause invited an invasion; the already high AR would mount enormously. The pessimists also denied NATO's ability to prepare for both conventional and nuclear warfare. Prior to an invasion, the Red army would concentrate its troops at selected points without having to fear inviting a nuclear attack. Would the troops be trained for both a conventional war and a nuclear war? Would the nuclear warheads be distributed only after conventional fighting was under way? In addition, to announce that we would refrain from firing TNW until later would give the Soviets an inducement to shoot first.

The most serious effect of deploying the TNW close to the border, where they were vulnerable to capture, was to increase the PR, and the planned pause did nothing to mitigate this problem; if the TNW were to be used at all, they had to be used quickly. The pause would only delay the firing of the weapons after they were in the hands of the combat units. Once fighting had started, troops would not restrain themselves for long, and command units would be unable to monitor their actions, to say nothing of controlling them. The unrealistic proposal was only an effort to gain political support for an unpalatable strategy.

The deployment of IRBMs in Britain, Italy, and Turkey also increased the PR. Their short flight time to Moscow increased the risk more than the U.S.-based ICBMs, which came later. Since NATO would be able to strike Soviet political leaders and military command centers within 12 minutes of launch, Moscow would be very tempted in a crisis to preempt an attack by striking these vulnerable weapons. The IRBMs were destabilizing, first-strike weapons.

Although the AR was small and the PR in a crisis was high, the Western Europeans insisted on deploying nuclear weapons to reduce the AR, and they ignored the resulting increase in the PR. The great risk was that a crisis would originate elsewhere in the world and erupt.

4
Kennedy and National Resolve

NATIONAL RESOLVE AND DEFENSE POLICY

National Resolve and Credibility

Kennedy's determination to show resolve drew the country down the nuclear slope. He accepted a higher PR to cut what he thought was a high AR. The policy was not inevitable. A cautious president who judged the Soviets also to be cautious would not have pushed Khrushchev to the limit in the Berlin and Cuban crises. Eisenhower, who estimated a small AR, did not try to show resolve by holding firm on West Berlin; he decided that the rise in the PR would be unwarranted. Kennedy's attitude was exactly the opposite. Unless we showed our resolve to fight, the Soviets would attack.

Kennedy firmly believed in the bogey. This belief, combined with his macho attitude toward risk, were the sources of the most dangerous episodes in U.S. history. It is hard to see how Arthur Schlesinger, Jr. could praise him for early steps toward détente after his vast nuclear buildup and his dangerous policy in the Berlin and Cuban crises. The bogey and Kennedy's dedication to national resolve also led the United States into Vietnam. According to Sorensen, Kennedy's major foreign policy goal was to stop the advance of communist power.[1]

Kennedy escalated the arms race. Strangely, Kennedy and McNamara expected the Soviets meekly to refrain from competing and allow the United States to gain the overwhelming superiority presumed by the counterforce strategy. Without such superiority, the strategy made no sense whatsoever—not that it was sensible under the most ideal conditions. The naiveté of the best and the brightest is hard to believe. The Soviets disappointed them. McNamara ordered the development of MIRVs and greater warhead accuracy in the now even stranger hope of retaining the lead by keeping the technologies secret. It was foolish to expect to hide a technology from competitors, who mined the journals, patent descriptions, trade magazines, and government contract solicitations, employed spies, and did their own research. Unfortunately, McNamara did not know that the Soviets had begun their research in rocketry and atomic physics as early as 1946 and had established design bureaus and bomb factories.

In 1961 Kennedy disingenuously wrote to Khrushchev that the Soviet Union's domestic policy was no business of the United States.[2] But its foreign activities were another matter, for, in Kennedy's view, even small tilts toward communism were dangerous. Seeing the Kremlin's hand in Cuba and Vietnam,[3] he warned that communist victories endangered the global balance of power. Kennedy worried as much about the appearance of strength, to which national resolve contributed, as he did about actual strength. Communist victories even in such nonvital regions as Indochina would damage the appearance of strength and invite attacks on friendly, weak governments. To avoid war we had to preserve appearances, which meant that we had to show resolve. We had to risk war, and in Vietnam we had to intervene in one. The policy was built on this paradox. It was the country's misfortune to have a macho president deciding the defense policy in these early years of the nuclear age.

Although the macho image appealed to Kennedy more than to other presidents, the nuclear defense policy's credibility problem preceded his administration. The credibility problem had contributed to Eisenhower's inconsistency and to his permitting the air force to proceed at full speed despite his own doubts. Kennedy believed that to reduce the AR the United States had to have a credible nuclear threat, which required raising the stakes in each conflict. We had to be willing to risk nuclear war to avoid one, or, in other words, to raise the PR. The argument only made sense if the AR was in fact higher than the PR. We could reduce the risk of nuclear war by increasing the PR only if it was less than the AR and if increasing the PR had the desired effect of reducing the AR.

Kennedy tied other problems to appearances. During the election campaign he attacked Eisenhower for damaging the nation's image by allowing the Soviets to gain the lead in the space technology race. Kennedy's attitude is revealed by Sorensen's report:

To [Kennedy, the space gap] symbolized the nation's lack of initiative, ingenuity, and vitality under Republican rule. He was convinced that Americans did not yet fully grasp the world-wide political and psychological impact of the space race. With East and West competing to convince the new and undecided nations which way to turn, which wave was the future, the dramatic Soviet achievements, he feared, were helping to build a dangerous impression of unchallenged world leadership generally and scientific pre-eminence particularly.[4]

If we think about the famous passage in the inaugural address,[5] in which Kennedy warned every nation, meaning the Soviet Union, that the United States would pay any price, bear any burden, meet any hardship, and so on, to assure the survival of liberty, its bellicosity becomes positively frightening.

Every confrontation was an episode in the grand game of Chicken, and, since the credibility of the vastly destructive weapons in nonvital confrontations was at stake, Kennedy would not swerve. Kennedy pledged West Berlin's security to signal his willingness to risk nuclear war when U.S. interests were modest. He took the risk because any confrontation was an incident in this century's struggle for world power; future Soviet aggressions had to be deterred. In addition, Kennedy judged that he did not have the strength to hold back the virulently aggressive Soviet Union in a conventional war. For Kennedy's policy to make sense, he had to believe that the Soviet Union was willing to take great risks in its drive for empire. Judging from the risks that Kennedy was willing to take, he had no doubts.

To contain communism and minimize the risk of war, Kennedy believed that we needed a cool, controlled nuclear strategy to resist minor aggressions. The greatest danger was the threat's lack of credibility. Assuming a high AR, he feared that a Soviet underestimate of our resolve would prompt some aggression, which would trigger a U.S. strategic attack. To reduce the risk, the United States had to play Chicken in the recurring crises. Kennedy inherited the Congo, Laos, and Vietnam crises; Cuba had fallen, and the Dominican Republic might be lost. The United States might be forced to issue a nuclear ultimatum to preserve the credibility of the deterrent. A continued string of communist successes would damage the deterrent's effectiveness, and the slide of world power into the Soviet grasp would accelerate. The Soviets had to be confronted even on small issues to discourage them from attacking a large and important territory. In crises over nonvital issues, the president had to slide a little way down the nuclear slope to show that in crises over vital issues the United States would not surrender. Credibility demanded a more confrontational posture than when armies did not threaten total devastation. Paradoxically, as the weapons became vastly more destructive, a higher PR had to be taken. Otherwise, the danger of war would increase.

The same logic was applied to nuclear war itself, for deterrence did not stop with its own failure. In a war the nation would have to inflict and be prepared to suffer some destruction to prevent either surrender or even worse devastation. To avoid launching attacks was equivalent to surrender and it encouraged the enemy to launch ever greater attacks. Deterrence did not even stop with limited nuclear attacks.

In short, a powerful U.S. arsenal reduced the high AR, and therefore the risk of war. In addition, a confrontational policy, which increased the PR, reduced the AR and, therefore, the risk of war. To the extent that a powerful arsenal raised the PR, it also reduced the AR. This reasoning was correct only if the AR greatly exceeded the PR. If the PR exceeded the AR, then the policy raised the risk of nuclear war.

We also had to take a high PR to win the worldwide conflict, according to Kennedy. The policy agreed with Schelling's theory of war bargaining that we had to persuade the enemy that we could and would hurt them badly. To stop communism we needed a large arsenal and to risk nuclear war.

Kennedy accepted this risk by adopting the policy of Flexible Response. The policy's fundamental fallacy was in its appraisal of the two risks. The policymakers were aware of the PR, but they dismissed it. All attention focused on the AR and how to minimize it. Since the principal risk was the PR, the policy that prescribed brinkmanship increased the danger of nuclear war; it did not reduce the danger. Flexible Response was another name for Chicken. Only if the Soviets were willing to risk nuclear war was Kennedy right. The argument here is that the major risk was the PR, not Soviet expansionism or the AR.

In pursuit of great superiority, Kennedy and McNamara undertook a large, rapid nuclear buildup. Starting with 12 Atlases, Kennedy ordered the deployment of 1,000 ICBMs. Under President Johnson, McNamara continued this pursuit by developing MIRVs and greater accuracy. We could still hope to eliminate all or most of the Soviet missiles while keeping some of our missiles in reserve to hold Soviet cities hostage.

McNamara took Daniel Ellsberg, Andrew Marshall, Charles Hitch, Alain Enthoven, and Henry Rowen away from Rand. Consultants included William Kaufmann, who had moved to MIT from Rand, and Albert Wohlstetter, who remained at Rand. Their systematic, logical analysis appealed to McNamara. One of their own kind, during World

War II in the Statistical Control Office of the army, he had applied economics, statistics, and the new operations research methods to logistical problems. The war over, he had organized a management consulting firm, from which he went to the Ford Motor Company and in due course became its president.

Dismayed by the plans for Massive Retaliation, Kennedy and Mc-Namara turned to Rand's strategy of limited destruction. The case for the credibility of the limited-war threat was persuasive. The administration adopted the variant of the counterforce strategy known as the "damage limitation" strategy, which also limited attacks to military targets. But this strategy did not call for bargaining by attacking a few silos at a time. It won its name by prescribing the destruction within a short time of as many of the enemy's silos as possible, which would limit damage by retaliatory attacks. Ideally, the objective was the complete elimination of the retaliatory capability, or a first strike.

At no time did McNamara publicly acknowledge the choice of the damage limitation strategy. Initially, the public statements emphasized the intention of limiting nuclear warfare, suggesting the counterforce strategy proper. The announcement of the shift to assured destruction signified the rejection of protracted nuclear exchanges; deterrence now was the sole objective. Under the alleged new policy, the arsenal had to be large enough to destroy only as much as necessary to deter a Soviet attack. However, very early the arsenal achieved a first-strike capability or nearly so, as required by either the damage limitation strategy or the counterforce strategy proper. The problem of a sensible defense policy confounded the Kennedy administration, as it had its predecessor. Under Eisenhower the policy was confused, going off in different directions. Although the Kennedy administration tried to address the problems more systematically, it had no more success. The administration announced two different policies and actually followed a third.

Thus, the confusion persisted. Although the declaratory policy shifted to assured destruction, the public discussion continued to emphasize the counterforce strategy. The debates over MIRVs and accuracy under Nixon, and over the MX more recently, have revolved around this strategy, to which we now turn.

The Counterforce Strategy

Kaufmann's influential 1956 article explained Rand's thinking.[6] Kaufmann chose the counterforce strategy after rejecting Massive Retaliation and without appraising other alternatives. He did not reject the communist threat in the following statement describing the assumptions of Massive Retaliation:

The first is that, while communism may take many forms and appear in a great variety of places, its actions are instituted from and controlled by the Soviet Union and Red China. The second assumption is that, although the leaders of the Soviet Union and Red China may have objectives quite different from our own, their cost-risk calculations must be roughly the same. The third assumption—and it follows from the first two—is that action on the periphery of the Communist empire can be forestalled by forecasting to the enemy the costs and risks that he will run, provided always that the costs and risks are of a sufficient magnitude to outweigh the prospective gain.[7]

According to Kaufmann, the Soviets would doubt that the United States would stake its own survival to keep South Korea or Indochina out of the communist bloc. Massive Retaliation was a credible deterrent only against actions posing a "clear and present danger to our society," which were difficult to categorize. The amplifying statement that such a danger threatened when "the United States has no real alternative than all-out war or ultimate surrender"[8] did not help much. How the enemy was to know what was forbidden was unclear, and Kaufmann opposed public, official definitions of vital interests. He described contingencies worthy of the threat of Massive Retaliation as the most "dangerous." The word can refer either to a highly probable, harmful event or to a highly improbable, disastrous one. Kaufmann obviously meant the latter—the worst possible, but highly unlikely attack. In short, Massive Retaliation deterred only highly improbable actions.

According to Kaufmann, deterrence needed proof of ability and willingness to intervene with strong conventional forces in the peripheral areas where communist aggressions were likely. Rating the Korean War a success, Kaufmann ascribed South Korea's independence and the end of the war to the communists' large losses.[9] However, Kaufmann destroyed his central argument by admitting that communist leaders—specifically those of the Vietminh—were not necessarily Soviet agents.[10] He no longer could justify U.S. intervention in nationalist revolutions or wars that had strong local roots.

Kaufmann's strategy, which required conventional forces for Third World interventions, had no place for Massive Retaliation. The arsenal was to threaten only limited nuclear retaliation. But when? This was the crux of the problem. When would the United States undertake a limited nuclear attack? Kaufmann refused to define the appropriate contingencies. He preferred that the Soviets remain uncertain. In the real world as in game situations, it is sometimes better strategy to leave the enemy uncertain, as Acheson was unhappy to learn after he announced that the United States would not defend South Korea. But it may be impossible to show determination to unleash nuclear retaliation without setting limits to aggression. Be that as it may, the best way to impress the potential enemy was to build a massive arsenal. However, to deter Soviet aggression in the Third World the United States also needed a clear policy toward revolutions in different parts of the world, which it did not have. Kaufmann's evasion of the definition of vital interests did not help.

Another influential theorist was Wohlstetter, who, Kissinger ventured to say, carried more weight with McNamara than any other strategist. In 1965 Kissinger's preface to Wohlstetter's article, "The Delicate Balance of Terror,"[11] praised the author for providing "the intellectual impetus for the recasting of American military strategy in the 1960's."[12] Wohlstetter first published the article in 1959 to challenge Eisenhower's assurances that rough parity would preserve national security. According to Wohlstetter, parity did not protect the United States against the enemy's future behavior. To quote Wohlstetter,

The most important conclusion is that we must expect a vast increase in the weight of attack which the Soviets can deliver with little warning, and the growth of a significant Russian capability for an essentially warning-less attack. As a result, strategic deterrence, while feasible, will be extremely difficult to achieve, and at critical junctures in the 1960s, we may not have the power to deter attack.[13]

Wohlstetter also warned that the Soviets might construct many hardened shelters, which were invulnerable to an attack by the low-payload and low-accuracy Polaris and Minuteman. Deterrence required the capability of destroying no less than half the population of many cities. Wohlstetter evidently feared that a smaller capability entailed a high AR. Assuming an average inaccuracy of two miles, he estimated that the SAC would need five half-megaton weapons to destroy half the unsheltered population of a city of 900,000 spread over 40 square miles. If the Soviets built shelters that could resist an overpressure of 100 pounds per square inch, 60 weapons would be needed, and deep-rock shelters would raise the number of weapons needed to 1,000,[14] making deterrence much more difficult. But Wohlstetter was speculating about the "possible"; he did not assess the likelihood of Moscow sheltering a large fraction of the population. Nor did he support the estimate of the destructive capability required for deterrence.

To shake the prevalent complacency, Wohlstetter listed two possible eventualities leading to a Soviet attack, again without saying anything about their likelihood. We can immediately dismiss one possibility: that the Soviets believed that they were taking preemptive action. Adding to our own arsenal increases the PR. The failure to distinguish between the two kinds of risk led him to recommend a policy that would raise the risk, not lower it.

The other possibility was so unlikely that it would hardly be worth mentioning were it not for the prominence of the author and the frequency with which it is given as a justification for a powerful counterforce capability. Wohlstetter contemplated that after a defeat in a peripheral area or a revolt in a satellite that threatened to spread to the homeland, the Soviet leaders might undertake an attack on the United States because it was the least risky option. According to Wohlstetter, the Soviets might go so far as to risk a nuclear war because they expected to recover, as they did after suffering more than 20 million casualties in World War II. Granted, a revolt in a satellite was not improbable, but the probability of such a revolt spreading to the Soviet Union was much smaller, and the probability that the Soviet Union then would attack the United States was smaller still. The scenario originated from the one depicting a ruler, threatened by revolt, trying to rally support by attacking another country. Some conventional wars allegedly began this way. But to risk nuclear destruction in order to block a revolt would be a poor exchange—the Politburo would have to be mad even to consider it. It goes without saying that a policy of deterrence against even improbable attacks is wise if it does not incur high costs. However, the policy is foolish if the price is a high PR.

Wohlstetter did not recognize the problem because he did not distinguish between the PR and the AR. For him, the only risk was the AR. Accordingly, credibility, willingness to retaliate, minimizing suffering in a war, and ability to inflict punishment were the desiderata for a good policy.

Economist Thomas Schelling was the one to provide a guide to fighting a nuclear war. He assumed that the goals would be to deter city attacks and a quick end to the war.[15] The basic ideas came from John von Neumann and Oskar Morgenstern's game theory, which sought to explain oligopolistic behavior. Economists had had difficulty predicting firms' competitive actions and responses in such oligopolistic markets as cigarettes, aluminum, tires, and light bulbs. Although the firms may dread a price war, they may be tempted to cut prices by the prospect of a complete monopoly. Game theory analyzed the behavior of firms before and during a price war. Schelling suggested that useful analogies could be drawn for nuclear war strategy. Game theory predicted that a risk-averse seller would refrain from large cuts in prices. By analogy, a nation would not unleash a full-blown nuclear attack. But to induce the enemy to surrender, the United States had to threaten great damage. To avoid surrendering itself or the destruction of its cities, the United States had to convincingly threaten the Soviets with the destruction of their cities. The analysis of market rivalry was suggestive. One way to signal readiness for all-out warfare is for a firm to retaliate against a small price cut by cutting even more. To signal restraint, a firm would limit its retaliation to actions inflicting only small damage on its rivals, such as increases in advertising expenditures, the introduction of new products, and small price cuts. An oligopolist's arsenal consists of cash. Analogously, the president might signal readiness for all-out war by retaliating against a conventional attack with a nuclear strike at a silo in a populated region. By contrast, he might signal restraint by destroying an isolated military installation. In this kind of bargaining, unleashing only TNW against military targets would be a restrained move, while striking a city would be severe escalation. The arsenal consists of nuclear weapons. Cautiously, Schelling avoided prescribing any specific strategy, in contrast to Herman Kahn, who later recommended a strategy of escalation. In any case, the analysis of strategy taught that a superior number of missiles gives a side more bargaining power by enabling it to expend missiles more freely. Other assets included invulnerability and greater accuracy. To win, a national leader required the ability to raise the stakes, whether or not he did.

In Schelling's game, both sides sought to "win," which was to say to secure certain political objectives. But political goals meriting a nuclear war were hard to imagine, and the strategists therefore evaded this critical issue. However, without political objectives, how was a government to decide when it had "won"? More important, it was difficult to decide when to use nuclear weapons. Kennedy offered a solution when he said that a series of small defeats would lead to the collapse of Western civilization. Since Western civilization was at stake, a risk of nuclear war was warranted in each conflict. He also equated the prevention of war with deterrence, which needed a strategy for war, that is, for its own failure. For this purpose, "winning" signified only denying victory to the enemy. Again, in any conflict some risk should be accepted to minimize the total risk over the indefinite future. But this approach did not warrant a high risk in any particular conflict. We needed a definition of victory. The United States might not be better off after a nuclear war that destroyed half rather than three-quarters of the cities. Schelling's contribution to this problem was negligible. Although he postulated the goals of a quick end to war and of minimizing damage, they did not affect the proposed counterforce strategy. The only goal was "winning," which meant the enemy's surrender.

The immediate practical advice was to develop an enormous counterforce capability. Since the object was to induce surrender, the nuclear threat needed credibility, which required the capability of destroying the enemy's counterforce capability and having some missiles to spare.

Game theory was not of much value. Applied to nuclear war, the theory defied common sense. The assumptions about communications, assets, goals, damage, and escalation were reasonable for oligopolists, and the theory might accurately describe bargaining by firms. But for nuclear war, equivalent goals were lacking. Missiles were not the equivalent of cash, communication between the two sides might be impossible, and perhaps no more than a single major nuclear exchange was physically possible.

The Policy

Without acknowledging it, Kennedy and McNamara adopted the damage limitation strategy, which superficially resembled the counterforce strategy. In public statements they gave the impression of having adopted the counterforce strategy by listing its characteristics and advantages. Thus, McNamara described the nuclear exchanges, envisioned by the counterforce strategy, as a form of bargaining.[16] He also argued that the counterforce strategy was superior to the strategy of assured destruction because it would result in fewer deaths. In May 1962 in Athens McNamara told the NATO ministers that Soviet attacks on targets limited to military forces and facilities would kill only 25 million in the United States and somewhat fewer in Western Europe, in contrast to attacks on urban centers, which would kill 75 million in the United States and 115 million in Western Europe.[17] He also said that to assure credibility the strategy needed a superior nuclear force. McNamara urged NATO to undertake the responsibility for destroying some Soviet targets;[18] the SAC would look after the others. Above all, he urged a strategy of limited warfare, which was how he characterized the U.S. strategy: "We in the U.S. are prepared to accept our share of the responsibility. And we believe that the combination of our nuclear superiority and a strategy of controlled response gives us some hope of minimizing damage in the event that we have to fulfill our pledge."[19]

Significantly, McNamara suggested that slaughter could be limited by a preemptive attack. But since a few surviving Soviet missiles could kill millions, reducing slaughter demanded enormous superiority. For this reason, marginal superiority would not ensure credibility. Without enormous superiority the United States would not retaliate against conventional aggression. To destroy the Soviet retaliatory capability in this period of inaccurate, single-warhead missiles when three or four were needed to strike a single missile required an arsenal that was several times as large as the potential enemy's. Indeed, deterrence required that we have sufficient superiority to retain some missiles with which to threaten Soviet cities after a Soviet attack and our counterforce retaliation. The Soviets knew that we would not retaliate with nuclear weapons against a conventional attack unless we could wipe out their retaliatory force and still retain some missiles. Repeating this argument before a congressional committee, McNamara emphasized the need for sufficient superiority to ensure such a surviving force.[20]

We have other evidence that McNamara adopted the damage limitation strategy. According to Nixon's defense secretary, James Schlesinger, McNamara had planned large missile salvos, not the varied menu appropriate for bargaining. Apart from demonstration shots, the SIOPs included only massive attacks. We also have the testimony of McNamara's strategist, Henry Rowen, who said that the strategy called for large attacks, and further, that the purpose was to limit damage.[21] McNamara had in mind a large preemptive attack. The attacks were intended to destroy silos, not to induce the Soviets to target our silos rather than our cities. In addition, we have Sorensen's report of Kennedy and McNamara's early budget review sessions. McNamara agreed that the planned 1,000-Minuteman force was more than enough for deterrence. Sorensen's report states:

In our budget review sessions, McNamara in effect acknowledged that he was agreeing to a nuclear force above the level of pure deterrence, but that the additions could be justified as forces to limit the Soviet's ability to do further damage should deterrence fail. He and Kennedy agreed, however, that to go further and seek a 'first-strike' capability—designed theoretically to render the enemy incapable of damaging us severely—the kind of capability advocated in some Air Force quarters—was not only unnecessarily expensive and provocative but not really feasible.

Sorensen continued as follows:

But these same calculations of deterrence also enabled Kennedy and McNamara to see clearly the folly of unlimited disarmament, and the irrelevance of complaints that we already had enough to 'overkill' every Soviet citizen several times. Because our safety as a second-strike nation required a great enough force to survive a first strike and still retaliate effectively, and because our strategy required enough weapons to destroy all important enemy targets, there was no absolute level of sufficiency. The concept of deterrence, moreover, required not only superior forces but a degree of superiority that would, when made known—and the Kennedy administration took unprecedented steps to make it known—convince all Allies and adversaries of that fact.[22]

Thus, Sorensen reported that the goal was damage limitation and that Kennedy and McNamara planned to acquire the very large number of weapons needed to destroy all important enemy targets after suffering a strike.

Kennedy and McNamara were curiously indifferent to the Soviets' reactions. According to one Soviet strategist, "A strategy which contemplates attaining victory through the destruction of the armed forces cannot stem from the idea of a 'retaliatory' blow; it stems from preventive action and the achievement of surprise."[23]

THE BERLIN CRISIS

Despite the large arsenal and the talk about national resolve, in the midst of the crisis the policymakers woke up to the great danger and refused to risk nuclear retaliation. The policymakers were not prepared to carry out the threat, thus devaluing the defense policy. Curiously, Nitze was the most outspoken opponent of undertaking an attack. Nevertheless, the administration's game of Chicken did risk nuclear war. The Soviets might have refused to back down, especially since Eisenhower had conceded their demands in 1958.

Further, the crisis demonstrated a high PR, not a high AR. Those policymakers who worried about the AR feared that the Soviets were testing the United States' willingness to risk nuclear war to save Western Europe; this was an episode in the grand struggle for the control of Western Europe. In fact, however, the Soviets were only seeking to prevent a mass exodus from East Germany (the GDR). Nevertheless, this was a game of Chicken, and the PR was high.

On entering office, Kennedy decided to confront the Soviet challenge on Berlin. The Soviets still insisted on a demilitarized, "free" city, with access controlled by the GDR and on a share in the control of West Berlin.[24] In March Kennedy sent Averell Harriman to Moscow with the message that he was withdrawing Eisenhower's concessions.[25] In June Kennedy told Khrushchev in Vienna that he would turn U.S. commitments to worthless scraps of paper by backing down.

Again leading the hawks, Acheson said that Western Europe was at stake, not mere legalities; small changes in Truman's hard won Berlin arrangements would signal surrender. To prevent the Soviets from eventually gaining dominance, Kennedy had to ensure that West Germany would remain in NATO and that Germany again would become unified, with the right to enter alliances and to organize an army. According to Acheson, to justify risking a war, to say nothing of a nuclear war, Kennedy had to inflate the immediate, nominal issues. An effective nuclear threat needed a big issue. Treating a change in the Berlin arrangements as minor would encourage the communists to disregard the threat and thus win.[26] To justify taking the risk of nuclear war over an intrinsically minor issue, he pressed for publicly representing the conflict as part of the basic struggle.

Acheson urged the administration to become more aggressive, not merely to resist a takeover of West Berlin. If they risked nothing, the Soviets would continue to make demands and would eventually defeat the West. To minimize the threat, the West had to challenge Soviet control of Eastern Europe. Berlin was an episode in the struggle.[27] Acheson urged Kennedy to terminate negotiations and to test Soviet will by sending a combat unit through East Germany to West Berlin. If the Soviets blocked the unit, then let there be war. We had to risk war to convince Khrushchev of our resolve to fight a nuclear war.[28]

The doves viewed the crisis quite differently. The freedom and prosperity of West Berlin in the heart of East Germany threatened Soviet control of that region. Thousands of professionals and skilled tradesmen were escaping East Germany through West Berlin, causing enormous economic damage. By the summer of 1961, about 3.5 million East Germans had fled, and in August the daily flow rose from hundreds to thousands.[29] To prevent war the doves urged minor concessions, which did not impede access to West Berlin.

This analysis was accurate, but Kennedy was determined to demonstrate resolve. As he saw it, the main problem was to avoid encouraging later Soviet aggression and to preserve the credibility of the nuclear deterrent in minor conflicts. This demanded some risk. In addition, Kennedy felt that Khrushchev thought him a coward for denying air support to the Bay of Pigs force.[30] Kennedy reinforced the message of resolve with his *"Ich bin ein Berliner"* address. Hearing that the Soviet ambassador doubted U.S. determination, Kennedy repeated his pledge. This was not mere bravado for, according to Sorensen, Kennedy foresaw having to choose between holocaust and humiliation.[31]

The incredibility of the threat of vast destruction, which entailed the willingness to risk nuclear retaliation, encouraged the administration to take greater risks than it would have done were only conventional weapons available. Paradoxically, the destructiveness of nuclear weapons invited a high PR. Only recklessness could make the nuclear threat credible. We needed a high PR to persuade the Soviets of our national resolve, especially when the stakes were small. Otherwise the problem would recur again and again in future conflicts over similarly minor issues. The Soviets would take advantage of any small issues to press their imperialist drive after they saw us retreat in the Berlin crisis. Interpreting a surrender as a sign of weakness, the expansionist Soviets would be encouraged to provoke and to be bold in future, similarly minor conflicts. Unless we were willing to risk nuclear war over the GDR's control of access to West Berlin, thereby warning the Soviet Union of our acceptance of a high risk, we would repeatedly have to go through the same agony. We had to accept a high PR as long as we depended on vastly destructive weapons and faced an aggressive and expansionist power. This was Kennedy's reasoning in the crisis.

This was why he chose a high PR. The strategy called for the response to the expected Soviet blockade to take the form of a probe by U.S. troops.[32] The intention was to warn the Soviets that turning back the allied divisions risked nuclear retaliation. Aware of the U.S. conventional weakness, the Soviets would know that the probes signaled a nuclear strike. Modest additions of troops were intended to impress the Soviets with our resolve. Eisenhower, it will be recalled, had rejected even sending a single division, since he saw it as provocative.

As in any game of Chicken, what the other side would infer was not easily forecast, and risks could not be avoided. Because the Soviets might mistake the operation as a bluff, Acheson recommended the more urgent measures of a declaration of a national emergency, calling up one million reserves, and extending terms of service.[33] Simply sending more troops without these more warlike measures might signal restraint—the U.S. intention not to use nuclear weapons.[34] However, Kennedy was unwilling to raise the PR much more. Afraid of forcing a dangerous response out of fear of humiliation, Kennedy only asked Congress for $3.25 billion to pay for a quiet, gradual defense buildup and for the rapid deployment of additional forces along the central front. Draft calls were tripled, some reserves were called, and the procurement of conventional weapons was increased.[35] Kennedy also gave a national address describing West Berlin as the "testing place of Western courage and will."[36] These were only gestures; they gave no indication of a strong resolve to risk a nuclear attack.

In fact, the administration was not ready to take the awesome risk. Some members of the administration resisted the adoption of a plan for a nuclear attack. In August Kennedy asked Carl Kaysen (McGeorge Bundy's assistant), General Maxwell Taylor, and Rowen to prepare such a plan.[37] The detailed study planned the bombers' altitudes and flight tactics, specified a list of targets; and it estimated the number of bombers and bombs needed, how much of the Soviet forces would survive, and how many Americans they could kill. At about the same time the administration received the National Intelligence Estimate, according to which the Soviets had no more than four ICBMs in place; a first strike appeared to be possible.[38] If the United States was not prepared to order a nuclear strike under these conditions, the effectiveness of the deterrent was doubtful. Nevertheless, Nitze, horrified, persuaded the administration that inaccurate and unreliable bombs could not guarantee a first strike. Surviving Soviet ICBMs and bombers plus a few SLBMs at sea would kill between 2 million and 15 million Americans, and the intermediate-range ballistic missiles (IRBMs) could kill tens of millions of Europeans.[39] When the chips were down, Nitze advised not exercising the threat, despite the damage to the deterrent. If the U.S. divisions were destroyed, and the United States had not launched its strategic weapons, the arsenal would have lost its ability to deter.

Nitze even opposed Schelling's suggestion to fire demonstration shots. At a war game at Camp David, Schelling proposed to target an isolated Soviet area. This was in line with his book, which had suggested that a demonstration shot was the least risky way of impressing the enemy with one's superior resolve. But even this risk was excessive, according to Nitze, who objected that the Soviets could follow suit. We might fire three, they could respond with six, and, sooner or later, one side would shoot to kill. Bundy also objected on the ground that in the early phase of the missile's trajectory Soviet leaders would not know the target.[40]

The same fear blocked another plan. Laying out the allied war strategy, Nitze, Rowen, Kaufmann, Seymour Weiss, and some Western European representatives set out the following scenario. After an initial phase, conventionally armed aircraft strike non-Soviet Eastern European airfields, three allied divisions invade East Germany, and then ten or 15 Warsaw Pact divisions destroy the allied divisions. Since Washington was not ready to carry out the declared policy of nuclear retaliation, the question of what would follow was left unanswered.

Apparently the Soviet retaliatory capability, small though it was, canceled the deterrent of a conventional response to a conventional invasion of East Germany by U.S. forces. But the planners were indecisive because the policy of deterrence did not fit the occasion. A war would have come as a result of a sequence of moves in a game of Chicken, not because of a deliberate Soviet attack that was part of a plan to conquer Western Europe. The Soviets might have harassed U.S. citizens traveling to Berlin, and the president might have blocked the construction of the wall. Despite the absence of any decision to go ahead with nuclear retaliation, the probability was high that the United States would have retaliated to the destruction of its divisions with a nuclear attack. The tensions resulting from such a defeat might have precipitated an attack. As long as we relied chiefly on the nuclear threat to back up a president's negotiations in a conflict, the risk was high. The policy was designed to deter only a deliberate attack intended to achieve a major political goal. In this case, a Soviet move intended to prevent migration from East Germany would have triggered conventional moves leading up to a nuclear war. The policy of deterrence would not have prevented a nuclear war; it would have been a cause, since it depended on nuclear weapons.

The history of the crisis reveals that we ran a considerable risk of nuclear war. The risk was high because in this situation the PR was high. The PR remained high regardless of whether or not any explicit decision was made in advance to resort to a nuclear attack in the event the enemy refused to concede.

Fortunately, the Soviets backed down by building the Berlin wall. Since the wall violated the guarantees of free movement within Berlin, Kennedy's victory was no more than nominal. In a curious reversal, Eisenhower said that since the four powers had guaranteed communication between the different parts of the city, "we had the absolute right to use whatever force we needed to eliminate walls."[41] By enhancing the problem of resolve, nuclear weapons exacerbated the crisis, especially since firmness was important for permanent rivals.

One other thing should be said. As most studies now agree, Moscow instigated the crisis to block the escape of East Germans, not, as the administration alleged, to further its imperialist drive westward. Nevertheless, the crisis might have resulted in a war and the Soviet occupation of West Germany. The Soviet Union might have defeated NATO, thereby expanding the territory under its control. A war to block Soviet expansionism might have had a disastrous effect. Later historians probably would have pointed to the resulting growth of Soviet controlled territory as further evidence of Soviet imperialism.

THE CUBAN MISSILE CRISIS

The substantive issue again was minor in the more dangerous Cuban missile crisis of October 1962. The danger arose, as before, out of the nature of the weapons and the related problem of resolve.

According to Sorensen's curiously frank report, Kennedy and the Executive Committee of the National Security Council (NSC), or ExCom, rejected the obvious theory that the Soviets sought military gains by attempting to place 42 IRBMs in Cuba. As before, Kennedy saw only a test of his resolve,[42] and he believed that to minimize the risk of nuclear war in the future we had to take some immediate risk. This reasoning was correct only if powerful expansionist ambitions drove Moscow to risky actions. Otherwise, the great risk came only from the game of Chicken and the effort to gain credibility.

The ExCom's theory 1 said that Khruschev was testing U.S. resolve. The IRBMs would yield no more military advantage than the deployment of SLBMs. The loss from backing down would damage the image of strong national resolve. The deterrent would lose its power, and the Soviets would take over West Berlin. The AR was high, so an apparently cautious policy really was risky. The Soviets had opened an episode in the game of Chicken, and to deter future Soviet aggressions involving more vital U.S. interests, the United States had to show resolve. Accepting the immediate PR reduced the future AR.

Theory 2 saw the Soviet venture as part of the complicated, continuing chess game over West Berlin. This theory got immediate support from Gromyko's appearance at the White House. While the ExCom was in session, Kennedy spent two hours discussing the Berlin issues with the Soviet foreign minister.[43] According to the theory, the Soviets wanted control of West Berlin badly enough to risk war. The negligible military advantage of missiles in Cuba did not merit the risk. Theory 3 simply and straightforwardly stressed the defense of Cuba. Theory 4, like theory 2, saw that Khrushchev still hoped to win the prize of West Berlin, and he wanted to trade the missile base for the withdrawal of U.S. overseas bases. Only theory 5 saw a military gain as the chief motive. Not only did IRBMs in Cuba cost less than ICBMs or SLBMs, but since they bypassed the north-facing warning system, Cuban missiles could strike U.S. bombers without any warning.

Kennedy, of course, was most attracted by theory 1, the Chicken theory.[44] Theories 2 and 4 deserved no more than mention. Cuba was not worth the risk nor was the strategic gain postulated by theory five. The discussion of the Jupiter missiles in Turkey also demonstrated Kennedy's attachment to the Chicken-game theory. Adlai Stevenson, who attended some of the sessions, urged Kennedy to retire these obsolete missiles in exchange for the removal of the Cuban missiles. Earlier, the president, McNamara, and Robert Kennedy had said that such a trade might be necessary, and McNamara had suggested that the United States might also have to offer to withdraw its missiles from Italy and even to abandon the base at Guantanamo. But, insistent on showing resolve, Kennedy refused to make such official concessions. Any concession would have to be made informally and secretly. According to Undersecretary of State George Ball, "In the end the President did obliquely promise Khrushchev that the Turkish Jupiters would be withdrawn, though only on condition that such a withdrawal would not appear as a part of the Cuban missile settlement."[45]

Apparently Nitze was the only member of the ExCom to judge the military motive to be important. Nitze said that the missiles would expose many U.S. strategic bombers to sudden attack, and the warning time for those based in the southeastern states would be cut from 15 minutes to two or three minutes.[46]

The two alternative courses of action were a naval blockade of military shipments and a surprise bombing attack on the missile installations, possibly followed by an invasion.[47] Acheson supported the high-risk latter choice, first, to enforce the Monroe Doctrine; second, because Kennedy had warned the Soviets against placing offensive weapons in Cuba; and, third, because Congress had authorized force to prevent a foreign military base in Cuba.[48] CIA Director John McCone, Treasury Secretary Douglas Dillon, JCS Chairman General Taylor, Assistant Secretary of Defense Paul Nitze, and McGeorge Bundy lined up with Acheson, while McNamara, Deputy Secretary of Defense Roswell Gilpatric, Robert Kennedy, Soviet expert Llewellyn Thompson, and Robert Lovett supported the less risky option.[49]

Nitze's theory of the Soviet motive probably was correct. The United States had deployed 28 ICBMs, many IRBMs in Turkey and in Western Europe, and 125 SLBMs. Including bombs carried by aircraft, the U.S. arsenal contained a total of 4,800 offensive warheads.[50] In the fall of 1961 the Soviets had only four ICBMs,[51] and their SLBM technology lagged far behind. Forty-two IRBMs in Cuba would have added an enormous strategic capability. Kennedy was so afraid he would have to order a nuclear attack that the issue of resolve blinded him to the obvious motive, and most of the advisers were similarly mistaken.

The nuclear arsenal itself was the source of the danger. The administration insisted on showing its determination to launch the weapons in future conflicts over minor issues. It feared that after a few victories the communists would dominate the world. Together, the bogey and the nuclear defense induced the Americans to take risks. On the other side, the arms race encouraged Moscow to take risks. The Soviets risked war to secure an effective deterrent—to provide themselves with the equivalent of an ICBM force.

In retrospect, some Americans ascribed the victory to superior conventional power in the Caribbean, not to the nuclear threat. But if the Soviets had had the more powerful arsenal, no amount of conventional power would have prevailed. The ExCom could rely only on conventional power because of the United States' overwhelming nuclear strength.

Both the Berlin and the Cuban crises demonstrated that it was the PR that we had to fear, not the AR. In neither crisis was the Kremlin attempting to expand the territory under its control. The Berlin crisis came because the Soviets wanted to block emigration from East Germany, and the United States interpreted the Soviet ultimatum to be a test of its national resolve. The United States risked nuclear war to deter the conquest of Western Europe. Nor did imperial ambitions prompt the Soviets to risk war by attempting to deploy missiles in Cuba. The attempt was merely an effort to gain the capability of matching the U.S. threat against the Soviet Union. Neither the Berlin nor the Cuban crisis demonstrated a high risk of a deliberate Soviet attack for imperial ends. The AR was low. On the other hand, the PR was high.

THE DEFENSE BUDGET AND THE NUCLEAR ARMS BUILDUP

Flexible Response's call for more conventional forces turned out to be only talk. Kennedy was no more eager to spend more for defense than was Eisenhower; and like his predecessor, Kennedy built up the nuclear arsenal. Eisenhower reluctantly accepted the nuclear defense policy for economic reasons. By contrast, Kennedy was persuaded by the strategists' case. However, while he agreed to expanding the conventional forces, in accord with the policy of Flexible Response, Kennedy allowed their strength to decline to less than their level under Eisenhower. Without saying so, Kennedy favored lower taxes and higher spending for social programs. Defense was a poor third. Unfortunately, the result was a massive nuclear arms buildup.

At the outset, when McNamara reported inadequacies in the number of combat-ready divisions, airlift capacity, and the ability to supply tactical air support,[52] Kennedy instructed him to disregard arbitrary financial limits in setting force goals. Later, the experience of the Berlin crisis reinforced the case for rebuilding the conventional forces. Showing support for a conventional defense policy, Kennedy appointed General Taylor, the advocate of Flexible Response, to be his military adviser and liaison with the JCS; later he appointed him chairman.

Increasing defense spending was consistent with the now reigning Keynesian economics. Faced by 6.7 percent unemployment and only a 1 percent rate of inflation, even fiscal conservatives did not insist on budgetary restraint. Kennedy pressed for additional expenditures for housing and slum clearance, highway and building construction, as well as for tax cuts.[53]

However, over the period 1961-65 the administration did not build up the conventional forces. The increase in military strength of 324,000, prompted by the Berlin crisis, was not maintained. Over the entire period, 1960 to 1965, total active military strength grew from 2,476,000 to 2,655,000, or only 7 percent. In 1965 total strength still was below the 1957 level. Although Kennedy had called for a stronger small-war capability, the U.S. Marine Corps grew from 171,000 to only 190,000. Moreover, the draft calls and the activation of some reserve units raised the forces in Europe from 379,000 to only 417,000 between 1960 and 1961, and there was no further increase in 1962.[54] The immediate threat ended, these forces came down to 363,000 in 1965, or below the low point under Eisenhower. Thus, the administration did virtually nothing to strengthen the conventional forces, for all its talk.

When he entered office, Kennedy knew that the Soviets had virtually no strategic arsenal, but he did not want to admit his campaign alarmism. Only in the fall of 1961 did Deputy Defense Secretary Roswell Gilpatric announce that the U.S. forces were vastly superior, so much so that those surviving a surprise attack would be superior to the *initial* Soviet forces; the U.S. second-strike capability exceeded the Soviet first-strike capability.[55] In December 1961 McNamara said that the Soviets had no more than 100 ICBMs,[56] but this upper-limit estimate gave a false impression, for, as already noted, the National Intelligence Estimate during the Berlin crisis was only four Soviet ICBMs. By July 1964 the United States had 834 ICBMs and 416 SLBMs, compared to the Soviets' 190 ICBMs and 107 SLBMs.[57] Table 4.1 reports the growth of the arsenal between 1961 and 1968. Kennedy ordered a vast buildup of the nuclear arsenal.

Low taxes and domestic programs came ahead of conventional forces. In this respect, nothing had changed since Eisenhower. The talk about deficits and recovery implied such growth in government expenditures that their share of the GNP would grow. But public spending grew more slowly than the GNP, and its share fell from 19.2 percent to 18.0 percent of the GNP. Unfortunately, the pressure for tax cuts reduced defense expenditures, as it had under Eisenhower. The tax cuts now were justified by Keynesian employment theory, not by attacks on government waste, but the effect was the same. More was spent on nuclear weapons and less on conventional defense. The resulting savings were passed on in tax cuts. Constant-dollar defense expenditures fell by 5.7 percent, and the defense share of GNP fell from 9.1 percent to 7.2 percent between fiscal 1961 and fiscal 1965. Kennedy turned out to be even more frugal than Eisenhower.

The nuclear weapons permitted the decline in defense expenditures, since after the buildup the arsenal required only small operating expenditures. Unlike under Eisenhower, the savings were not the

Table 4.1
U.S. Nuclear Missiles, Strategic Bomber Squadrons, and Total Offensive Nuclear Warheads, 1961, 1965, 1968

	1961	1965	1968
Missiles			
ICBMs	28	854	1,054
SLBMs	80	464	654
Strategic bomber squadrons	125	88	40
Total offensive warheads	4,800	6,230	4,500

Sources: 1961: *Setting National Priorities* (Washington, D.C.: Brookings Institution, 1974), p. 294. 1965 and 1968: Henry Owen and Charles Schultze, eds., *Setting National Priorities: Next Ten Years, 1976* (Washington, D.C.: Brookings Institution), pp. 86-7.

reason for the policy, only the result. The apparent motive was to stop Soviet aggression. In the first days of the administration, at McNamara's request, Hitch, Enthoven, and Martin Stern drafted a paper advocating an arsenal large enough to provide a reserve for threatening cities after having destroyed the enemy's military forces. In addition, JCS Chairman General Lyman Lemnitzer argued that the theory that called for withholding missiles after having been attacked required very large forces.[58] Kennedy and McNamara agreed, and so the damage limitation strategy was implemented. The first Defense Message provided for doubling the production of the Minuteman missiles and for increasing the rate of construction of the Polaris submarines by 50 percent.[59] The defense program also provided for increasing the number of TNW in Europe by 60 percent.[60] Again in the opposition, General Taylor reminded Kennedy of the great destructive power of the TNW.[61]

In February 1962, to justify the new strategy, McNamara said that nuclear weapons were for bargaining in a war. The United States would seek to prevail by threatening future attacks.[62] The following June McNamara announced, first, that the administration assumed that a Soviet attack on a member of NATO would open the next general war. Second, the administration was seeking to induce the Soviets to refrain from striking U.S. cities. Third, for this purpose, the United States would confine its attacks to military targets. Fourth, the U.S. nuclear force had to be large enough to carry out this strategy even after a massive surprise attack.[63] The statement conformed to the counterforce strategy; nothing was said of damage limitation. However, as we have seen, it was only the declaratory policy. The actual policy envisaged the quick destruction of all or most Soviet missile silos.

The administration was divided. Carl Kaysen said that although the U-2 evidence revealed a small Soviet arsenal and slow growth, McNamara had adopted the air force goal of an unlimited missile force.[64] Agreeing with Kaysen, Taylor said that the diversion of expenditures from conventional forces to the nuclear arsenal increased the risk of nuclear war.[65]

A limit to the arsenal was difficult to set. McNamara was stymied by Senator Mahon's request for an estimate of the number of land-based missiles necessary for a second-strike capability.[66] The problem was that the required number rose with the Soviet arsenal, which itself would grow in response to the U.S. arsenal's expansion. Only a vulnerable ICBM force would supply the *counterforce* capability, prescribed by the damage limitation strategy, and to ensure a second-strike capability this force had to be far superior to the enemy's. However, the Soviets, who were forced by a primitive SLBM technology to rely on ICBMs, might interpret such overwhelming superiority as constituting an intolerable first-strike capability. Nevertheless, the administration acted on the premise that the Soviets would accept vulnerability to a first strike.

Sensitive to the criticism concerning the required size of the arsenal, McNamara announced the new policy of assured destruction, but, in fact, the policy did not change. The declaratory goal now was the capability of inflicting unacceptable damage, which was defined as the destruction of 20 to 25 percent of the population plus 50 percent of the industrial capacity. Although "unacceptable" suggests that the department had sought to assess the maximum devastation the Politburo would tolerate, this was not the basis of the estimate. Moreover, it was absurd to believe that the Politburo was so eager to gain territory as to accept the slaughter of up to 20 percent of the population and the risk of much more as the fair price of the potential gains from aggression. Not surprisingly, the so-called estimate of unacceptable damage was based on the cost to the United States of inflicting more damage, not on a reading of Soviet intentions. The cost per thousand killed rose rapidly above the defined level because to destroy the less dense nonurban population would require many more bombs.

To apply the policy, the administration built an arsenal of 1,054 ICBMs plus 656 SLBMs, and after 1966 developed accurate, MIRVed missiles. When historians report a shift in policy to assured destruction, they accept official policy statements too readily,[67] disregarding the continued enhancement of the arsenal.

Nothing stopped the buildup, not even new, much lower estimates of the Red army's strength. Since the estimates implied unlikely masses of manpower, Enthoven and K. Wayne Smith suspected that they were wrong. Moreover, Soviet officials were unlikely to find the money for 175 divisions, if U.S. expenditures on a mere 22 divisions were any guide. The new estimate of the Warsaw Pact's strength, which took account of cost, firepower, combat personnel, number of artillery pieces and other equipment, was 619,000, which was approximately equal to NATO's strength of 677,000 in the central region, including five French divisions. NATO had little more than half as many tanks as the Warsaw Pact, but in other respects the allies were stronger.[68]

Despite questions about the new estimate, it shattered the illusion of overwhelming Soviet strength. One objection was that the French troops, who were not integrated with the other members' forces, would not help much in the early fighting. Another was that the Soviet combat troops were better prepared for a short war. On the other hand, the new estimate may have exaggerated the Warsaw Pact's strength by assuming that non-Soviet troops were reliable. In any case, if the Soviets had an advantage, it was small; a conventional defense of Western Europe was not hopeless. Since the chief concern was the risk of a deliberate attack, absolute certainty of a successful defense was not essential to security. Unless the Soviets had high expectations of an easy victory, they would not undertake an attack.

Trying to exculpate Kennedy, Arthur Schlesinger, Jr. found the villain in the air force, which estimated between 600 and 800 Soviet ICBMs. But, as Schlesinger himself reported, Kennedy also had the CIA's estimate of 450 and the navy's of 200. (Even this estimate turned out to be much higher than the four of the National Intelligence Estimate.) To settle the matter, Kennedy spent Thanksgiving weekend with his defense experts at Hyannis Port, where, after much argument, the low estimate won out. Nevertheless, Kennedy went ahead with the massive ICBM buildup. Schlesinger decided that even McNamara was innocent, for he too opposed acquiring a large arsenal. Poor fellow, he had to concede to the air force, with which he was battling over the cancellation of the program to build B-70s, which he judged to be obsolete. Kennedy was not to blame because he found it difficult to overrule McNamara.[69] Thus, if we believe Schlesinger, neither the president nor the secretary of defense was responsible for the huge ICBM arsenal.

However, we have the report of Sorensen—who was Kennedy's closest adviser and actually participated in the Oval Office defense budget sessions—that Kennedy and McNamara not only made the decision, but they did so enthusiastically. Sorensen praised Kennedy for the largest and fastest military buildup in U.S. history, and he presumably was echoing the president's own enthusiasm. Moreover, he reported that this buildup "provided [Kennedy], as he put it, with a versatile arsenal 'ranging from the most massive deterrents to the most subtle influences.' "[70] Sorensen's report (see pp. 77–78) said that Kennedy and McNamara's goal was a damage-limiting capability.

Contrary to any reasonable expectation, Kennedy and McNamara assumed that the Soviets would not make the effort to match the U.S. arsenal that would invalidate the policy's rationale. In 1965 McNamara said that he had believed and continued to believe that the Soviets would acquiesce to their inferiority: "the Soviets have decided that they have lost the quantitative race, and they are not seeking to engage us in this contest. . . . There is no indication that the Soviets are seeking to develop a strategic force as large as ours."[71] This was no casual, off-hand statement, for in 1968, about to resign from the Cabinet, he gave the same description of his attitude in the early sixties in *The Essence of Security*.[72]

The primary goal was a better hard-target capability to carry out the damage limitation strategy. In 1963 in SIOP-63 McNamara approved the strategy and thus a powerful counterforce capability, which had to grow with the Soviet arsenal.[73] In the discussion of a successor to the Minuteman I, McNamara insisted on a missile that carried several accurate and high-yield reentry vehicles (RVs) capable of destroying hardened silos, and that would contribute more to the capability of a preemptive strike than would the large single-warhead missile proposed by SAC.[74]

In December 1964 McNamara reported to President Johnson that a MIRVed missile would be able to strike three geographically separate targets with MK-12 warheads. Also, a new inertial guidance system was being developed that would raise the probability of destroying silos hardened up to 300 psi overpressure to over 90 percent. The next year McNamara informed Johnson of the progress of the Minuteman III, which promised greater accuracy and a heavier payload.[75] In addition, the *New York Times* reported that the more accurate, MIRVed Minuteman III was intended to have the capability of destroying the new, hardened Soviet silos.[76] In 1967 McNamara announced that the successful development of MIRVs made it possible to strike more targets with the same number of missiles.[77] In October 1969 Air Force Chief of Staff John D. Ryan said that the Minuteman III program was designed to achieve a hard-target capability. The following year he reported the new missile's capability of destroying the enemy's time-urgent strategic weapons.[78] "Time-urgent" was a euphemism for "preemptive."

Many members of Congress had become concerned about the risks the strategy entailed. They began to fear that the Minuteman III would raise the PR. According to testimony presented before the House Committee on Foreign Affairs in 1969, the self-contained guidance packages on MIRVs would eventually achieve accuracies of between 50 and 100 feet.[79] In 1970 Herbert F. York, a former director of defense research, reported that "since the ICBM programs were initiated 15 years ago, we have already achieved an improvement in accuracy of tenfold." He warned that accuracy could be improved sufficiently for the United States to be able to destroy "virtually all their silo-based missiles in a surprise attack."[80] The fear was that in response to the new U.S. weapons, the Soviets would raise the PR many times by adopting a launch-on-warning policy.

The damage limitation strategy was not the only reason for the administration's decision to develop the Minuteman III. We have Wohlstetter's word for it that a second reason was the economies that MIRVs would offer. Since satellites had located many new targets, the goal of maximizing the number that could be struck per dollar spent had become more urgent. As Wohlstetter testified, in 1969 the availability of numerous dispersed, vulnerable targets made MIRVs attractive.[81] To cover the thousands of targets listed in the SIOPs with single-warhead missiles would have entailed the cost of many launchers and associated underground facilities.[82] To carry out the damage limitation strategy required the capability of destroying thousands of targets, and the Defense Department was concerned with the costs. Evidently, the declaratory policy of assured destruction was a smoke screen.

Publicly, McNamara emphasized the third purpose—that of penetrating the ABM system then being developed. Surveillance photographs revealed radar sites in Leningrad and Moscow and a surface-to-air missile system near Tallinn in the northwest part of the Soviet Union. The Defense Department said that MIRVs were needed to get through Moscow's ABM system.[83]

But the ABM was only the official excuse. As the Defense Department knew, the Soviets were slowing down the Moscow program and not building a nationwide system.[84] The Defense Department also knew that a good ABM system was difficult, if not impossible, to develop. In 1962, expressing his skepticism, Kennedy had said that the Soviets could not hit a thousand missiles traveling at enormous speeds and accompanied by decoys.[85] The technology had not improved significantly since then. Nevertheless, the administration preferred publicly to discuss the ABMs rather than damage limitation, since assured destruction, which had no use for MIRVs, still was the *declaratory* policy. Only General Ryan, in unguarded statements, admitted the intention of improving the hard-target capability.

The programs were needed to maintain the validity of the damage limitation strategy. As long as the Soviets had only a few, vulnerable ICBMs, the theory had easier sailing. Not that it was ever free of doubts; even overwhelming superiority did not guarantee an effective first strike. McNamara hoped that accuracy and MIRVs would save the damage limitation strategy.

DEFENSE VERSUS OTHER PUBLIC EXPENDITURES
IN WESTERN EUROPE

Social expenditures still growing, the Western European governments continued to resist adding to their burdens by increasing conventional forces. The British, French, West German, and Italian rightwing governments had to move to the left to retain support. In 1964 Labour recaptured the British government, and at the end of the decade the Social Democrats took over in West Germany. The governments welcomed the free nuclear umbrella offered by the United States.

NATO governments' share of total GDP grew rapidly (Table 4.2). In France, for example, it increased from 33.5 percent in 1955-57 to 39.4 percent in 1967-69. The growth in West Germany accelerated under the Social Democrats after 1969. All of the growth in the government share was for nondefense purposes; the share of GDP spent on defense by Western European governments declined. In France it dropped from 5.9 percent to 4.7 percent (Table 4.3). Only West Germany maintained the share spent on defense.

The rise in public expenditures resulted in a sharp rise in the tax burden. In the UK personal income and social security taxes combined rose from 11.5 percent to 16.9 percent of the GDP (Table 4.4). Consumption taxes also rose. In Denmark, which introduced such taxes in this period, receipts amounted to 7.6 percent of GDP in

Table 4.2
Public Expenditures as a Percentage of GDP,
Various NATO Countries, 1955-57, 1967-69, 1974-76

	1955–57	1967–69	1974–76
Belgium	NA	35.6	43.0
Canada	25.1	33.0	39.4
Denmark	25.5	35.5	46.4
France	33.5	39.4	41.6
Germany	30.2	33.1	44.0
Italy	28.1	35.5	43.1
Netherlands	31.1	42.6	53.9
Norway	27.0	37.9	46.6
United Kingdom	32.3	38.5	44.5
United States	25.9	31.7	35.1

NA = not available.
Source: OECD, *Public Expenditure Trends.* June 1978, p. 14.

Table 4.3
Defense Expenditures as a Percentage of GDP,
Various NATO Countries,
1955-57, 1967-69, 1974-76

	1955–57	1967–69	1974–76
Belgium	3.3	3.1	2.6
Canada	5.4	2.5	1.7
Denmark	3.0	2.9	1.6
France	5.9	4.7	3.8
Germany	2.9	3.0	3.1
Italy	2.7	2.4	2.2
Netherlands	5.7	4.3	3.0
Norway	3.7	3.6	3.1
United Kingdom	7.4	6.1	5.0
United States	9.5	8.4	5.8

Source: OECD, *Public Expenditure Trends.* June 1978, p. 14.

Table 4.4
Individual Income Tax Receipts Plus
Social Security Tax Receipts as a
Percentage of GDP, Various NATO Countries,
1960, 1970, 1980

	1960	1970	1980
Belgium	12.5	19.6	27.4
Canada	10.2	13.5	14.7
Denmark	11.5	21.1	24.0
Germany	15.7	18.7	23.8
Italy	14.3	13.5	18.1
Netherlands	16.2	24.6	29.7
Norway	15.1	20.1	23.3
United Kingdom	11.5	16.9	16.7
United States	12.5	16.4	19.4

Source: OECD, *Long-Term Trends in Tax Revenues of OECD Member Countries, 1955-80* (Paris, 1981), p. 14.

1970. To keep the tax burden within tolerable limits, the governments reduced the defense share of GDP. The only exception was Germany, whose defense effort was initiated only in the mid-fifties.

NATO AND NUCLEAR DEFENSE

The West Germans distrusted the U.S. shield, but other Europeans still would not allow them to acquire nuclear weapons. Continuing to insist on the TNW along the East-West border, the West Germans attempted to minimize their fear of PR by reassuring themselves that in a war the superpowers would destroy only each other. Since they foresaw no hope for themselves in an extremely destructive conventional war, they regarded a high risk of such a war as not worth a lower PR. As a consequence, to win West German support, the United States adopted a high-PR strategy. The United States accepted a high PR in return for reducing the AR; it maximized deterrence.

In the bitter debates, the PR–AR tradeoff was central without becoming explicit. TNW advocates argued that a credible deterrent required quick readiness to fire the weapons and a low nuclear threshold. In other words, a high PR in any crisis would reduce the number of crises. The Soviets would not dare threaten the West with troop movements to bring pressure to bear in future conflicts. In the view of the premier hawk, FRG Defense Minister Franz-Josef Strauss, the Soviets were greedy for more territory. Norstad's proposal was unacceptable because in the period of grace, which it permitted, the Soviets could advance without risking nuclear retaliation. Worse, the distinction between 'minor' and 'major' allowed launching attacks below some vaguely defined threshold of violence. Nor did Strauss want stronger conventional forces, which would permit a delay in nuclear retaliation. In short, reductions in the PR raised the already high AR.

Although Strauss welcomed a high risk of superpower strategic exchanges, he said that credible deterrence required the threat of increasing violence in which the firing of TNW came early and represented a low level of violence. The Soviets would not expect a conventional attack to provoke the United States immediately into inviting its own destruction. A sequence of escalating violence leading to a strategic attack was more credible. Moreover, the firing of the TNW would destroy troop concentrations before the attack got under way. Immediate nuclear retaliation was a good defense.[86]

Helmut Schmidt, later the Social Democratic defense minister, opposed Strauss. He advocated more troops to minimize the PR, which was the greater risk.[87] U.S. IRBMs in Britain, Italy, and Turkey not only could strike Moscow in less than 15 minutes, but they were vulnerable. The combination of a first-strike capability and vulnerability was destabilizing.[88] Moreover, endangered combat units could not be trusted to refrain from firing nuclear weapons.[89] Schmidt supported planning nuclear retaliation to deter only a Soviet *nuclear* attack.

Although the idea of a hierarchy of violence, with the TNW inflicting only local damage, was essential to the defense policy, the TNW were as destructive as strategic weapons. Enthoven and Smith pointed out that since nuclear shells did not improve accuracy, artillery units would continue to fire barrages as before. Excluding distant targets and using only low-yield weapons would have little effect.[90] In addition, artillery units in a battle would seek the advantage of first use. Moreover, the Red army had only high-yield missiles; short-range, low-yield strikes at well-defined targets were not possible. Indeed, with their nuclear capability in their own country, the Soviets could not fight a limited, tactical battle. TNW strikes would be indistinguishable from those by strategic bombs.

Schmidt rejected the vague and unsupported cost arguments.[91] As General Gavin had said much earlier, a nuclear defense would entail high casualties, complex logistical support, and the operation of conventional as well as nuclear weapons.[92] In addition, the new estimates of the Warsaw Pact's strength were much lower than earlier ones, and according to T. W. Stanley, a conventional defense was not excessively costly. Stanley judged that 60 divisions, half of which would be in ready reserves, could stop an attack by 90 Warsaw Pact divisions, the equivalent of 60 or 70 U.S. divisions. Acheson's estimate, made about this time, was similar.[93] Stanley estimated NATO's additional annual manpower cost at $1 billion and that it would have to spend between $8 billion and $10 billion on additional equipment. Over five years the additional total costs would come to $15 billion, or $3 billion per year. The cost of "maximum insurance," which, according to Stanley, required 40 active and 40 reserve divisions, would come to between $5 billion and $6 billion annually.[94] Even this higher estimate was not excessive for all of the NATO countries together to carry.

However, social programs still had a higher priority, and the choice between these programs and a nuclear defense policy was not presented directly. Leaders preferred to discuss the effectiveness of conventional deterrence, the likelihood of the superpowers striking only each other, the destruction that conventional war would inflict, and the size of the Soviet army. The cost of a conventional defense would have been small, but the governments judged the current tax burden to be excessive.

THE PREEMPTION RISK

The administration ignored the PR. According to Kennedy, credibility demanded great risks. Moreover, the strategy of attacking nuclear installations and command centers called for a first strike in a crisis. The high PR entailed by this strategy was raised further by continuing advances in warning and intelligence systems. Satellites, ground-based radars, and communication intelligence systems transmitted information to processing centers, which sent it on to political and military command centers.[95] The information helped to protect bomber units, IRBMs stationed in Western Europe and in Turkey, and command units. Normally, such systems reduced the PR because unconfirmed signals of an attack were more likely to be dismissed. Under a high alert, however, false signals became more dangerous, particularly after the hostile command centers could read each other's messages. A burst of radio messages between Soviet command centers and missile bases would set off an alarm within the U.S. warning system. Under a high alert, the two systems' interactions could set off an attack.

In the 1950s the United States developed the Semi-Automatic Ground Environment (SAGE) system to supply bomber and missile crews with radar warning information,[96] and it expanded the radio monitoring capability. Posts on the Black Sea; at Samsun, Turkey; and in the Elburz Mountains of Iran listened for signals of movements of forces;[97] and U-2 flights, which also were intended to detect signs of an impending attack, began a little later. The SAC planned a swift preemptive strike at Soviet bombers after a warning had been received but before they had taken off.[98] To warn of impending SLBM attacks on bombers and command centers, the navy deployed underwater acoustic sensors. The plan was to match the noises of ships and submarines against known noise patterns and to send information to air bases and attack submarines, which then would pursue enemy submarines.[99]

A few months before the Cuban crisis Kennedy secured links to the warning system and to the forces. He established the National Military Command Systems (NMCS) in the Pentagon to send him detailed information, and through which he could send commands to the nuclear forces. In addition, Kennedy gained access to intelligence information with a direct reporting channel from the Natoinal Security Agency (NSA) in the White House. Communications and electronic intelligence (COMINT and ELINT) now went directly from NSA to the president. According to Paul Bracken, in a crisis the resources of COMINT, ELINT, and of satellite photography would be alerted to provide warnings of an impending attack.[100]

The invulnerable SLBMs usually are regarded as stabilizing, but this is not certain. Although "use them or lose them" does not apply to submarines at sea, they may raise the PR. After 1969 the new Soviet Yankee submarines could strike command and bomber centers within four to 15 minutes of launching their SLBMs. A few submarines could, with depressed trajectory launches, destroy the central command in Washington within five minutes.[101]

The Soviets also developed an elaborate warning system. Hitler's surprise attack made Soviet military leaders aware of the advantage of preemption, which the advent of missiles increased. General Daniel O. Graham, former director of the U.S. Defense Intelligence Agency, reported that in the mid-1960s the Soviets adopted a launch-on-warning policy.[102]

It is difficult to overestimate the danger under a high alert, when the president will be besieged by many conflicting warnings and intelligence messages. A sequence of small events may set off a disaster. The information also flows into subordinate command centers which may misinterpret the signals. The danger increased with gains in the two countries' warning systems' sensitivity to each other's signals. The U.S. system can detect movements of Soviet equipment, ships, or other forces almost immediately, and the president may not risk waiting to understand their significance before ordering protective measures, and the Soviets may react in turn. Messages that do not signal an attack may prompt a preemptive attempt. The intelligence systems can initiate a mutually reinforcing alert. When Nixon said that the North Koreans shot down a U.S. reconnaissance aircraft, which both they and the Soviets knew was in international air space, he inadvertently revealed this ability.[103] The interactions did not precipitate a crisis because the commanders retained control. Human judgment also prevented the false alarm set off by a flock of Canada geese in the 1950s from causing a disaster. However, under a high alert we may not be as fortunate.

CONCLUSION

Kennedy's rapid buildup initiated the arms race and increased the PR. The administration did not expect a rapid Soviet reaction to its nuclear buildup, and even after the Soviet missile program was under way, McNamara hoped to maintain superiority with MIRVs and greater accuracy.

Kennedy took great risks. Khrushchev might easily have judged the risks in the Berlin crisis to be greater than a rational president would take and that the Soviet stakes were greater than those of the United States, especially after Eisenhower had conceded. Nevertheless, Kennedy was not entirely to blame. He had inherited the nuclear defense policy. The weapons themselves presented a problem of credibility.

The danger in future confrontations may be much greater. Efforts to avoid crises may not avail. Neither country may be able to avoid lining up with one of the sides in a revolution in Iran or in Saudi Arabia. A leader, in danger of immediate destruction and receiving confusing and frightening warnings, may panic.

5
Nixon
the Negotiator

LIMITED NUCLEAR OPTIONS = COUNTERFORCE STRATEGY

Nixon has been hailed as a realistic, tough, pragmatic negotiator by that dove George McGovern, while the hawks cannot understand how the former Red-baiter could negotiate the Berlin agreement, the SALT Treaty, and the Vladivostok agreement. But the hawks should invite Nixon back into the flock. By now they should realize that the negotiations only camouflaged a great counterforce buildup. By ordering the replacement of 550 ICBMs with the same number of MIRVed Minuteman III missiles, which he represented as a mere qualitative improvement, Nixon multiplied the United States' counterforce capability several times. At the time, Kissinger made his bows as the great peacemaker, but his protestations to the Reaganites that he did not give anything away are closer to the truth. Historians have been deceived by Nixon's pretended goal,[1] and it is hard to believe Kissinger's more recent claim that he hinted to the Soviets of the U.S. interest in a ban on MIRVs.[2]

Fearful of the effect on the PR, many in Congress opposed the deployment of the MIRVed Minuteman IIIs. But the opposition did not stop Nixon from continuing Kennedy's will-o'-the wisp chase of superiority. After McNamara had managed the development of MIRVs the Democrats were in a poor position to put up a strong fight against them, and some who were deeply involved in defense matters supported the policy.

The SALT delegation knew that it was the number of warheads that mattered, but, since Nixon prohibited any discussion of this

100

issue, the negotiations centered on the number of missiles. The days when the number of missiles had been important passed with the birth of MIRVs. In the late sixties, after the United States lost its overwhelming superiority but before the deployment of the Minuteman III, neither side could wipe out the other's retaliatory capability. The missiles were inaccurate, and on average it took more than two to destroy one. Games of Chicken were played, as we have seen, so it is an exaggeration to say that we were safe. But there was no danger of the mutual fear of preemption setting off the holocaust. The attacker would have lost more missiles than the victim. Invulnerable SLBMs made us even safer. The coming of greater accuracy plus MIRVs deprived us of this safety by giving the attacker a dangerous advantage. Perversely, the SALT Treaty made things worse. It increased each side's vulnerability to MIRVs by reducing the number of missiles and thus the number of targets. Indeed, by fixing the number of Soviet targets, the treaty, as Kissinger realized later if not at the time, facilitated Nixon's pursuit of superiority.

As we see in this chapter, Kissinger found it difficult to keep on mouthing the fiction of a Soviet military threat. The Soviet hordes in East Germany had supplied a convenient rationale for the nuclear arsenal for two decades, but it became difficult to continue crying wolf. Therefore, Kissinger turned to a political rationale. Influence came with missiles now, as it had with tanks and troops in the old days.

Nor were the Democrats innocents who yearned only for peace, for, like the Republicans, they feared losing world leadership more than nuclear war. The Democratic military strategists, who suddenly became political experts, proclaimed that the most powerful arsenal won world leadership;[3] the arms race was a struggle for influence. Soberly, they expressed the incredible doctrine that teetering nations would not drop into the communist net only if they were sure of a U.S. victory in a nuclear war. The Russian bear was no longer under their beds, but Democratic strategists still insisted on the lead in weapons. Adhering to Kennedy's apocalyptic view of the struggle of the age, they believed that influence ultimately rested on military power. The bogey was more ephemeral, but it did not disappear. The Democratic strategists agreed with Kissinger.

The counterforce strategists still dreaded a full-bodied bogey. Brezhnev's adventurous impulses might run riot; he might risk a preemptive attack. Because an attack on Western Europe remained the perennial worry, the central task was how to achieve deterrence. The counterforce doctrine, which offered a more credible deterrent than the alternative of assured destruction, continued to prevail.

The more extreme damage limitation strategy now out of reach, Nixon implemented the limited nuclear options strategy (LNO), or the counterforce strategy relabeled, by deploying the full Minuteman III force and 448 Poseidon SLBMs in a short five years.[4] Publicly Nixon advanced the bargaining chip argument, but to bargain effectively he would have had to deploy a few missiles while threatening to deploy many. However, fearing the AR, he refused to sacrifice the United States' principal advantage.

As his *The Real War* revealed, Nixon's chief article of faith was the bogey:

The Soviet goal is, reversing Woodrow Wilson, a world made unsafe for democracy: a world in which the Soviet state is secure and all others respect Soviet control and pay Soviet tribute. The Soviet ambition has been to control economic, political, and strategic affairs directly from Moscow. The Chinese communists accuse the Soviets of seeking 'hegemony,' and the word aptly describes Soviet aims.[5]

That Nixon, from the beginning, intended to build up the arsenal was demonstrated by his selection of Kissinger as national security adviser. So much did *Nuclear Weapons and Foreign Policy* appeal to him, that Nixon went so far as to draw his principal foreign policy adviser from archrival Nelson Rockefeller's camp. The book thus demands more attention than it received in Chapter 3. The book rejected the possibility of fruitful negotiations. It said that avoiding the risk of nuclear war gave the Soviets a blank check, and imitating Kennan, Kissinger traced their foreign policy to the same fundamental domestic conditions:

Because harmony between different social systems is explicitly rejected by Soviet doctrine, the renunciation of force will create a vacuum into which the Soviet leadership can move with impunity. Because the Soviet rulers pride themselves on their ability to 'see through' our protestations of peaceful intentions, our only possibility for affecting their actions resides in the possession of superior force. For the Soviet leadership has made every effort to retain its militancy. It has been careful to insist that no technological discovery, however powerful, can abolish the laws of history and that real peace is attainable only *after* the triumph of communism. "We will bury you," Nikita S. Khrushchev has said, and the democracies would have been spared much misery had they not so often insisted that dictators do not mean what they say.

Kissinger went on to say, "the refusal to run any risks would amount to giving the Soviet rulers a blank check. At a time when we have never been stronger, we have had to learn that power which is not clearly related to the objectives for which it is to be employed may merely paralyze the will."[6] Kissinger saw little hope in the new Soviet regime. The dogma of the still revolutionary and imperialist state both motivated and justified conquest. The flow of power to the communists was becoming a flood, as their victories in Southeast Asia and elsewhere shifted the balance of power, and the already high AR was growing.[7] The United States could not surrender its nuclear weapons without paralyzing its will to resist aggression.

The book failed to support the thesis of Soviet expansionism. Kissinger's evidence consisted of the growth of the Soviet atomic stockpile, the triumph of Chinese communism, and the consolidation of Soviet control over Eastern Europe.[8] We must remind ourselves that at the time of the book's publication in 1957 the Soviets had little nuclear power, Dulles was still threatening devastation, and the West's hostility to communism had not diminished.

The growth of the Soviet atomic stockpile before 1957 was no evidence of expansionism. It was only a reaction to the growth of the U.S. arsenal.

Allegedly, Moscow's evil hand was behind the Chinese Revolution. However, by 1957 it was no secret that out of fear of creating a powerful rival within the Marxist camp the Soviets had refrained from helping the native, peasant revolution. Mao Zedong was a Marxist but not a puppet.

The harsh Soviet oppression of Eastern Europe did not demonstrate ambitions for more territory. Stalin's successors preferred Eastern Europe under foot to free, but the Soviets were not about to attack the strongly defended West. Kissinger harkened back to Hitler's *Mein Kampf* when he pointed to the Marxist doctrine of the inevitability of a socialist-capitalist war. However, theoreticians' journal articles, which were a poor vehicle for whipping up popular war frenzy, hardly warranted a high-risk policy. Moreover, he did not support his characterization of totalitarian regimes as expansionist. Kissinger also inferred an imperialist drive from the concentration of troops in East Germany, but the Soviets could very easily believe that these troops protected their hold on Eastern Europe. They could reasonably say that the West would take the opportunity of a revolt in the region to invade it. Acheson and Dulles had urged such intervention, and revolts there had shaken Soviet control. The United States could not convincingly claim that under no circumstances would it invade Eastern Europe. Moreover, advocates of a dangerous, nuclear defense policy are hardly in a position to describe Soviet fears as fictitious.

Like his predecessors, Kissinger defended a high-risk policy by pointing to the Soviet bogey. But Kremlinologists, who knew the Soviets well, saw no threat. Studies of Soviet foreign policy by Adam B. Ulam, Thomas W. Wolfe, Joseph L. Nogee and Robert H. Donaldson, David Holloway, Robin Edmonds, and Marshall D. Shulman do not warn against a military threat.[9] They agree that the Soviet Union will support revolutions, but to call this a policy of "expansionism" is misleading. The Soviets will not attack a region of vital interest to the United States. In short, Soviet policy does not warrant a high-risk, provocative buildup of a preemptive, hard-target capability and of a large TNW force to trigger a nuclear war. Nevertheless, Kissinger urged the deployment of the Minuteman III and of the TNW. Not bothering with such messy details as the Red army's strength and readiness, he argued only from references to Soviet doctrinal writings and flimsy history.

Nixon, who could not bear to discuss nuclear strategy,[10] had other experts on call, as well as Kissinger. Among them were the strategists at Rand, whose former director of strategic studies, James Schlesinger, became his third defense secretary. Neither Rand nor Kissinger dared to rate a Soviet attack on Western Europe as probable; this was not why they recommended MIRVs. They spoke only of a *possible* attack. Following the same logic, all of us should rush to gun dealers because a neighbor might attack. The Soviets were not threatening the West. Their newspapers welcomed détente. Their routine condemnations of capitalism were no more intended to whip up a war hysteria than were Reagan's equally routine denunciations of communism. A real threat would have been obvious and would not have to be inferred from dubious bits of evidence.

Avoiding a flat prediction, the strategists claimed only that it was common sense to believe that a strong counterforce capability was the most effective deterrent. But the advice was pointless without a high AR; the strategists may as well have predicted a Soviet attack. They gave this advice because they restricted their thinking to the problem of effective deterrence. Their self-imposed problem was how to deter a first strike and, failing that, how to deter subsequent strikes. The strategists did not realize how absurd it was to raise the PR to deter an unlikely attack. The strategists said that they wanted to deter a *possible* attack, but their prescription was worse than the disease. Their recommended strategy raised the risk of nuclear war. In their formal analysis the only risk was the AR. In this formal context they either did not see the consequences for the PR or chose to ignore them. Informally the strategists wrote war scenarios depicting a higher PR than AR, which suggested that they were aware of the PR. But these scenarios were inconsistent with the logic of their policy recommendations.

One popular scenario goes as follows. Soviet troops try to suppress East German riots; the fighting spills over into West Germany, setting off a Soviet-U.S. clash; larger forces become involved; NATO fires its TNW, and either the Soviet Union or the United States unleashes a strategic attack. Contrary to their policy rationale, the strategists do not envisage ambitious Soviet leaders ordering an attack. What is most startling about the scenarios is that they show the nuclear weapons initiating a nuclear war, not deterring an attack. In the scenarios, the big risk is the PR. The policy recommendations were appropriate only for a high AR and a low PR.

The counterforce strategists now warned that the Minuteman III was essential for responding to a limited Soviet attack. This was the big danger only because we had no credible deterrent. The basic thesis was that without an adequate deterrent, we risked a deliberate attack by an expansionist Soviet Union. Kissinger later justified the position in *White House Years* by saying that McNamara agreed; the deployment of MIRVs did not mark a change in policy. Kissinger quoted McNamara as saying that, while pretending to implement assured destruction, he really had sought strategic options consistent with the counterforce strategy.[11] However, that McNamara had followed the same policy was no justification. Kissinger also smugly gave his dovish former academic colleagues the back of his hand by castigating assured destruction as impressive sounding in an academic seminar but unworkable in the real world and potentially dangerous.[12]

According to Kissinger, deterrence required a high-risk nuclear defense policy.[13] Nixon had to threaten the Soviets with dangerous actions:

Until the day he left office, Nixon retained an international reputation for being willing to stake American power and prestige swiftly and ruthlessly. Adversaries did not dare to test, under the pressure of short crisis deadlines, to what extent his authority had been impaired. No country took us on frontally until the Soviets prompted our alert at the end of the Middle East war, when one of its clients found itself in desperate straits. And even then the Soviets subsided as soon as we showed our teeth. We were thus able to use the crisis to shape events and reverse alliances in the Middle East in defiance of the pressures of our allies, the preferences of the Soviets and the rhetoric of Arab radicals.[14]

Kissinger was referring to the U.S. nuclear alert during the Yom Kippur War of 1973, about which more later.

Further, he argued that to refrain from seeking nuclear superiority in the face of the Soviets' superiority when they also possessed conventional superiority was to disarm unilaterally. In addition, limiting the United States to a second-strike antipopulation capability also was equivalent to disarmament, since we needed a countersilo capability that could survive an all-out Soviet attack and still threaten Soviet cities.[15] At the time, the administration denied that its goal was "superiority," and it appealed instead to the euphemisms of "greater flexibility," "selectivity in targeting," and "sufficiency." But to be "sufficient," a countersilo capability had to be able to survive a duel—to exceed the enemy's capability.

These arguments are taken from Kissinger's memoirs, and no hawk could object to what Kissinger then said he had advocated. But the memoirs, written when Reagan's shadow loomed, may not have been accurate. They may have advocated a more extreme policy than Kissinger did in the White House, where he gave a confusing impression of his position by moderately describing the Soviet Union as only protecting its own interests and seeking 'geopolitical' gains[16] and by minimizing the significance of the Trident and the B-1 programs.[17] He left it to Schlesinger to be the strong advocate for the administration's counterforce strategy. Detecting his apparent ambivalence, the strategy's opponents, Senators Thomas McIntyre and Walter Mondale, sought his support.[18] In his memoirs Kissinger admitted having had doubts, which led him to want a reexamination of the strategy, but he did not urge one because the massive Soviet buildup prohibited procrastination.[19] Kissinger may have been ambivalent or trying to play on both teams, but his warnings against small Soviet gains in the Third World were unambiguous. Evidently, he had a very accurate scale to weigh shifts in power. On the other hand, he also said that confrontations now were less dangerous, since neither Angola nor Ethiopia was worth a holocaust.[20]

After Kissinger had enjoyed Brezhnev's summit hospitality, it would have been bad manners to continue calling up the bogey. Kissinger filled the gap left by its abandonment with the political argument that said that we could expect political blackmail after the Soviets won parity.[21] His memoirs did not concede that the Soviets were not expansionist; quite the opposite. But expansionism now denoted political blackmail, not the threat of invasion. "Expansionism" had become an open-ended word referring to Soviet efforts at gaining influence. The upshot was that nuclear superiority was the formula for preventing the spread of communism. The moderate sound of this political argument should not fool us, for it demanded the capability of playing Chicken over a variety of issues. The argument did not specify the political goals meriting the high risks. In office, Kissinger might have feared repeating Acheson's error of expressly saying what the United States would not defend. But, once out of office, this was no excuse. Ultimately, however, the theory that the Soviet Union and the United States are permanent rivals in a worldwide conflict justifies great risks even in minor conflicts. The problem has been to measure the risk appropriate to each of the many potential conflicts. Kissinger probably would agree that the Soviet Union would not tolerate any threat to its control of Eastern Europe, even at the risk of total war. He would not risk a challenge to Soviet hegemony there. On the other hand, judging from Kissinger's behavior in the Yom Kippur War of 1973, he was willing to play nuclear Chicken to keep the Soviets from gaining influence in the Middle East. Kissinger's view of the Soviet Union as a great power nibbling away the balance of power suggests that he was prepared to take big risks to preserve the balance. Moreover, even without the ideological excuse, the stakes did not have to be as big as the balance in the Middle East. He was prepared to have the United States compete for influence in other regions with the biggest weapons available, regardless of the effect on the PR.

Kissinger neglected alternative avenues to influence, despite the expected longevity of the rivalry. Nuclear weapons were likely to pay smaller political dividends than investments in other, obviously more appropriate areas, including the education of future Third World leaders in U.S. schools and the expansion of the Peace Corps. It is hard to believe that its nuclear weapons won allies in Africa and in Southeast Asia for the Soviet Union.

Because Kissinger's theory was based on prenuclear defense technology, it was inconsistent. According to the theory, we had to build a powerful arsenal to prevent the Soviet Union from upsetting the balance of power by gaining new allies. But any allies would contribute only troops under arms, artillery pieces, and so forth. Even in this conventional arms calculus, shifts of minor Third World countries from one camp to the other would hardly affect the balance of power. Indeed, China's becoming a Soviet rival has shifted the balance more than any likely future Soviet successes. In any case, Kissinger's premonitions were unwarranted. Any war between the superpowers is likely to become a nuclear war in which alliances will have no effect on the outcome. Influence has no significance for such a war, and it does not warrant a high risk.

The truth of the matter is that Kissinger, like his predecessors and successors, wanted a powerful counterforce capability with which to play Chicken. Although he repeated the strategists' war scenarios, it is unlikely that he believed them to be realistic. Kissinger had no illusions about winning a nuclear war. However, anticipating crises, he wanted as strong a hand as possible, which now required a powerful counterforce capability. He expected confrontations in unstable regions, most notably in the Middle East. A revolution in Iran might give the Soviet Union the opportunity to invade that country. To stop the Soviet Union from gaining control of a region, the United States needed the nuclear threat to deter Soviet military actions. A landing of U.S. troops would be ineffective without the ultimate deterrent because the United States could not project enough conventional forces to rely on them alone. But a credible nuclear threat required the ability to conduct counterforce warfare. The United States did not need a counterforce capability to credibly deter an attack on it; the SLBMs were sufficient. Credibility was a problem, however, when the United States needed to invoke its nuclear weapons to deter attacks elsewhere. A strong counterforce capability supported the needed credibility.

According to the scenario, the United States had to threaten doomsday to keep the Soviets out of vital areas. Kissinger advocated that the United States inform the Soviets in advance of any confrontation in the Middle East that a Soviet invasion would trigger a nuclear war. Indeed, Nixon's deployment of the Minuteman III may have reduced the AR by deterring the Soviets from taking a more active role in the Middle East. However, since the PR already was much higher than the AR, it was wrong to reduce the AR in exchange for a rise in the PR. This is not to say that the Soviets were prepared to risk becoming involved in a major war in the Middle East; the evidence suggests that any Soviet intervention in the Yom Kippur War would have been minor, in any case. Moreover, more powerful nuclear weapons would not reduce the AR over any extended period, since the Soviet Union would match the growth in counterforce capability. Over a long period, growth in counterforce capability does not increase deterrence when it is part of a race.

The high cost of conventional defense was another argument. Nixon would have met more resistance to higher defense expenditures than either Kennedy or Eisenhower. The risk entailed by the TNW did not frighten members of Congress into voting for appropriations for larger conventional forces.

If Nixon insisted on Minuteman III, then why the Strategic Arms Limitation Talks (SALT)? At best it was a useless diversion, and negotiations risked cutting off options. Kissinger's *White House Years* answered the question directly. Nixon hoped that SALT was the road out of Vietnam. Since the cost of the arms race was a burden to the Soviets, Nixon hoped to extract concessions in exchange for an arms limitation agreement. He thought that the Soviets might moderate Hanoi's intransigeance. Kissinger was quite straightforward:

The new Administration wanted to use the Soviet concern about its intentions to draw the Kremlin into discussions on Vietnam. We therefore insisted that negotiations on all issues proceed simultaneously. The Soviet leaders were especially worried about the impact of a new arms race on the Soviet economy; they therefore gave top priority to arms limitation.[22]

President Carter would not hear of "linkage"; for him, arms control came first. But he was not entrapped by Vietnam. Thus, Nixon's top priority was not reaching an arms control agreement, and to build up the arsenal was not inconsistent.

In his memoirs, Kissinger denied that he had conceded anything, contradicting earlier statements. According to the memoirs, the United States no longer was acquiring strategic missiles, in any case. Additional ICBMs were a hopeless cause in Congress, and the chiefs did not want more missiles: they only wanted to replace the Poseidons with Tridents. What was more, the agreement made no allowance for the French and British nuclear weapons, and it did not limit the number of strategic bombers, the forward-based aircraft, and aircraft carriers in Europe and in the Pacific. According to Kissinger, not only did SALT I not force the United States to give up a single offensive weapons program, but the freeze was essential for the United States to catch up. He pointed out that a substantial modernization of the strategic forces followed SALT I.[23] "Modernization" referred to the deployment of the Minuteman III. Kissinger also said in his defense that the ABM program passed the Senate by only one vote. According to Kissinger, in 1970, 40 Senators signed an appeal to stop MIRV testing. Further, in 1973 the Trident program, which was the only strategic offensive program ready for production, escaped cancellation by one vote.[24]

In *Years of Upheaval* Kissinger said that SALT strengthened the opposition to the new weapons systems, which were needed to match the "relentless" Soviet buildup, and he apologized for demoralizing the Pentagon by describing the new programs as mere bargaining chips.[25] According to Kissinger, nothing less than nuclear superiority was essential to national security. Without superiority, the United States could not have contained Soviet power in the Berlin,

Korean, Middle Eastern, and Cuban crises. It could not have credibly threatened to initiate a nuclear exchange. The new parity deprived the United States of its bargaining power, and the Soviets would be more aggressive. They could now more easily threaten NATO with a conventional attack. This was as hawkish a position as the Reaganites could have wanted. Not only did the Soviets' expansionist ambitions have to be checked by nuclear forces, but they threatened to invade Western Europe. The United States needed superiority to play Chicken, and he predicted greater Soviet aggressiveness with parity.

From the outset, Nixon pressed for a flexible and selective capability, relying on the counterforce arguments:

A different strategic doctrine is required in this decade when potential adversaries possess large and more flexible nuclear forces. The threat of an all-out nuclear response involving the cities of both sides might not be as credible a deterrent as it was in the 1960s. An aggressor, in the unlikely event of a nuclear war, might choose to employ nuclear weapons selectively and in limited numbers for limited objectives. No President should ever be in the position where his only option in meeting such aggression is an all-out nuclear response. To deal with a wide range of possible hostile actions, the President must maintain a broad choice of options.

Credible deterrence in the 1970s requires greater flexibility.

Lack of flexibility on our part could tempt an aggressor to use nuclear weapons in a limited way in a crisis. If the United States has the ability to use its forces in a controlled way, the likelihood of nuclear response would be more credible, thereby making deterrence more effective and the initial use of nuclear weapons by an opponent less likely.[26]

Since only with a very large arsenal could the United States, while under attack, afford to withhold some missiles, the message made a disguised appeal for superiority, while, at the same time, implicitly condemning McNamara's plans for massive attacks.

The administration conducted an alarmist campaign for the approval of the Minuteman III program by Congress, which preferred cost-of-living allowances for the elderly. Projecting dismal trends, Defense Secretary Melvin Laird predicted that by the mid-seventies the current rate of building would give the Soviets 2,500 ICBMs, or two and one-half times the U.S. number. The Soviets already had 230 of the ominous 25-megaton (mt.) SS-9s deployed or under construction, and by the mid-seventies they would have 400, some of which would be very accurate. They were testing these missiles armed with three 5-mt. warheads. If the number of SS-9s increased to 420 and their accuracy to a quarter of a mile, these missiles alone would be able to destroy 95 percent of the Minuteman force, leaving only 50 surviving. Laird concluded, "They are going for a first strike capability. There can be no question about that."[27] These projections were unwarranted alarmism. As with any stockpile, a high rate of acquisition was unlikely to persist, unless, of course, U.S. improvements induced the Soviets to change their goal.

The campaign for a limited-war capability continued in March 1974, when James Schlesinger, the new defense secretary, warned,

Since we ourselves find it difficult to believe that we would actually implement the threat of assured destruction in response to a limited attack on military targets that caused relatively few civilian casualties, there can be no certainty that in a crisis, prospective opponents would be deterred from testing our resolve.[28]

In Schlesinger's view, although the number of warheads was enough to destroy several optional sets of targets, it was inadequate. In 1974 the United States had 4,500 missile warheads and about 800 on B-52s. Since 800 warheads could destroy all significant civilian targets in the Soviet Union and China, more than 4,000 were available to strike military targets.[29] Surely, this was more than enough to permit the National Command Authority (NCA) in a limited nuclear war to execute a flexible and selective strategy. However, Schlesinger did not think so.

Congress was more upset by the PR than the administration, as it continues to be. Beginning with Kennedy's, every administration has striven for superiority, while many in Congress have opposed strengthening the counterforce capability. More sensitive to the public fear of war, Congress has been more attracted by the nuclear freeze proposal, and some members sponsored the proposed build-down agreement and the Midgetman program to reduce the PR.

We now turn to a description of the growth of the counterforce capability.

THE OFFENSIVE POWER OF THE ICBMs GREW FIVEFOLD

Since offensive capability is proportional to the number of warheads (N), the three-warhead Minuteman IIIs, which replaced all the Minuteman I and some Minuteman II single-warhead missiles (Table 5.1) between 1970 and 1975, added the equivalent of 1,100 older missiles.

Table 5.1
Number, Warheads per Missile, Yield, and CEP
of U.S. ICBMs and SLBMs, 1970 and 1975

	Number		Warheads	Yield mt.	CEP nm.
	1970	1975			
Minuteman I	490	0	1	1	.5
Minuteman II	500	450	1	1.2	.34
Minuteman III	10	550	3	.17	.12
Titan II	54	54	1	9	.8
ICBM Total	1,054	1,054			
Polaris A-2	128	32	1	.8	.5
Polaris A-3	512	176	3	.2	.5
Poseidon	16	448	10	.04	.25
SLBM Total	656	656			
Grand Total	1,710	1,710			

Source: John M. Collins, *U.S.-Soviet Military Balance: Concepts and Capabilities, 1960–1980* (New York: McGraw-Hill, 1980), App. 2.

More significant was the improvement in accuracy. Measured by the Circular Error Probable (CEP), the Minuteman III had four times the accuracy of the Minuteman I. If many Minuteman IIIs were fired, then 50 percent of them would fall within .12 nautical miles (nm.) of the target, or 720 feet. Since it increased with the square of accuracy (A^2), the new warhead's offensive capability was 16 times that of the Minuteman I's warhead for the same yield.

The new warhead's lower yield or explosive power resulted in only a small loss in this capability. Since much destructive power is wasted at the point of impact, it grows less than proportionally with yield. A bomb with a yield of one mt., which represents the equivalent of one million tons of TNT, is only 100 times as destructive as one with a yield of one kiloton (kt.), or 1,000 tons, not 1,000 times. Destructive power increases proportionally with the two-thirds power of the yield. For this reason, strategists refer to equivalent megatonnage (EMT), which is yield to the two-thirds power ($Y^{2/3}$). No wonder McNamara opted for accuracy and multiple warheads instead of competing with the Soviets in yield. It was only when the Soviets used their large throw-weight capability to mount MIRVs and improved their accuracy that Senator Henry Jackson began to worry about the potential enemy's offensive capability.

The effects of changes in the three dimensions of offensive power are summarized in the following formula for offensive power:

$$K = NY^{2/3} A^2$$

where K = offensive power, N = the number of warheads, Y = yield, and A = accuracy. I substitute A for $1/(CEP)$ to simplify the formula. Recall that CEP stands for Circular Error Probable.

Applying the formula, we learn that the administration increased the offensive power of the land-based force over fivefold between 1970 and 1975, or by the equivalent of 3,260 Minuteman IIs. This huge expansion in the counterforce capability, and thus potentially in the PR, went through without raising any great furor in Congress. There was some opposition, but not as much as the more obvious equivalent increase in the number of Minuteman I or II missiles would have provoked. Nixon succeeded in concealing the significance of the enhancement.

There was also a large increase in the sea-based arsenal's power. The deployment of the Poseidons more than doubled the sea-based offensive power. The strategists may have had little use for the inaccurate SLBMs, but they did not dismiss some less accurate Soviet land-based missiles. Nevertheless, it is true that the offensive power depended mainly on the ICBMs.

Nixon said that MIRVs were needed to keep the United States from falling behind. By 1970 the Soviets were ahead in the number of land-based missiles (Tables 5.1 and 5.2), the total number of strategic missiles, and in offensive power. In land-based offensive power, they led by 62 percent; in total offensive power, by 23 percent. The number of the much-feared SS-9 missiles, each with a yield of 20 mt., increased from 228 to 298. The USSR now also deployed the four-warhead SS-17, the six-warhead SS-19, and the giant SS-18 with a yield of 24 mt. A MIRVed SS-18 could carry a large number of warheads; only 200 or 300 of these monsters were needed to wipe out the U.S. land-based force. However, by 1975 the United States again was in the lead by a substantial margin. The Minuteman III more than offset the Soviet additions. In 1975 the offensive power of the U.S. land-based force exceeded that of the Soviet Union by 68 percent. Including the SLBMs, the U.S. lead was even larger. In 1975 the total offensive power of the United States was as much as 84 percent greater than the potential enemy's. Reagan to the contrary notwithstanding, between 1970 and 1975 the United States hardly stood still. In that period the offensive power of the United

Table 5.2
Number, Warheads per Missile, Yield, and CEP
of Soviet ICBMs and SLBMs, 1970 and 1975

	Number		Warheads	Yield mt.	CEP nm.
	1970	1975			
SS-7	190	190	1	4	1
SS-8	19	19	1	3	1
SS-9	228	298	1	20	.4
SS-11	970	960	1	.95	.76
SS-13	20	60	1	.6	1
SS-17	0	10	4	.75	.24
SS-18	0	10	1	24	.23
SS-19	0	60	6	.55	.21
ICBM Total	1,427	1,607			
SS-N-4	27	21	1	1	1.5
SS-N-5	54	60	1	1	1.5
SS-N-6	208	528	1[a]	.75	.7
SS-N-8	0	132	1	.75	.8
SLBM Total	389	741			
Grand Total	1,816	2,348			

[a] 3 MIRVs in 1974 and later.

Source: John M. Collins, *U.S.-Soviet Military Balance: Concepts and Capabilities, 1960-1980* (New York: McGraw-Hill, 1980), App. 2.

grew more than twice as fast as the Soviet Union's. The U.S. offensive power grew four and one-half times, while the Soviet power doubled.

COUNTERFORCE THEORY

Two articles expounded some of the policy's underlying ideas. One was published in January 1973 by Rand alumnus and director of the Arms Control and Disarmament Agency (ACDA) Fred Iklé,[30] who is undersecretary of defense under Reagan. At the time, Senators Edward Brooke and Thomas McIntyre were attacking the program to strengthen the arsenal, and the SS-9 was the new threat.

Iklé advocated improving the arsenal for deterrence. Logically, a policy of deterrence had to assume that the AR exceeded the PR, but Iklé's list of eventualities referred to the latter. Judging from his list, Iklé only echoed the statement of the goal of deterrence in routine fashion without giving it much thought. He feared commanders' errors, faults in communication, and the irrationality of political leaders, not deliberate Soviet aggression. The list did not include the possibility of a leader seeking political advantage or territorial gain, perhaps because Iklé could not imagine a rational leader deliberately ordering a nuclear launching. Not every Soviet leader was certain to be rational, assured destruction might not deter a Hitler in his final bunker, in a crisis even otherwise rational leaders might not calmly appraise the risks, an accident or incompetent military leaders might initiate hostilities, Japanese leaders irrationally attacked Pearl Harbor, and Soviet leaders might decide that the least risky option was to eliminate the U.S. land-based arsenal, while sparing cities. The last possibility might be associated with a political goal, but it need not be.

A war strategy was needed. To be consistent, Iklé should have dropped the goal of deterrence, since in most of his contingencies it was not attainable. Iklé's more serious statement of purpose was that a nuclear strategy would minimize slaughter. He rejected assured destruction, which he said was unlimited destruction, because, if it failed, it would kill more people than the counterforce strategy. Iklé's major goal was to minimize slaughter; he advocated a limited-war policy to achieve this goal. To carry on a limited war, the United States needed to enhance its counterforce capability. An accurate low-yield warhead could destroy silos with minimum collateral damage, and MIRVs could strike many military targets.

Concerning the PR, Iklé proposed investigating sinking land-based missiles deep underground. Missiles, which did not have to be launched on warning, eliminated the incentive for a preemptive attack. Inaccurate SLBMs were not a good alternative because they did not provide a counterforce capability, and communications with the submarines might break down. Thus, the author was an early advocate of the so far fruitless search for a survivable land-based force. Although Iklé acknowledged the PR, his support for a powerful counterforce capability was not conditional on invulnerability. The PR was not his primary concern, despite his list of contingencies that argued that this was the major risk.

Iklé's minimum-slaughter case assumed unrealistically that in a war the Soviets would refrain from striking cities. This becomes obvious when we realize that the counterforce strategy pertained to only the first 15 minutes or so after the Soviet commanders received a warning. Knowing the U.S. strategy, they were more likely to launch immediately than if cities were the expected targets. The Soviets would not know how many or which missiles had been fired. To strike still loaded U.S. silos, the Soviets would have to unleash many missiles. The vision of an attack on a few silos to which the Soviets would retaliate in similar fashion was unrealistic. Thus, the high PR resulting from the counterforce strategy was not worth the small prospect of mitigating the devastation.

The other article, by William R. Van Cleave and Roger W. Barnett, appeared in fall 1974.[31] Van Cleave, a former member of the SALT delegation and a special assistant to the defense secretary, at the time was director of the Defense and Strategic Studies Program at the University of Southern California. Later, President Ford appointed him to the B Team, which became famous for judging the CIA estimate of Soviet capabilities as optimistic. Navy Commander Barnett had been on the JCS staff and the SALT delegation.

Van Cleave and Barnett adhered closely to the standard counterforce argument. They had no use for the strategy of assured destruction, which, they said, sought only deterrence and therefore was self-defeating. The United States could not expect to deter an attack by seeking to avoid launching nuclear weapons. Contrary to Iklé, they could easily imagine a rational leader risking a nuclear war for even a small gain because a U.S. policy of assured destruction implied a small risk. Knowing that a president would not condemn the American people to mass destruction, a leader might deliberately fire his TNW, certain of inflicting only a small number of fatalities. A limited strike entailed little risk when the only available response was a massive attack. Thus, assured destruction was deterred from deterring a limited strike. In our language, it did little to reduce the high AR. The nation needed a powerful arsenal. But Van Cleave and Barnett merely assumed a high AR. They recommended raising the PR only because a leader *might* fire nuclear weapons, but they did not assess the probability of such a decision. To justify raising the already high PR, they had to show that the AR was high. It was not enough to refer to a possibility.

Van Cleave and Barnett asserted, as have other writers, that an uncertain deterrent was ineffective, and they therefore have dismissed the sea-based force as a deterrent. A president might not retaliate against cities. When the actual probabilities are not assessed, the reasoning is appropriate to a game, not to policy in the real world. In a game, with sufficient superiority, side A might undertake a limited attack. Expecting victory in an all-out war, it would not expect retaliation. Thus, superiority on one side entailed a high risk of a limited attack or the threat of one. But, in the real world, the

Soviets would not take even a small risk of retaliation. They would be uncertain about their own destructive capability as well as about the reaction of the United States. No political goals merited these risks. The Soviets were unlikely to take even a small risk of retaliation.

Moreover, the game of Chicken was much more complicated than the authors imagined. Knowing that a strike might be only the first in a series, the full consequences of which could not be foreseen, no Soviet leader could be confident that exchanges would remain limited. He might expect a pessimistic president to order an all-out response to a limited Soviet attack because if a strike was the first of several, the best strategy might call for the immediate elimination of as much of the other side's counterforce capability as possible. The view that a flexible and selective capability reduced the risk of an attack more than a retaliatory capability did was derived from an overly simplified game.

Finally, a limited war is impossible. A sequence of limited, orderly actions requires that both NCAs survive, keep strict control over the forces, receive accurate damage assessments, and that each NCA negotiate with the other. However, as Bracken has argued, a single warhead can destroy the central command, the centralized structure imposes an excessive information burden on the NCA, and the central command cannot communicate directly with hundreds of missile silos, SSBNs, and bomber commands.

This unrealistic theory provides the foundation for the continuing defense policy based on the counterforce strategy. Recognizing the problems of communication during a war, the actual plans specify a decentralized command system. In the 1950s under the new National Military Command System (NMCS), the president was to communicate with a few primary command centers, which in turn controlled lower centers. Moreover, control would be taken over by the next lower level of authority as each one was destroyed. When the NCA was eliminated, the primary command centers would take over. Control would cascade down the succeeding echelons until only the operational groups survived. At that point they would be self directed. The decentralization was intended to assure a continuing retaliatory capability. If retaliation cannot be ordered without the NCA, then Washington indeed becomes a sitting duck, and the primary command centers are few enough also to be destroyed in a single, coordinated attack. However, independent commands that have lost contact with each other as a result of an electromagnetic pulse (EMP), and have little damage information, cannot conduct an LNO strategy. They cannot carry out a coordinated series of limited attacks in response to similar Soviet attacks. The vision of the NCA controlling weapons closely enough to bargain with a similarly functioning Soviet NCA is unrealistic.[32]

The fear of the new Soviet counterforce capability, which was expected to grow to the Vladivostok limits, supported the demand for a more powerful arsenal. Part of the Soviet arsenal could destroy the U.S. land-based force, even at the Vladivostok level.[33] The agreement allowed each side 2,400 strategic delivery vehicles; the subceiling for MIRVed missiles was set at 1,320. John D. Steinbrunner and Thomas M. Garwin assumed that the CEP of the Soviet SS-18 was between .20 and .29 nm., its yield was between 1 and 3 mt. per warhead, and each missile carried 8 warheads. After making allowance for unreliability, the authors estimated that the Soviets would need only 300 MIRVed missiles to destroy the U.S. land-based force. If each side had the maximum number of ICBMs possible, which meant no SLBMs or bombers, then 600 ICBMs could destroy the enemy's entire land-based missile force. Potentially, the Soviets were in a worse position than the Americans, since they depended much more on ICBMs.

However, the estimates may have exaggerated Soviet power by not allowing sufficiently for unreliability. Rocket engines may fail in the boost phase; warheads may not explode; the explosions of leading warheads may destroy or deflect following warheads; and dust, atmospheric turbulence, and large-scale electromagnetic disturbances from previous explosions may reduce counterforce capability. The success of peacetime space launchings after much advance notice, careful preparations, and many postponements, did not warrant assuming wartime reliability. In addition, the accuracy estimates were based on flights over a test range, but different gravitational pulls over other parts of the earth might cause large errors. The proponents of the Minuteman III may have exaggerated Soviet power.

The counterforce strategists assumed the high probability of a limited Soviet attack against which the deterrent was ineffective. This argument, advanced by the Nixon, Carter, and Reagan administrations to justify a powerful counterforce capability, posits an incredible willingness of the Soviets to take great risks. The policy is ludicrous unless it is shown that the Soviets indeed are intensely ambitious for empire.

SOVIET VS. U.S. DEFENSE EXPENDITURES

The bogey's awesomeness grew with the CIA's estimates of the size and growth of Soviet defense expenditures. The CIA adds up bullets, manpower, SS-9s, and tanks in dollar or ruble aggregates, which are not easy to interpret. We must consider the method of estimation.

Toward the end of the Nixon-Ford administration, the estimate of Soviet defense expenditures rose from between 6 and 8 percent of the GNP to between 10 and 15 percent. Only the CIA estimate had changed, not Soviet expenditures. But they now appeared to be very high. The Soviet Union apparently was spending 40 percent more than the United States, or double the previously estimated gap of 20 percent.[34] Since President Ford suspected that even the new estimate was too rosy, he appointed the B Team, which prepared a much gloomier estimate.

Wohlstetter added to the gloom in two alarming articles,[35] which said that defense expenditures had been declining "nearly exponentially" since the period 1956-61. The resulting fall in the strategic forces' power had produced a dangerously vulnerable arsenal and greater "instabilities that could lead to nuclear war."[36] The destructive capability, or the explosive yield of the arsenal, had reached a peak in 1960, when it had been as much as two and one-half times the level of 1972.[37]

The articles were grossly misleading. Wohlstetter measured "power" by yield, neglecting accuracy and ignoring the shift from bombers to missiles. The appropriate measure of power—offensive capability—had increased greatly when missiles replaced bombers. The fall in the quantity of available explosive power did not signify less offensive capability because more of the initial stockpile now could strike the targets. Bombers would be shot down on the way to their targets and bombs were inaccurate. The missiles could not be shot down and they were more accurate. Wohlstetter again ignored this shift when he warned about the decline in the number of warheads and in equivalent megatonnage (EMT), or yield adjusted for the waste of destructive power at the point of impact.[38] He also again ignored accuracy. A tenfold increase in warheads increased the offensive capability ten times, the same increase in yield multiplied the capability only 4.64 times, but the same increase in accuracy multiplied it 100 times. The hawks should have been reassured, not frightened.

Nor should Wohlstetter have warned against the decline in constant-dollar expenditures on the strategic forces from the end of the Eisenhower administration, when they were three times the level of 1974.[39] The lower expenditures did not signify less power. The offensive capability of the ICBMs did not fall when their number stopped growing. Moreover, during the Nixon administration, despite lower expenditures, this capability grew five times. MIRVs and accuracy were cheaper than additional missiles and launchers.

Nevertheless, which country was spending more had become a perennial issue. According to Lawrence J. Korb, later assistant defense secretary under Reagan, the CIA did not allow sufficiently for the Soviet soldiers' low pay, which permitted the Soviets to buy a larger army while spending only 30 percent of their budget on manpower, compared to the U.S. share of 60 percent. The savings in pay allowed the Soviets to spend twice as much as we did on weapons, R&D, and combat training.[40] They were improving their missiles much more rapidly, and the Red army was ahead in combat readiness.

The validity of the estimates thus is a primary issue. Because Korb's estimates were based on dollar prices, they exaggerated Soviet expenditures. As Korb said, U.S. pay scales were high, but he did not also point out that U.S. equipment prices were low. Since the Soviets bought large amounts of manpower and relatively little equipment, estimating their expenditures at U.S. prices, including the pay rates, exaggerated them. If the CIA had applied the equally valid Soviet prices, it would have exaggerated U.S. expenditures by valuing equipment at high Soviet prices. As it turns out, Soviet expenditures were higher than U.S. expenditures even when ruble prices were applied, but the difference was smaller.

However, this is not the whole story. Even the ruble-based estimates exaggerated the Soviet-U.S. gap because the quality of U.S. equipment was superior. The CIA did estimate quality differences for many pieces of equipment, but when estimates were not possible, it assumed no difference, resulting in a large overestimate of Soviet quality. Franklyn D. Holzman, a Soviet specialist at Tufts University, estimated the quality differences from available data on non-military equipment. The export prices of Soviet machine tools, transformers, land turbines, and compressors were set 30 to 50 percent below those of other countries' competitive products to offset quality differences.[41] Thus, if, as was likely, military equipment was similarly inferior, a correct estimate easily might reveal that in 1976 the United States spent more on defense. In any case, it is unlikely that Soviet expenditures were significantly higher.

Moreover, the United States probably outspent the Soviet Union in the decade ending in 1977. Taking quality into account and balancing the dollar and ruble estimates, Holzman concluded that the expenditures in the two countries were approximately equal in 1977. If, as the CIA judged, Soviet expenditures had been climbing more rapidly, then the United States outspent the Soviet Union in the preceding decade.[42]

Further, Korb disregarded the obviously more relevant comparison between NATO and the Warsaw Pact. Britain's International Institute of Strategic Services estimated that, measured even in dollars, NATO's expenditures in 1978 exceeded those of the Warsaw Pact; the NATO members other than the United States spent $75 billion compared to only $12 billion by Warsaw Pact members other than the Soviet Union. Further, Korb ignored the portion of Soviet expenditures that was for defense against China, which Defense Secretary Harold Brown's report for fiscal 1979 estimated at one-fifth the total.

SALT

Adamant about the U.S. lead in MIRVs, Nixon turned SALT into a farce. His appointee, Gerard Smith, the head of the Arms Control and Disarmament Agency (ACDA) and of the SALT delegation, said, "Too late was it realized that no stable agreement to limit offensive strategic arms could exist without stringent MIRV control."[43] This respectable former adviser to Dulles was exasperated.

The United States missed a great opportunity. To reduce the PR, SALT should have banned or limited MIRVs, not the number of missiles. This perversion was consistent with the administration's goal of superiority and its hope that the Soviets would fail or take a long time to develop the MIRV technology.

From the beginning, the administration opposed a significant limitation on offensive weapons. According to Kissinger, at the first official session of SALT in Helsinki on November 17, 1969, Smith was afraid that since he favored a ban on ABMs and a moratorium on MIRV testing, he would not like the president's instructions. To curb any dangerous enthusiasm, the administration instructed the delegates to refer any proposals on MIRVs to Washington. Kissinger also reported that the administration planned to kill any move for a MIRV ban by raising the problem of verifiability.[44]

Ten years later, Smith's book, *Doubletalk*, accused Nixon of bad faith.[45] Smith's complaint that the Soviets refused to renounce the right to test MIRVs was less persuasive. He described their demand for a prohibition of the production and deployment of the weapons as one-sided. But it was unreasonable to ask the Soviets to surrender access to a technology already mastered by the United States.

The Soviet bogey reinforced the administration's stone wall on MIRVs, contributing to the failure of SALT, as will become obvious. We first consider the agreements. The administration gave up nothing. It wanted to ban the hopeless ABMs, but, as a negotiating tactic, it proposed to allow only a minimal deployment. Surprisingly, the

Soviets agreed right off, and the ABM Treaty permitted only one system, to be located either at the national capital or at an ICBM field.

Since Nixon wanted only "qualitative" improvements in the ICBMs, the prohibition of additional launchers and their relocation was no sacrifice. Nor did the prohibition of the upgrading of light- to heavy-ICBM launchers cost anything. Another provision limited the number of SLBMs unless those added replaced ICBMs up to a maximum of 710. This, too, cost nothing since the plans called for Tridents to replace Poseidons, not more Poseidons.

Despite the knowledge that the ABMs were useless, the United States was slow to agree to a ban or a restriction. Dr. Wolfgang Panofsky, the director of the Stanford Linear Accelerator, had told a Senate subcommittee that the Safeguard system's radars were less than one-tenth as blast resistant as the silos they were supposed to protect. After small missiles knocked out the radars, the silos would be undefended.[46]

As always, deterrence was at the center. Because he believed the AR to be high, Senator Frank Church was willing to raise the PR to ensure deterrence. He therefore made the shocking proposal that the United States threaten a launch on warning, despite the risk of a false signal setting off a nuclear war.[47] Others would not go this far. Kissinger, among others, saw the ABMs as a bargaining chip.

The opposition was widespread. Nixon wrote to Kissinger that if Gerard Smith persisted in opposing the ABMs, he should resign his post at the ACDA. The president's General Advisory Committee on Arms Control and Disarmament, headed by John McCloy, agreed with Smith. In the Verification Panel, Secretary of State William P. Rogers, Undersecretary Elliot Richardson, and Nitze, who was a member of the SALT delegation, urged that the United States propose limiting any deployment to the capitals. On the other hand, Kissinger was reluctant to see torn down the ABM systems that were being built.[48]

But the policymakers knew that the ABMs were of little use, so eventually Nixon went along. Indeed, in November 1975, only one month after it was installed, the United States abandoned its single Safeguard system, consisting of 100 Sprint missiles at the missile base near Grand Forks, North Dakota. Nor did the Soviets have much more confidence in their system. In October 1980 they dismantled half of the Galosh system, comprising 64 launchers in four sites around Moscow. According to John Collins, the system could easily be saturated.[49] It was not a great negotiating feat to limit the deployment of defensive systems that both sides were almost ready to abandon in any case.

Unfortunately, the negotiators had much more trouble with offensive weapons. In June 1969 Smith urged the administration to give up the destabilizing MIRVs in exchange for a halt to Soviet deployment of ABMs, ICBMs, and SLBMs.[50] At the same time, the public debate over MIRVs caught fire. Many members of Congress feared the effect of the MIRVs on the PR. Senators Clifford Case and Edward Brooke introduced bills to stop their testing, over 100 members of Congress supported a moratorium on further tests, and a House subcommittee urged that the SALT negotiators give a MIRV ban a high priority.[51] In April 1970 a resolution, sponsored by Senators Brooke and Sherman Cooper, calling for the immediate suspension of deployment of all offensive and defensive strategic weapons was passed by the overwhelming majority of 72 to 6. The majority included Senate Republican leader Hugh Scott and Senator Henry Jackson.[52] Even the president's General Advisory Committee on Arms Control and Disarmament favored a suspension of MIRV testing. Smith hoped to get the support of Defense Secretary Laird, who was worried that the Soviets would install MIRVs on their large missiles, but the secretary's solution was a stronger offensive capability. Optimistic as usual, the JCS would not give up the technological advantage.[53]

Nixon opposed taking the risk of using MIRVs even as a bargaining chip, but the idea of a ban had great popularity. To appear to be on the right side and at the same time shift the blame for failure to the Soviets, he fabricated the issue of verification. The opportunity came when JCS Chairman General Wheeler raised the verification problem at the National Security Council. The NSC set up the Verification Panel with Kissinger as chairman. Assuming responsibility for all issues relating to SALT, the panel superseded ACDA and the SALT delegation[54] and became Nixon's and Kissinger's instrument for blocking a ban on MIRVs.

The demand for onsite verification was bound to be rejected by the Soviets, who feared spies permanently stationed at missile bases. Serious inspection required many foreign engineers to enter the USSR. They would have to remove casings from missiles to look for MIRVs, some would have to be stationed at production facilities, and the inspection unit would have to include guards to watch over inspected missiles. The Soviets might have tolerated a few untrained sergeants, but not platoons of experts who would learn the details of Soviet operations. The U.S. Air Force probably would have no more tolerance for Soviet inspectors. Aware of the Soviet attitude, the Senate adopted a resolution for a ban of MIRVs, which specified only national verification. Onsite inspection was unnecessary since, with satellites and aircraft, Americans could count the number of warheads on missiles being tested at target ranges and measure the limits of the size of the missiles contained in silos. At Vladivostok the negotiators overcame the problem by simply assuming that any missile observed to carry multiple warheads in the tests was in fact so armed. The conciliatory Senate even refrained from demanding that the Soviets accept their technological inferiority; it proposed only a ban on deployment, not of tests. However, Nixon insisted that the SALT delegation counter any call for a ban with a demand for on-site inspection.

The JCS relied on the tactic of raising an unlikely possibility, saying that the United States would need MIRVs if the Soviets abrogated the ABM Treaty. The chiefs also tried to minimize the consequences for the PR. Ignoring the large number and accuracy of the Minuteman III warheads, the JCS said that the low-yield MIRVs could not achieve a first strike.[55]

Cleverly, Nixon proposed a ban conditional on onsite inspection.[56] To ensure that no agreement was reached banning MIRVs, he demanded onsite inspection of Soviet surface-to-air missiles (SAMs), as well as of ICBMs and IRBMs, giving the reason that they might interdict single-warhead missiles. He argued that the Soviets would violate a MIRV ban and gain a first-strike capability if the SAMs were secretly improved to reduce the retaliatory damage. This farfetched argument justified Nixon's demand for the dismantling of the large Soviet radars used to aim the SAMs.[57] He ignored studies by the State Department, the ACDA, and the CIA demonstrating the impossibility of secretly improving the SAMs. The Pentagon also advanced far-fetched arguments, insisting that without the Minuteman IIIs enough secret improvements could be made to threaten the U.S. retaliatory capability. The Defense Department rejected offering an exchange for a ban on Soviet testing because the Soviets might use short-range or space tests and then secretly deploy MIRVs.[58]

Accordingly, the administration resisted indirect and unofficial Soviet bids for negotiations. In the summer of 1969 Soviet academician Millionschikov told Senator Hubert Humphrey that he saw no obstacle to a ban on tests in exchange for one on deployment. In the fall Counselor Vorontsov of the Soviet embassy in Washington said that the Soviets were developing MIRVs only in response to the United States; a suspension by the United States would be followed by one by the USSR. But by the spring of 1970 the Soviets were no longer willing to surrender the right to make tests; they proposed a ban on only the deployment and production of MIRVs.

Contrary to the widespread impression, Kissinger actively fought any concessions. In a letter to Nixon, he opposed a moratorium because it risked ending the Minuteman III and Poseidon programs. Ignoring the evidence that the ABMs were ineffective, he said that the programs were a useful negotiating tool for removing the ABM system that the Soviets already had deployed.[59]

The Ford-Brezhnev Vladivostok summit in 1974 produced a sub-ceiling for MIRVed missiles of 1,320 under an overall ceiling of 2,400 ICBMs and SLBMs. With so many MIRVs permitted, the limit on the number of strategic missiles increased the PR.

In December 1974 a reporter asked Kissinger whether he now regretted that the United States had deployed MIRVs. His inexcusable reply was that he wished he had thought through the implications of a MIRVs world more carefully in 1969 and 1970 than he had.[60]

Nixon and Kissinger stubbornly opposed any limitation on MIRVs until the Soviets mastered the technology, when they changed their minds. Later, Kissinger kept shifting. As we have just seen, in 1974 he expressed some regrets about MIRVs; in his memoirs, Kissinger said that he had not given in to the Soviets; and in March 1983 in *Time*, again revising his memory, he blamed the Soviets for ignoring the administration's hints to open the subject of a MIRV ban in the SALT talks.[61] Kissinger now was seeking to join the group that saw MIRVs as the chief danger. The proposal to replace the Midgetman IIIs with single-warhead mobile missiles had won considerable support in Congress. Kissinger went so far as to say that we should go ahead with the shift unilaterally if the Soviets are unwilling to negotiate mutual deMIRVing. Once out of office, he joined the disarmament crowd along with other former administration officials. He no longer argued that we needed MIRVs to conduct nuclear warfare.

A LITTLE BRINKMANSHIP

We may gain a clearer idea of what Kissinger meant by the political payoff of a powerful nuclear arsenal from a description of the sequence of events leading up to the U.S. nuclear threat during the Yom Kippur War of 1973. Apparently, keeping the Soviets out of the Middle East was worthy of great risk. With Nixon incapacitated by Watergate, Kissinger and the Washington Special Action Group (WSAG) made the critical decisions. The incident also illustrates how confrontation may lead to a catastrophe—how misunderstandings or deliberate attempts to strengthen a country's position may start a war.[62]

The Israeli Army had trapped the Egyptian Third Army along the Suez Canal.[63] In Moscow, on October 20, 1973, Kissinger agreed to demand a cease-fire from the Israelis, and although Golda Meir reluctantly accepted the conditions two days later, there was some confusion about the 12-hour deadline. Under the impression that the United States would not insist on strict observance of the deadline, the Israelis tried to complete the encirclement of the Third Army. On October 23 Brezhnev accused Kissinger of having deceived him.

By the 24th Brezhnev had placed Soviet airborne divisions with a total strength of 40,000 on alert, and an airborne command post was set up in the southern Soviet Union. At Belgrade and several other airports the air force made preparations for departure, Soviet amphibious assault vessels and two helicopter carriers were deployed in the Mediterranean, and the United States heard rumors of a Soviet ship carrying nuclear missile warheads in the Mediterranean. U.S. intelligence could not locate the Soviet aircraft that had been flying weapons and supplies to Egypt and Syria. Intercepts of Soviet messages indicated changes in flight plans, and there was a surge in Soviet communications.

After President Sadat asked the United States and the Soviet Union on the afternoon of the 24th to send a peace-keeping force, several UN delegations drafted a resolution for a cease-fire imposed by the superpowers. Pointing to the danger of superpower rivalry in the region, Nixon's reply to Sadat rejected his request. In the evening a note from Brezhnev warned that the Soviets might take unilateral action.

Late the same evening Kissinger chaired a meeting of the WSAG, which requested that the SAC be placed in defense readiness condition III (DEFCON III), with DEFCON I representing a state of war, and the lowest state being DEFCON V. With the president's consent, the JCS chairman ordered this state of alert to take effect by 2:00 A.M. the following morning. At 5:40 A.M. a note to Brezhnev via Ambassador Dobrynin threatened "incalculable consequences" of Soviet unilateral action. At the same time, to press the Israelis, Kissinger informed them of the Soviet preparations and of the U.S. response. In the early afternoon of the 25th the Soviet ambassador to the UN stopped pressing for a U.S.-Soviet peacekeeping force, and the Israelis began to observe the cease-fire. Shortly after, the Security Council sent a force, which did not include U.S. or Soviet troops.

The crisis went no further than threats and counterthreats, but it demonstrated the dangers of relying on nuclear forces. Fortunately, the Soviets did not have much at stake, and, since they gained the nominal objective of saving the Egyptian forces from annihilation, they were not forced to accept a humiliating defeat. The United States only had to move part of the way down the slippery slope.

Confrontations will recur, Reagan and his successors may be quicker to see vital interests being threatened, and a confrontation in a period of hostility will be more dangerous than in one of détente. Moreover, after this experience, a bomber alert may not be effective. We slide a little further down that slope each time a threat is made.

6
Carter and
the MX

SOVIET EXPANSIONISM VS. THE PSYCHOLOGY
OF POWER

The Soviet Buildup and the MX Decision

After the Minuteman III was deployed the Soviets raced ahead
with their counterforce capability (Table 6.1). By the end of 1979
they had deployed 240 SS-18s, each carrying eight warheads with a
yield of between 500 and 900 kt., in contrast to the Minuteman III,
which carried only three warheads with a yield of only 170 kt. More
frightening still, the Soviets were catching up in accuracy; the CEP of
the SS-18 was about the same as the .12 nm. of the Minuteman III.
An SS-18 was the equivalent of five Minuteman IIIs in offensive
power, and it became the major threat, accounting for nearly two-
thirds of the combined Soviet ICBM and SLBM capability. There
were also the SS-19s carrying six warheads, each with a yield of 550
kt. and a respectable CEP of .19 nm. Since 1975 the Soviet land-
based force had quintupled in offensive power; it now had approximately three times as much power as the U.S. land-based force. The
Soviets had come a long distance.

Carter may have realized that the SS-18s and SS-19s were the
latest chapters in a race. As we will see, he made a half-hearted effort
to negotiate some reduction. Worse, the improvement in the Minuteman III missiles, the Pershing II, and the MX decisions accelerated
the race. Carter ordered the replacement of the warheads on 300
Minuteman III missiles with Mark 12A warheads, which had twice
the yield and possibly also greater accuracy. This was no minor

Table 6.1
The Buildup of Soviet ICBMs and SLBMs, 1975–1979

	Number			Yield	CEP
	1975	1979	Warheads	mt.	nm.
ICBMs					
SS-7	190	0	1	4	1.0
SS-8	19	0	1	3	1.0
SS-9	298	68	3	3.5	1.0
SS-18	10	240	8	.7	.14
SS-11	960	650	3	.75	.75
SS-13	60	60	4	.75	.24
SS-17	10	140	4	.75	.24
SS-19	60	240	6	.55	.19
SLBMs					
SS-N-4	21	3	1	1	1.5
SS-N-5	60	57	1	1.5	1.5
SS-N-6	528	468	3	.75	.7
SS-N-8	132	289	1	.75	.8
SS-N-17	0	12	1	.5	.75
SS-N-18	0	160	3	1	.75

Note: Mid-point substituted for range of yield when Collins provided only the range.

Source: John M. Collins, *U.S.-Soviet Military Balance: Concepts and Capabilities, 1960–1980* (New York: McGraw-Hill, 1980), pp. 449, 453.

"qualitative improvement." According to Raymond L. Garthoff, "The Minuteman III with the Mk-12A warhead is said to have ten times the lethal potential of its predecessor, with an accuracy [CEP] of 250 meters, half the miss radius of its predecessor, while its warhead of 335 kilotons is more than twice that of its predecessor." Further, 300 missiles could theoretically target 900 Soviet ICBMs.[1] The enhancement did not attract much attention in the United States, perhaps because it was only a change in the warheads, not a new weapon system. But according to Garthoff, Carter had decided to add the equivalent of about 1,000 Minuteman III missiles.

In 1979 the administration decided to deploy in West Germany the accurate Pershing II missiles, which could strike targets in or close to Moscow within 15 minutes of launching, raising the PR much more than the equivalent ICBM counterforce capability. The Pershing IIs were not in place before 1983, but the Carter administration made the deployment decision.

In the same year the administration proposed the MX program, which Reagan has partially implemented. With ten warheads, each with a yield of 335 kt. and a CEP of .05 nm., a single MX will have 30 times the offensive power of a Minuteman III; 200 MX missiles would be the equivalent of 6,000 Minuteman IIIs. If these figures do not boggle the mind, then perhaps a comparison with the entire land-based Soviet force will. The proposed 200 MX missiles would have had no less than 4.7 times the counterforce capability of the entire Soviet ICBM force at the end of 1979, or 2.4 times as much as in 1983. The MX decision expressed the policy, as declared by Presidential Directive 59 (PD-59), to prepare for protracted limited nuclear warfare. Carter hoped to have an invulnerable land-mobile basing mode, but he planned to go ahead without one.

The policy, which hardly suited Carter's rhetoric, showed much confusion. It was inconsistent with his election campaign attacks on SALT I for allowing too many missiles and with his efforts to negotiate large arms reductions.[2] Soon after taking office, Carter sent Secretary of State Cyrus Vance to Moscow with a list of proposed cuts which were much deeper than those in the Vladivostok agreement.

The president was not the only confused dove in the administration. When the chips were down, Walter Mondale, formerly an ardent MIRV opponent, switched sides.[3] Vance was another dove who joined the majority at the June 1979 NSC meeting.[4] We know little about Carter's own attitude. His memoirs' two short references to the MX only reveal a reluctance to say anything.[5] However, the hawkish advisers, National Security Adviser Zbigniew Brzezinski, Defense Secretary Harold Brown, and Nitze, were more outspoken.

Brzezinski and the Democrats on the MX and the Perception of Power

One would think that the Russian bear had gone wild and the administration was greatly frightened. The MX missiles alone would multiply the offensive capability 800 times. But the proposed huge multiplication of forces was intended only to preserve U.S. political influence. The complex psychopolitical argument for the proposal concerned the balance of power and bargaining. Brown was the only Cabinet member publicly to contemplate a nuclear war. But he too felt more comfortable with the political argument that the MX would restrain the Soviet demands in confrontations. The ephemeral case said nothing about the specifics of U.S.-Soviet conflicts. Chicken was the whole game. The administration expected confrontations of one kind or another, and the members felt that winning the rivalry in counterforce capability would keep them from blinking first. The

MX also was needed to keep friendly countries within the camp. Clearly, the Democrats wanted superiority as much as the Republicans, but their reluctance to appeal to paranoid fears left them with only the ephemeral political case and the other fall-back, the bargaining-chip argument.

National Security Adviser Brzezinski, who exercised influence daily by briefing the president, qualified as an expert with a Harvard Ph.D. in political science and previous appointments as professor and director of the Research Institute on Communist Affairs at Columbia University. His support of the Vietnam War, while a member of the State Department's Planning Council under President Johnson, had won him a reputation as a hawk.

Brzezinski did not come right out and say that the Soviet Union would attack Western Europe or some other vital region. As we will see, he may have since changed his mind. But before he reached the inner White House sanctums, his published views of Soviet policy were much more restrained. An article on U.S.-Soviet relations neither referred to expansionism, nor expressed any fear of Soviet-instigated revolutions. Having furled its revolutionary flags, Moscow only sought recognition as the "preeminent global power." By now the bogey was taboo for students of U.S.-Soviet relations, and the psychopolitics of power was the rage. Brzezinski did not even argue, as Kissinger had, that the leader in the arms race gained world influence. He dismissed the prospect of the Soviets instigating revolutions with the remark that the Politburo members were too old and tired. All Brzezinski could think of saying was that the Soviets "may find increasing gratification in 'big power chauvinism,' "[6] adding another to the list of new chauvinisms.

But power has strange effects, and when Brzezinski wrote his memoirs the Soviet leaders were young and dangerous once more. In some way Soviet nuclear superiority would promote revolution. The argument is hard to follow. Brzezinski did not actually say that the Soviets would instigate more revolutions or that they would more actively support revolutionary groups. He said that superiority would embolden the Soviets in tests of will. Presumably if the United States decided to blockade Nicaragua, as it did Cuba in the missile crisis, the Soviets now would run the blockade.

The bogey remained the issue, and in his memoirs Brzezinski was willing to go farther out on the limb. He inched toward saying that the Soviet leaders would promote revolutions. As his authority for the Soviet leaders' intentions, Brzezinski cited a Soviet journal article that said that détente would help communists to instigate revolutions.[7] The equivalent source for Reagan's ideas would be an article of opinion in *Foreign Policy*! Moreover, as Brzezinski himself reported, the Soviet article only claimed that the conditions for revolution were better, not that they were good.

At the critical NSC meeting that made the administration's MX decision on June 4, 1979, Brzezinski's words carried much weight, Carter having chosen him to make the opening statement. His main argument was political. He tossed aside the heretofore major argument for a powerful counterforce capability by recognizing that NATO's conventional forces were superior to the Warsaw Pact's, and the regional military balance was improving. But he said that strategic inferiority would cause "damaging political perceptions and encourage assertive Soviet behavior." The vulnerability of our nuclear forces was depriving us of bargaining power, and the strategic balance was fast deteriorating because the Soviets had been outspending the United States for defense since the late 1960s. Thus, Brzezinski went back to Kissinger's argument that implicit nuclear threats would win political concessions, not that the Soviets would attack. Since it was difficult to divorce the threat from the prospect of an attack, Brzezinski advanced the standard counterforce argument about a "spastic, apocalyptic war." He concluded that the threat of controlled warfare could gain political ends.[8] This muddy reasoning underlay the MX decision.

Discarding the bogey and then persuading anyone that the risk of war increased with Soviet strength was a difficult feat. References to big power chauvinism, Soviet recklessness, and bargaining power were a weak substitute for the bogey. In addition, giving up the bogey might lead us to admit that the Soviets feared an American attack. The recognition that the danger came from the symmetry of Soviet and U.S. concerns would challenge the rationale of our policy, which Brzezinski refused to do.

Brzezinski's argument for the MX and more specifically for the bigger version was as follows:

In a cover memo to the President, I urged him to approve in general the construction of a new missile with solid hard-target kill capability in order to avoid the possibility that at some point in the future the Soviets would have more strategic military options than we did. I feared that if such a situation were to arise, the United States could be forced into significant political concessions in the course of a protracted crisis with the Soviets.[9]

Thus, Brzezinski advocated accepting a high PR to ensure bargaining strength, despite his reluctance to accuse the Soviets of expansionism.

How many more games of Chicken could we survive now that Soviet inferiority was finished?

In his recent book, *Game Plan*, Brzezinski described the U.S.-Soviet relationship as a "classic historical conflict between two major powers." Now he was ready to call the Soviets expansionist, but perhaps to show balance and objectivity, he also characterized the United States as imperialist. According to Brzezinski, "It is also a struggle between two imperial systems. And it involves—for the first time in history—a two-nation contest for nothing less than global predominance."[10] Nowhere did he emphasize ideological origins for the conflict, and indeed he said that Soviet ideological fervor had waned. His list of the important origins of the conflict does refer to ideological differences, but they are one item among many. First, the collapse during World War II of the British-dominated international system left a vacuum. The Soviet Union naturally viewed the United States as the principal obstacle to its quest for greatness. Second, this was the current version of the old geopolitical conflict between the great oceanic powers and the dominant land powers. Third, the two nations differ in "the imperatives of their respective geopolitical situations," in their historical experience and therefore in their "political subconscious," in ideology, in political organization, in the relationship of the spiritual to the political, in economic organization, in life-styles, and in the nature of the ideological appeal to other nations. In addition, the Soviet Union aspires to supremacy, while the United States is at its peak in vitality and power; and the Soviets desire to surpass the United States, while the United States yearns only for peace.[11]

Brzezinski supported his argument concerning the Soviet quest for supremacy with a history of Russian imperialism. Here he distinguished Russia proper from the Soviet Union as a whole. Like Kissinger, he regarded the Soviet rulers as only the tsars' heirs. Brzezinski was no longer as inhibited as he was in his pre-White House years when he had refrained from accusing the Politburo of imperial ambitions. He emphasized Russia's dominance of the Soviet empire, including the satellites, and its unrelenting expansionist drive over the last 300 years. Persistently the aggressor, Russia was motivated by territorial acquisitiveness.[12]

For evidence of the Politburo's territorial ambitions, Brzezinski went back to the 1920 Comintern Congress, which called for the Soviet Union to establish a link with the revolution in Germany by taking control of Poland. Later the Soviet leaders also called for revolution in Asia and throughout the world. Brzezinski also referred to Stalin's ambitions. In 1939 Hitler and Stalin divided Poland between them; the next year eastern Finland and the Baltic republics were annexed. In discussions with the Nazis, the Soviets demanded a base in the Dardanelles, acknowledgement of their dominance of Finland and Bulgaria, and control of areas around the Persian Gulf. After Hitler's attack, Stalin strove for a weak postwar Germany, U.S. disengagement from Europe, and the absence in Western Europe of any major power. In addition, he demanded control of Norwegian Spitsbergen and Bear Island and a share of Italy's colonies. After the war he again demanded a base in the Dardanelles. As the price for Soviet intervention in the war against Japan, Stalin wanted to take over Sakhalin Island, the internationalization of the Chinese port of Dairen, a naval base at Port Arthur, and control of the Kurile Islands. Brzezinski also listed as evidence of Soviet imperialism the occupation of Eastern Europe and of North Korea, the attempt to maintain domination of occupied areas in Iran through satellite revolutionary governments, the communist-led Greek revolution, the Berlin blockade, and the invasion of South Korea.[13]

According to Brzezinski, military strength is the key dimension of power, not socioeconomic conditions, which become irrelevant in war. Moreover, military power affects the rivals' political conduct. In Brzezinski's view, the most important current questions are whether the military balance and therefore nuclear deterrence are endangered by the possibility of a disarming first strike; whether local conflicts will grow into a general war; and whether the nuclear stalemate will encourage the assertion of Soviet conventional power.[14] Its continuing strategic buildup may give the Soviet Union greater flexibility in the use of both strategic and conventional power, inducing a U.S. strategic paralysis. In the face of Moscow's buildup of a war-fighting nuclear capability, the United States has remained content with only a deterrence capability. Resulting superiority may encourage Soviet expansionist efforts with either conventional or strategic power.[15] About the European conventional balance, Brzezinski evidently had changed his mind since 1979. Now he saw the Warsaw Pact as far ahead of NATO.[16] Consequently, the U.S. nuclear forces are essential to deter a Soviet conventional attack. The danger that a war would escalate into a strategic engagement deters a conventional attack.[17] To extend Brzezinski's reasoning, the Soviets would enter more readily into a conventional war and thus risk nuclear war if they had nuclear superiority. Brzezinski asserted that further deterioration in relative strategic strength might deter the United States from responding to a major Soviet conventional attack with TNW. It follows that the Soviet Union might launch a conventional attack on some contiguous area.[18] Again completing Brzezinski's argument, the United States would more readily fire its TNW, thereby initiating a nuclear war, if it had nuclear superiority. A superior nuclear arsenal therefore would be a more effective deterrent of conventional aggression than would an inferior one. At best, the probability of Soviet political intimidation has increased.

Brzezinski also prescribed strong conventional forces, which would be integrated with TNW, and sufficient power to control the seas and space. National security required a massive force of MX and Trident II missiles and a strategic defense system. The current arsenal and the prospects for additions were inadequate, and Reagan was wise to urge the development of strategic defenses. The only acceptable but unlikely alternative was an arms limitation agreement that would substantially reduce Soviet strategic weaponry.[19]

Brzezinski did not argue that the Soviets' territorial acquisitiveness was so acute that the West was in danger. We should also note that the Russian aggressions cited by Brzezinski took place too far in the past to pose a future threat. Nor is the Soviet buildup an effort to gain global preeminence. It may be difficult for Americans to admit the possibility that the Soviets also feared an attack. However, a better case can be made for the proposition that they wanted to deter an attack by the United States, which had armed itself first and had brandished the nuclear weapons, than for the alternative that their aims were imperialist. Moreover, if Brzezinski got his way, the Soviets had even more reason to ensure their capability. This is not to say that crises will not recur. The Soviets may take advantage of instability in the Middle East to expand the territory under their control. The Soviets do not instigate the instability, and their nuclear and conventional strength will have little effect on events there. However, they may exploit post-Khomeini turmoil to invade Iran, and we cannot deploy sufficient conventional strength to block such an invasion. Brzezinski suggested that with a sufficiently large arsenal the United States could deter a Soviet conventional attack. Perhaps so. This would be tantamount to threatening to commit suicide and to destroy the Soviets at the same time, which we can do now without additional nuclear forces. The threat will be no more effective after we have a large MX force and strategic defenses. Brzezinski believed that strategic superiority would enable us to counter the Soviet threat of protracted nuclear warfare. But victory in a nuclear duel will be meaningless. Moreover, superiority, however defined, is unattainable. Moscow will not allow it. We should also keep in mind that the effort to achieve superiority has produced a high PR and continues to raise it.

Differing little from Nixon's, Brzezinski's and thus presumably Carter's world consisted of the United States and its allies and of the Soviets and their communist followers. The Third World and the Middle East had replaced Western Europe as the points of danger. The MX was the universal prescription against communist takeovers. Brzezinski urged the United States to take suicidal risks in future games of Chicken to prevent Soviet gains in world power. The MX was necessary to embolden the president in future crises.

Brookings' military expert, Barry M. Blechman, also prescribed a politically oriented defense policy: "The military establishment helps to set the image of the U.S. as a great power. The mere existence of large military forces is evidence of the nation's ability and its *willingness* to underwrite its announced role in the world."[20] (Emphasis in original.) Recognizing the small military advantage gained with nuclear superiority, the strategists turned themselves into political experts. Essentially agreeing with self-acknowledged hawks, the Democratic experts preferred expressing ambiguous, vague views concerning political power to adopting the illusions of the warlike writers and imitating their harsh language. The difference was only in style, not in substance, for the recommendations were the same. With experts like these advising the administration, it is no wonder that the hawks cheered its policies. The administration's dovish language was a cover for a dangerous policy.

Disagreements over priorities added to the confusion. The administration feared losing in recurrent confrontations, not hypothetical future breakdowns. Brzezinski wanted a strong hand in bargaining. Unworried by the PR, parity appeared to be less dangerous than Soviet superiority. But one party had to relent to prevent a confrontation from erupting; bilateral stubbornness was the condition for a breakdown. Congress sensibly feared the PR above all else. Thus the debaters never confronted each other directly. To do so would have required a comparison of the two risks and the associated priorities involving the Chicken game and bargaining power, which neither the administration nor Congress was willing to face.

Brown and the Bogey

In *Thinking About National Security*, cautious and thorough Defense Secretary Brown tried to make a good case by relying on both the bogey and the political argument. The quintessential nuclear expert, Brown had been director of the Livermore Laboratory, which developed nuclear weapons; then McNamara's director of Defense Research and Engineering; and, after a stint as Johnson's air force secretary, when he had a hand in the development of MIRVs, he was technically better equipped than any previous defense secretary. But when it came to major decisions there were no experts, as can be seen in his disagreement with that other so-called expert, James Schlesinger, and in his own inconsistency over time. Experts are not experts when they disagree or are inconsistent. In 1977 Brown disagreed with Schlesinger about the possibility of a limited nuclear war. He reversed positions between 1964, when he advocated a hard-target capability with MIRVed SLBMs, and 1975, when he said that a counterforce strategy was impossible to carry out. In his own defense report of February 1978, Brown doubted the possibility of controlling the firing of nuclear weapons to avoid a full-blown eruption. Nevertheless, shortly thereafter he advocated the MX as a counterforce capability.[21]

Brown's inexpert judgment on Soviet intentions mattered most, and although the choice between the 92-inch and the 83-inch missile raised many technical issues, it turned more on political questions. While Brzezinski confined himself to the banality that the two countries were rivals, Brown, who was not handicapped by professional claims in this field, had fewer inhibitions. But the MX was too dangerous to acquire on the basis of a dubious judgment of Soviet aggressiveness and of its effect on political power.

Brown rehashed the decades-old argument featuring Soviet internal problems, the Politburo and world revolution, Soviet recklessness, and the Soviet troops in Eastern Europe.[22] In his historical judgment, earlier U.S. strategic superiority had saved Western Europe.[23] Surprisingly, Brown did not consider the recent Afghanistan invasion worth mentioning.

Brown also dragged in the perception and bargaining argument. According to Brown, if the United States relied on vulnerable land-based ICBMs or abandoned them while the Soviet ICBM force remained much less vulnerable, this would be both a political and a peacetime military defeat. It would send a signal to the world that the United States lacked the skill, the judgment, or the determination to preserve a strong strategic deterrent in the face of a massive Soviet strategic buildup.[24]

As for Brzezinski, "deterrence" had become a catch-all, including the prevention of Soviet intimidation of other countries, which easily translated into efforts to enhance U.S. influence. According to

Brown, the Soviets might win even in adversarial and nonconfrontational situations, as he called them.[25] What Soviet "intimidation" meant is not clear. In short, Brown could think of no good reason for acquiring the MX, but it was the only hope of reasserting U.S. superiority.

The prescription remained the same, whatever changes were made in the concept of deterrence. With everyone believing that deterrence was prudent, but not many staying awake nights fearing a Soviet attack, the thing to do was to stuff every other pro-MX argument that one could think of into the deterrence bag. The change in the meaning of deterrence made little difference to the prescription. Only a flexible and selective capability could ensure that in a war the Soviets suffered more damage than they inflicted. Otherwise the Soviets would carry on their intimidation. Brown maintained the Strangelovian image of the president watching a large screen showing which missile silos had been hit. The United States needed a more powerful arsenal than it already had to ensure the capability of destroying conventional ground forces, as well as silos. We had to prevent the Soviets from dominating Europe and the Chinese border region after a nuclear war.[26] Some would wonder what there might be left to dominate. In any case, the old bogey would have done just as well, for Brown's answer to the Red army still was the threat of a strategic attack. The political argument provided a complicated and unpersuasive case for the MX. It was hard to believe that the outcome of political crises involving unimportant or even important interests depended on the assessment of the chances of victory in a nuclear war.

Brown did wonder about the significance of the strategic balance in an actual war, as in the following statement:

But both the inherent uncertainties of predicting the detailed outcome of a thermonuclear war and the high degree of certainty that it would result in the destruction of both the superpowers as functioning societies lead to a single conclusion—that differences in analysts' estimates of fatalities in a strategic war of two or even three times are unlikely to play so large a role in the evolution of such a crisis as the simple fact of the immense destructiveness of thermonuclear war.

Why bother, then, about the strategic balance? Because in circumstances of confrontation and crisis, or if conventional warfare between the superpowers has already broken out, decisions might be made that would seem quite irrational under most normal circumstances.[27]

Here he shifted away from the problem of political power to the prospect of an actual war triggered by a confrontation. Brown refused to evaluate the effect of the MX on this risk—the PR. Not only did he ignore this effect, but he insisted the United States had to stand firm. According to Brown, a reduction in the ability to penetrate Soviet defenses or uncertainty about the ability of the United States to retaliate in a strategic war would have two deleterious effects during a crisis. He dismissed the first effect, which was on the likelihood of a Soviet decision to make a preemptive attack. Although the alternative to preemption might appear to the Soviet leaders to be more damaging, it still appeared to him that such a decision was unlikely.[28] Brown then went on to what he thought was the more likely effect:

But a second, more likely occurrence would be an erosion of the determination of US decision makers, helped along by an avalanche of pressure from within the United States and from allies. Such pressure was substantial even during the Cuban missile crisis, when both the strategic balance and the local conventional balance were relatively favorable to the United States. Soviet perceptions of such a lack of determination could lead to the worst result for everyone: a Soviet miscalculation that the United States would not respond, when in fact the United States would—and does—so that a Soviet action sets off an all-out nuclear war.[29]

Brown's case for a stronger counterforce capability assumed a low PR. This was the basic fallacy. According to Brown, a preemptive attack was less likely than a Soviet underestimate of U.S. determination to retaliate with nuclear weapons. The idea was startling in view of the well recognized danger of a preemptive attack in a state of two-sided simultaneous alert. As for the problem of resolve, even a small risk of its own destruction by SLBMs and a few surviving ICBMs would deter the Kremlin from a deliberate attack.

The reasoning was very fuzzy. Brown did not say that the probability of an attack was high, but only that in a confrontation the best option for the Soviets might be to attack. Here again everything turned on a mere possibility, not on a probability. But the superior deterrence effectiveness of the MX over the SLBMs did not merit the added PR. Again we have to bear in mind the magnitudes of the two risks and the PR effect of additional counterforce capability. Even a small probability of retaliation by SLBMs will deter a planned attack, and any additional deterrence by the MX is more than offset by the PR effect. Unfortunately, for Brown nuclear war remained a chess game between NCAs in full control.

Conceivably, the Soviets might underestimate U.S. resolve to retaliate to an attack on an ally. But to deter a conventional attack with nuclear weapons entailed an excessive PR, one which far exceeded the AR. Without any basis, the argument assumed that the AR exceeded the PR.

Moreover, a strong case against the MX can be made even without the comparison of the two risks. Suppose that we are wrong. Suppose that we admit the hawks' worst fears and agree that the AR exceeds the PR. We still should not raise the PR by strengthening the counterforce capability, if the other less dangerous option of strengthening the conventional forces is available.

Brown did not compare the risks associated with each option. A loyal Kennedy man, Brown feared only that in a crisis the Soviets would expect us to swerve. His disregard of the PR, combined with an eagerness to show stubbornness in confrontations, was dangerous.

Nitze, the Committee on the Present Danger, and the Bogey

In 1976 Nitze helped to found the Committee on the Present Danger, which became a rich source of policymakers for Reagan. At one time or another, the committee's Board of Directors included Reagan himself, Nitze, National Security Adviser Richard V. Allen, Assistant to the President Martin Anderson, CIA Director William J. Casey, Defense Undersecretary Fred Iklé, arms control negotiator Max M. Kampelman, UN Representative Jeane J. Kirkpatrick, Navy Secretary John F. Lehman, Jr., Defense Assistant Secretary Richard N. Perle, Secretary of State George P. Schultz, Undersecretary of State W. Allen Wallis, ACDA Director Eugene V. Rostow, and his successor, Kenneth L. Adelman.[30]

Nitze clung to the bogey. In January 1976, to show that the Soviet Union's threat was continuing, he cited its aid to the North Vietnamese while they were violating the recently negotiated agreements, and the threat to intervene in the Yom Kippur War.[31] Other evidence consisted of two Soviet journal articles forecasting a favorable shift in the correlation of forces in Europe.[32] But a favorable trend in the "correlation of forces," a phrase embracing political and economic conditions as well as military strength, implied nothing about Soviet military plans. It only meant that the opportunities had improved.

Unlike Brzezinski, for whom Moscow was a great power that was willing to bargain, Nitze condemned the Politburo as the fanatical communist world leaders in the twentieth century's religious war.[33] This was an uninhibited call to arms. Summoning Americans to the cause, Nitze rejected unilateral restraint as surrender. Hawks have always called for more arms in the name of peace, and he was no different. His appeal was that to prevent a nuclear war we had to show resolve by acquiring the biggest weapons. Otherwise, the calculating and ever dedicated enemy might risk a deliberate, limited attack. This extreme image represented Moscow as a dangerous threat, not an adversary from whom concessions could be wrung at the bargaining table. Although this view was at odds with his later business-like negotiations in Geneva, it was why he urged augmenting the arsenal. The effect of the MX on the PR was ignored. The bogey was essential, and since the AR was so high, one could ignore the PR. If the probability of a deliberate attack was high, what else could the United States do but acquire more powerful weapons?

The statement by the Committee on the Present Danger in April 1977 was even more portentous:

Notwithstanding its vast territory and rich mineral resources, the Soviet Union can only with difficulty support its population. Its extreme northern latitude makes for a short agricultural season, a situation aggravated by the shortage of rain in areas with the best soil. . . . These factors have historically been among those impelling Russia—Tsarist and Soviet alike—toward the conquest or domination of neighboring lands. No empire in history has expanded so persistently as the Russian.[34]

Referring to the ruling elite, the statement went on:

This elite can enjoy its monopoly of advantages only so long as it is able to keep the deprived population under effective control—a significant relaxation of that control could spell the end of its favored status and advantage. The elite, however, is not guided merely by self-serving motives. The Soviet leadership asserts that it is the vanguard of a revolutionary society which has discovered the fundamental laws of history. The openly stated ultimate Soviet objective is the worldwide triumph of communism. This triumph would give the Soviet elite ready access to the world's resources, both human and material; it would also do away with all external challenges to its privileged position by eliminating once and for all alternative political and social systems.[35]

The statement also described the Soviet "grand strategy," which involved the use of a great variety of means to reduce any potential opponent's ability to resist. These means include economic, diplomatic, political, and ideological strategies, supported by military strength.[36] The only evidence was the military buildup.[37]

Nitze called attention to the vast Soviet expenditures for civil defense[38] and the dispersal of new industry to small and medium-size towns.[39] But the warning was misleading alarmism. Through much of the sixties, without a strong deterrent, a civil defense system was the best the Soviets could provide. As the Soviets saw it, Dulles, unprovoked, had threatened devastation, and the Americans, who had built up a powerful first-strike force, said that they planned to use nuclear weapons. Western leaders, who described the Soviets as cruel and unjust oppressors, might intervene in Polish and East German nationalist revolts. Indeed, defense may not have been the chief motive for the dispersal of industry. Economic considerations may have been primary, and Soviet planners may have hoped to reduce the overcrowding of Moscow. Look at what has happened in the United States, where industry has shifted from the big cities of the snowbelt to the sunbelt. We also heard a repetition of Wohlstetter's and McNamara's old argument that Soviet leaders would risk millions of deaths for territorial gains because the country had recovered from the slaughter of World War II. The implication of this statement is absurd. Are we to believe that only if the country had not recovered would the Soviet leaders be unwilling to risk millions of deaths?

Ensconced in well-paying, safe jobs, only mad bureaucrats would have gone about igniting revolutions, even if at the missile alarm they could rush into nearby deep caves. It was absurd to think of Soviet bureaucrats as revolutionaries, however much they repeated hackneyed doctrines. As Brzezinski said, the Soviet Union now resembled the U.S. Post Office more than Lenin's religious revival.[40] Led by Brezhnev in a dark business suit, the bureaucrats gained little from foreign Marxist victories. They had to send troops to control Eastern Europe, Cuba had to be paid off with massive aid, and Vietnam has proven to be a burden. What was more, Yugoslavia, China, and Albania had shown that, far from endowing Moscow with filial devotion, Marxist revolutions might produce dangerously independent governments.

With extreme views running wild in Washington, it would be a wonder if Moscow did not seek security from a first strike by building a powerful arsenal. The U.S. strategists' public discussion of the attacker's advantage might well have worried Moscow that the United States was planning a first strike. Brzezinski and Nitze were worried by two obscure Soviet journal articles, which only described an improvement in the conditions for revolution. The Soviets had more reason to be alarmed by the scores, perhaps hundreds, of articles by Nitze and his fellow strategists. Indeed, NATO planned the first use of nuclear weapons in what would begin as a conventional war. Any one of the conflagrations in the Third World or the Middle East might turn into a major conventional war. Worse, the proposed Pershing IIs might allow the United States to take preemptive action. Soviet leaders could hardly be blamed for building up their arsenal as rapidly as possible.

THE SOVIET THREAT TO THE ICBMs

According to Nitze, the deterrent was weak because a Soviet first strike would increase the Soviet margin in throw-weight, even if it were followed by a U.S. response.[41] This new term essentially referred to yield. To be adequate, the arsenal had to be able to match the Soviet counterforce capability, as measured by yield, after an exchange. It will be recalled that, unlike the Soviets, McNamara had opted for accuracy instead of yield. Now we learned that McNamara had made the wrong bet. Only throw-weight mattered, since after an exchange accuracy would not be needed to hit the cities, which would be the only targets left.

Nitze also made the case for the MX and the Trident by considering alternative policies and rejecting them. This was easy to do because any policy entailed risks, and there was always some possible combination of events against which a policy could not provide perfect protection. Nitze listed five deterrent postures: minimum deterrence, massive urban retaliation, flexible response, denial of nuclear war-winning capability to the Soviets, and a nuclear-war winning capability. He rejected right off the last one as unattainable. Minimum deterrence, or a capability of attacking a few cities, would not do because the Soviets could hold our cities hostage. Equally unacceptable was massive urban retaliation, which included massive retaliation and assured destruction, since it too placed the population at risk. Moreover, McNamara's shift to assured destruction did not put a stop to the Soviet buildup. Nitze was willing to agree that the weapons deployed by the Soviets in the late sixties were intended only to achieve parity, but not after 1971. Nitze chose his words carefully:

One cannot prove that this was the Soviet reasoning. But the programs they set under way about 1962—above all the new family of weapons systems embodying not only numbers and size but also greatly advanced technology, the development and deployment of which began to be evident beginning in 1971 but which must have been decided upon some years earlier—seem to reflect a fundamental state of mind on the Soviet side that contains no doubt as to the desirability of a war-winning capability, if *feasible*. [42] (Emphasis in original.)

Nitze ignored the development of the Minuteman III, which came well before 1971. McNamara's policy was hardly consistent with assured destruction. Aware of the Minuteman III program, whatever the Soviets did to enhance their arsenal may have been a reaction. The history of this program, described earlier, indicates that McNamara was pursuing a damage-limitation strategy. Moscow had good reason to fear a first-strike capability.

According to Nitze, without a large capability, Flexible Response was no better than minimum deterrence. I quote Nitze:

In this form of deterrence the United States would have the capability to react to a Soviet counterforce attack without going immediately to a counter-city attack. It would thus increase the credibility of deterrence. The question of military or political victory if deterrence fails would depend on the net surviving destructive capacity of the two sides after the initial counterforce exchanges. If the net surviving capacity after such a flexible response were grossly to favor the Soviet Union or if each limited exchange placed the United States in a progressively weaker relative position, we are back to the minimum deterrence or massive urban/industrial retaliation situation, depending on the amount of surviving effective nuclear capability on the U.S. side. [43]

Two things had to be kept in the forefront: the threat of a Soviet counterforce attack and the net surviving destructive capacity on both sides after a limited U.S. response. Unless the United States could continue to execute its countersilo strategy, we would be forced into the minimum deterrence strategy of attacking cities. Without a powerful counterforce capability, we could not be certain of deterring a first strike directed at our own counterforce arsenal.

Our goal had to be to deny the Soviets a war-winning capability, and the MX and Trident II were essential. Moscow would not dare attack if, after U.S. retaliation, it could expect only parity in throw-weight. According to Nitze, if current trends continued, after 1976 a Soviet attack would gain an advantage as measured by throw-weight. It could destroy more cities. Why this advantage would matter after an initial exchange is difficult to understand. Is it much of an advantage to be able to destroy 20 large cities rather than only ten? This argument is even more specious than that the side with the greatest offensive capability, for which accuracy counted more than yield, would win a nuclear war because its surviving weapons would threaten cities.

Nitze built his case by examining and rejecting all but the favored strategy. The only ground for judging the probability of outcomes was the expansionist argument. Moreover, Nitze projected trends; current strengths were unimportant. Although the current U.S. hard-target kill capability was four times as large as that of the USSR,[44] the United States was moving to minimum deterrence. By the 1980s the potential enemy would have 25 times our capability. To achieve this goal, assuming the United States did nothing, the Soviet Union would have to increase its capability 100 times.

The importance given to rates of growth was truly shocking. A larger arsenal was not enough; our lead had to grow. In 1950 the same view led Nitze in NSC-68 to advocate a large arsenal when the Soviets had no more than the bare beginnings of an arsenal; a potential arsenal was enough to alarm Nitze. In 1957 Nitze helped draft the Gaither Report, which again sounded the alarm when the United States still was far ahead. In the seventies safety could be assured only by a lengthening lead. Following Nitze's formula for safety would trigger a rapidly accelerating race.

To continue Nitze's argument, forgetting his assertion that only surviving throw-weight mattered, he said that the United States had to make up for its throw-weight disadvantage by reducing the CEP of its weapons. Nitze based his hopes on the maneuvering reentry vehicle (MaRV), which he expected to achieve a CEP as small as .02 nm. (120 feet), or virtually pinpoint accuracy. Aware of the problem of crisis stability—of the PR—he offered the mild assurance that greater accuracy did not necessarily result in greater crisis instability since the Soviets might dismantle their ICBMs and acquire less vulnerable SLBMs. To count on the sensible Soviets to save us from our recklessness was not a strong recommendation for a destabilizing policy. Nitze also said that the United States would enhance stability by accelerating the development of the Trident and the B-1 bomber, and by deploying the MX in the invulnerable multiple-protective-shelter (MPS) basing mode. Although the invulnerability of the Trident and an MPS basing mode for the MX might reduce the PR, Nitze supported Reagan's request for the authorization of 100 MX missiles in vulnerable fixed silos. Moreover, the accuracy of the MX and the Trident II would increase the PR. Nitze emphasized the invulnerability, but the package as a whole would not reduce the PR.

Nitze failed to demonstrate that a large increase in counterforce capability would give the United States the victory in a strategic duel that he said deterrence required. Further, to obtain Nitze's adequate retaliatory capability meant gaining a first-strike capability or nearly so, which the Soviets would not permit. Nitze also failed to consider the effect on the PR of the growth of the counterforce capability on both sides. The Soviets would not quietly accept inferiority, and any gain in deterrence did not merit the increase in the PR.

Even the combination of a strong counterforce capability and invulnerability was of dubious merit. Since the United States was not to strike first, the counterforce capability served no purpose. Faced by an invulnerable land-based force, the Soviets could strike only other military and industrial facilities or cities. If, as Nitze argued, the goal of an invulnerable basing mode was a low PR, the ICBM force was superfluous.

It becomes apparent that a superior counterforce capability was intended to provide a first-strike capability. Successive administrations have repeatedly denied that this has been and remains the objective of efforts to achieve superiority, but no other goal makes sense. A superior capability might deter a retaliatory attack by surviving Soviet missiles, and invulnerability would add to the deterrence of retaliation. Thus, standing Nitze's analysis on its head, the United States might attempt to do what he feared from the Soviets. If they feared a preemptive attack, then the argument suggests that the hawks wanted the capability of carrying one out. Nitze tried to deal with this doubt by predicting that the Soviets would remove the danger by also building an invulnerable capability. However, the Soviets were unlikely to achieve this goal quickly, and the United States would retain its superiority for some time. Future technology is uncertain in any case.

SALT II

The goal of arms control negotiations should have been to cut the number of accurate warheads on each side relative to the number of launchers on the other. A reduction in the warhead/launcher ratio would reduce the PR. One approach was to raise the limit on launchers while maintaining the limit on warheads. Instead, the negotiations reduced the number of launchers. Carter did not recognize that such a cut raised the PR. Another reason for the failure was the high priority the administration assigned to strengthening the U.S. counterforce capability.

The United States was reluctant to give up the Trident II and the MX even in exchange for a reduction in the number of SS-18s. The package might have included a prohibition on SSBNs closely approaching a capital city and canceling deployment of the Pershing IIs in Western Europe. The requirement of verifiability also conflicted with the major goal. Mobility enhanced the survivability of land-based missiles and therefore reduced the PR, but it also reduced verifiability, which had a higher priority. Finally, the agreement should not have limited the number of strictly retaliatory weapons, including cruise missiles and bombers. Nevertheless, since they were bargaining chips, cruise missiles were covered by the SALT II agreement.

The administration had no interest in reducing the PR, as Brzezinski's and Strobe Talbott's reports on the debates reveal. In a simple-minded way, Carter wanted deep cuts because missiles were dangerous. The universal fear of their destructive capability lent support, as the birth of the nuclear freeze movement testified. The thoughtless protests obscured the important goal, for to reduce the number of launchers on both sides gained nothing. In addition, the goal of an agreement for its own sake interfered. For some in the administration, reaching an agreement came first, not a low PR. Also, Carter wanted an important place in history. The finishing touches on Kissinger's Vladivostok agreement would earn nothing more than a footnote. Only deep cuts would give him a special claim, and they were simple enough for voters to understand.

As we saw earlier, the services reckoned that manned bombers advanced their interests best. The JCS was more than happy to concede long-range cruise missiles in exchange for the B-1 bomber.

Carter pressed for deep cuts immediately after he was in office. At a meeting of the Special Coordination Committee (SCC) of the NSC, he attacked the Vladivostok agreement for setting a ceiling of 2,400 strategic launchers and a subceiling of 1,320 MIRVed missiles. He was so insistent that neither Brzezinski nor Secretary of State Cyrus Vance, who were more concerned about Soviet receptiveness, objected. Six years later, Brzezinski still thought that Carter was naive. He said flatly, "I favored modest cuts as the most attainable goal."[45] Responsible for the negotiations, Vance was especially concerned. He knew that Kissinger had conceded a high limit to MIRVed missiles so as not to have to accept a restriction on the number of forward-based U.S. missiles, nor the inclusion of British and French missiles in the number of strategic launchers. Brown's position appears to have been ambiguous.[46] In any case, no one at the meeting mentioned the warhead/launcher ratio or stability.

The goal of "deep cuts" did not deal with outstanding issues and defined no priorities for the negotiators. Kissinger had left unresolved the Backfire and cruise missile issues. According to the Soviets, the Backfire, which was not a strategic bomber, did not belong on the agenda, and they wanted to limit the number and range of cruise missiles. Without guidelines, Carter made concessions that were attractive to the Soviets and did not repel Senator Jackson. He also allowed the counterforce strategists and the services to influence the U.S. negotiating position. Since the cruise missiles were not a counterforce weapon, the strategists were willing to give them up, and the air force preferred a new manned bomber.

For the chief negotiator and former member of McNamara's Defense Department, Paul Warnke, SALT II was an opportunity to improve U.S.-Soviet relations. His primary goal was an agreement, not reducing either the PR or the AR. Fearing that Warnke would concede too readily, Nitze fought his confirmation by the Senate. Moreover, Warnke's casual dismissal of the vulnerability issue earned him a black mark in Nitze's book.

Warnke had to negotiate with the Soviets and with Senator Jackson, neither of whom worried much about the PR. Accordingly, at the SCC meeting of March 10, 1977, Warnke suggested softening up the Soviets by conceding a limit to the range of GLCMs. He argued that they feared that the West Germans would eventually acquire these weapons. He also warned that the weapons' range should be limited before the Soviets caught up with the technology, and while they were still willing to agree to their control. He reminded the others that the United States now would have less to fear than they would have had MIRVs come under control earlier.[47] Nobody at the meeting saw any harm in the proposal.

The JCS's bureaucratic interests dominated their view of the cruise missiles, which were the B-1's chief competitor. The B-1 was to be a much more expensive ALCM carrier than the B-52, which could do just as well. Without the cruise missiles, the B-1 program would have easier sailing. The JCS proposed a cruise-missile range limit of 1,500 km., low enough to prevent GLCMs coming within striking range of the Soviet Union. This limit would also force cruise-missile carrying aircraft and vessels to approach the Soviet Union more closely and become more vulnerable.[48] The range limit would help protect the career opportunities of officers.

Other policymakers promoted the search for superiority. Secretary Brown and David Aaron, Brzezinski's deputy and Mondale's adviser on foreign policy, advocated limits on modernization as a way to constrain the Soviets. Aaron's chief worry was the increasing vulnerability of the U.S. ICBMs to the Soviet heavy ICBMs.[49]

The achievement of Carter's apparently idealistic goal would not reduce the PR. To cut the arsenals from 1,320 MIRVed launchers to only 1,200 would make no difference. Indeed, it would make no difference to the AR as well. The proposal was only a gesture. Carter's lack of interest in the PR also was demonstrated by his acceptance of a low limit for the range of cruise missiles.

Not everyone neglected the PR. NSC staff member Roger Molander suggested banning new types of ICBMs, including the MX. Brown, who later changed his mind, had said that the United States did not need another ICBM.[50] Brown himself proposed to slow down the introduction of new missiles by limiting the number of tests per year. However, the Soviets might have suspected a trick to maintain the U.S. lead in accuracy.[51]

The SCC meeting of March 19, 1977, decided that Vance was to propose a cut in the Vladivostok aggregate total of 2,400 strategic delivery vehicles to 1,800-2,000 and in the ceiling of 1,320 MIRVed, strategic missiles to 1,100-1,200. These reductions would not have been enough to prevent the threat of a first strike. Not even the suggested cut to 550 MIRVed weapons would have been adequate. With ten warheads per ICBM, the number was more than enough to destroy all the ICBMs permitted by the agreement on each side. A third proposed limit of 150 would have cut the number of Soviet heavy missiles by half; the United States put in this category both the 272 Soviet SS-9s and the 36 SS-18s (as at the end of 1976), adding up to 308 missiles. Since the United States had none, the Soviets were expected to reject this proposal.

The agreement finally signed on June 18, 1979, did not depart significantly from the one reached at Vladivostok. The limits were: 2,250 launchers, including heavy bombers; 1,320 launchers for MIRVed missiles, including heavy bombers equipped with long-range cruise missiles; 1,200 launchers for MIRVed missiles, not including heavy bombers; 820 launchers for MIRVed ICBMs; no mobile launchers for heavy ICBMs; no increase in the number of warheads on existing ICBMs; the flight testing or deployment of no more than one new type of light ICBM, carrying no more than ten warheads, with new heavies prohibited; no flight testing or deployment of SLBMs carrying more than 14 reentry vehicles. The prohibition of new heavies, together with the freeze of launchers, limited the Soviets to their present 308 heavies, and the United States could have none. The three-year protocol prohibited the flight testing or deployment of mobile ICBMs and the deployment of GLCMs and SLCMs with a range of more than 600 km. The last provision would have sacrificed some stability had it been included in the agreement proper.

The invasion of Afghanistan in December 1979 provoked Carter to withdraw his request for ratification. The lack of a legal bind did not prevent the parties from observing the agreement, which they continue to do.

Unfortunately, the agreement became the springboard for another potentially huge and dangerous addition to the arsenal. In an effort to win Senator Jackson's support, Carter promised to push the MX program. The bargaining with both the Soviets and the Senate accelerated the arms race and increased the PR.

THE MX AND ITS VULNERABILITY

Neither the deployment of the MX nor the proposed number of such missiles troubled the administration. The debates were over the basing mode and the size of the missile. To prevent the issue of the basing mode from becoming an insuperable problem, Carter separated it from the deployment issue. Of course, a vulnerable basing mode for so lucrative a target added enormously to the PR.

The choice between the 92-inch and the 83-inch diameter revolved around the issue of counterforce capability versus survivability. The 83-inch missile might be small enough to be land-mobile and therefore more survivable, and it also had the advantage of fitting the Trident II's launch tubes. In addition, it could accommodate the ten warheads permitted by SALT II.

Brzezinski led the fight for the larger missile. He had no illusions about winning a nuclear war, but the perception argument allowed him to join the hawks without also having to accept their vision of victory in a nuclear war. Political power, as he saw it, simply increased with the missile's counterforce capability. True, SALT II prohibited more than ten warheads, but if the Soviets abrogated the agreement, their large missiles would have the lead in silo-killing capability. We needed the larger missiles to win this contest for political power.

For Brown, Senator Jackson, and the air force, survivability was not essential. What mattered, as the Ford administration had said, was that the United States needed the missile to attack hardened "time-urgent" targets.[52] Despite their denials, it is difficult to see any grounds for their support of the MX other than the view that the United States needed a first-strike capability. Few fixed-silo missiles would survive a Soviet attack, so "time-urgent" could mean only "first strike." Even if we remove the "time-urgent" requirement, it is still hard to see any other objective. The MX's silo-killing capability would be useless after a Soviet first strike. It was highly unlikely that a Soviet attack would be limited to a few MX missiles if the surviving missiles could destroy most of the Soviet land-based force. The air force wanted no fewer than 300 missiles, which would have been able to destroy between 1,800 and 3,000 hardened targets.

According to Brown, the countervailing strategy, as he called it, sought to deny the Soviets victory, however defined, in any stage of a war. The strategy is difficult to distinguish from one in which the United States seeks a first-strike capability. As Brown said,

the United States seeks a situation in which the Soviets would always lose more than they could reasonably expect to gain from either beginning or escalating a military conflict. . . .

The countervailing strategy is less of a departure from previous doctrine than is often claimed. It keeps deterrence at the core of U.S. policy. And it implies no illusion that nuclear war once begun would be likely to stop short of an all-out exchange. But it does acknowledge that such a limited war could happen, and it seeks to convince the Soviets that if a limited nuclear attack by them somehow failed to escalate into an all-out nuclear exchange, they would not have gained from their aggression. . . .

The plans to carry out the countervailing strategy could require increases in accuracy to attack hard targets, and they will certainly require improvements in command-and-control. The evolution from the criteria in National Security Study Memorandum 242 in 1974 (which calls for targeting plans, including options to threaten Soviet military targets, based on available weapons systems) to those of Presidential Directive 59 of 1980 (which makes flexibility in targeting options a factor in systems acquisition) could also provide a justification for an expansion of U.S. counterforce capability.[53]

On September 7, 1979, the president announced plans for 200 missiles, each of which would move among 23 hardened sites along a closed loop, or "racetrack," between 15 and 20 miles in length. Each launcher was to be parked horizontally to facilitate rapid shifting. A launcher could move to another site after a warning of an imminent attack and continue to move. A first strike would be unable to destroy most of the 4,600 aim points. If the agreement limiting the number of Soviet MIRVs did not hold up, then more shelters could be added.[54]

In July 1980 PD-59 stated the policy of preparing for a limited, prolonged war. The United States planned to target missile silos and the command-and-control capability, including the Soviet political leaders. According to Brzezinski, the strategy's most articulate proponent, PD-59 marked a shift away from preparing for a brief conflict to preparing for a protracted war.[55] According to Brown, who disagreed, the document only declared a refinement of long established policies.[56] But James Schlesinger went even further than Brzezinski; he saw the policy as fundamentally new and as more extreme than the defense policy had been earlier. Schlesinger said that Nixon's policy had sought only the capability of making limited, selective attacks, while Carter sought victory. Herken reported that Schlesinger based his view on the increase in the number of weapons and in the number of potential Soviet targets from 25,000 to 40,000, as well as on the document. According to Herken, "Schlesinger concluded that PD-59 'took logic too far' by spinning out theoretical concepts 'in a way that was still barely plausible on paper, but in my guess is not plausible in the real world.' "[57]

Curiously, policymakers have planned a nuclear war while doubting its feasibility. Schlesinger was not the only one to express skepticism about nuclear war plans. As we have seen, Brown and Brzezinski also had doubts. Brzezinski probably thought of PD-59 as a warning to the Soviets against dangerous moves, not as a serious plan. Nevertheless, the plans added to the PR. Military actions will be guided by such documents. If and when a war breaks out, commanders will look to PD-59 to supply direction. Moreover, some policymakers did expect at least an effort to conduct a war in the prescribed manner. Thus, Brown would not have said that PD-59 reflected long-standing policy unless he took it seriously, and Schlesinger would not have disagreed so strongly. They did not view the planning as mere show.

Carter was unable to implement the new weapons program over the opposition of the designated host states of Nevada and Utah. These states objected to being selected as targets and to the expected environmental damage and growth in demand for water.

SS-20s vs. Pershing IIs and GLCMs

Carter's decision in December 1979 to deploy 108 Pershing IIs in Western Europe showed little concern for the PR. His decision to deploy 464 ground launched cruise missiles (GLCMs) did not raise the same problems. The Pershing IIs threatened Soviet command centers with destruction within 15 minutes and, with some modification, they could strike Moscow itself. Doubts concerning the need for the Pershing IIs were raised by Deputy Undersecretary of Defense Walter Slocombe's testimony that SLBMs and ICBMs already covered these targets.[58] However, advocates said that the weapons made Soviet strategic and tactical command-and-control centers more vulnerable; they could strike with little warning. Not even a launch-on-warning policy would protect Soviet ICBMs. Apparently, Carter did not regard this capability as dangerous enough to offset the gain in the contest for bargaining power. The decision was a response to the Soviet threat to Western Europe posed by the new SS-20s. These missiles carried three warheads, each with 150 kt. yield, a CEP of .2 nm., and a range of 2,700 nm. With a solid propellant, they were more reliable than the old liquid-fueled missiles, the SS-4s and SS-5s, which they replaced.

Two decades earlier Helmut Schmidt, whose top priority had been to reduce the PR, had vigorously opposed the deployment of the IRBMs. Now, as chancellor, he was worried more by Soviet political power. He sparked the move to deploy the Pershing IIs by raising the alarm that the SS-20s had eliminated the U.S. shield:

SALT codifies the nuclear strategic balance between the Soviet Union and the United States. . . . SALT neutralizes their strategic nuclear capabilities. In Europe this magnifies the significance of the disparities between East and West in nuclear tactical and conventional weapons. . . . strategic arms limitations confined to the United States and the Soviet Union will invariably impair the security of the West European members of the Alliance vis-à-vis Soviet military superiority in Europe if we do not succeed in removing the disparities of military power in Europe parallel to the SALT negotiations. So long as this is not the case we must maintain the balance of the full range of deterrence strategy.[59]

Schmidt, who expected more pressure on Western Europe, not an actual attack, now wanted bargaining power above all. He did not mention any difficult, unresolved issues, but only undefined pressures. His view now was that if Moscow canceled U.S. power, Western Europe would become its vassal. The weighing of political influence entailed predictions of the outcome of counterforce engagements and thus estimates of the balance of power. The Soviets' ability to conduct limited warfare against Western Europe without fear of limited retaliation gave them great leverage. To prevent the Soviets from gaining power, NATO had to have an independent counterforce capability to win such a war, or, in the more moderate version, to deny victory to the Soviets. Credible deterrence required the capability of graduated escalation, which inaccurate and high-yield SLBMs did not provide.[60] A more complicated analysis depicted the threat of a conventional attack, which, unless the Soviets faced a nuclear counterattack, would sweep through Western Europe. The Pershing IIs were essential to counter such a threat, and their vulnerability enhanced deterrence and therefore helped to offset Soviet power. It was Chicken all over again, for the Soviets would not dare destroy the Pershing IIs.[61] Schmidt had joined his former opponent, Strauss. That Strauss warned against an actual attack and Schmidt only against the threat of one made little difference. The weapons policies recommended were the same. Although Schmidt did not fear the AR, he advocated accepting a high PR to protect Western Europe against vassalage. Although he did not expect an attack, he had to develop a persuasive attack scenario to argue that without the Pershing IIs the Soviets would turn Western Europe into another Finland.

But the idea of an independent NATO deterrent was unconvincing. NATO could not independently order the Pershing IIs fired. The United States was to exercise control, which meant that the Soviets would react accordingly. The Pershing IIs would be no more effective as a deterrent than the ICBMs. Moreover, limited warfare in densely populated Western Europe was even more of an illusion than limited, strategic warfare. Worse, in a crisis the threat to command centers by vulnerable weapons would be dangerous. Any additional deterrence would come at the price of a higher PR. Again, the question came down to weighing the AR against the PR.

It is a mistake to entangle the Pershing IIs with the GLCMs, which do not raise the same problem. The low speed of the GLCMs made them good retaliatory weapons, and substituting them for ICBMs and IRBMs therefore reduced the PR. Cruise missiles were small, unmanned, air-breathing, and fuel-consuming jet aircraft, with a maximum speed of 550 miles per hour. Relying on terrain contour matching (TERCOM) periodically to correct the course selected by inertial guidance and to find the target, they were expected to achieve a CEP as small as 30 meters. Estimates of their range varied between 2,000 nm. and 3,000 nm. At a cost estimated at $814,000 in 1977, they were relatively cheap.[62] Small and flying at 150 feet above land, they could avoid radar detection better than manned aircraft. Requiring as long as three hours to strike Soviet targets, the GLCMs were retaliatory weapons only, not preemptive ones.

We again heard the old themes of national resolve, the psychology of power, the need to implement Flexible Response, and the need to win support for SALT II. To gain in the psychological power struggle, the United States had to be able to match any escalation of violence. The Pershing IIs were the necessary match for the SS-20s, whose range put them one rung below the ICBMs on the ladder. Of course, the credibility refrain was repeated. And Washington had to assure the allies that SALT II was not desertion. An arms control agreement again excused an increase.[63]

The controversy revived doubts about the United States' commitment to Western Europe. In September 1979 Kissinger regained prominence by questioning the credibility of the commitment without strategic superiority. I quote an important passage:

While we were building assured destruction capabilities, the Soviet Union was building forces for traditional military missions capable of destroying the military forces of the United States. So that in the 1980s we will be in a position where (1) many of our own strategic forces including all of our land-based ICBMs, will be vulnerable and (2) such an insignificant percentage of Soviet strategic forces will be vulnerable as not to represent a meaningful strategic attack option for the United States. Whether that means that the Soviet Union intends to attack the United States or not is certainly not my point. I am making two points. First, that the change in the strategic situation that is produced by our limited vulnerability is more fundamental for the United States than even the total vulnerability would be for the Soviet Union because our strategic doctrine has relied extraordinarily, perhaps exclusively on our superior strategic power. The Soviet Union has never relied on its superior strategic power. It has always depended more on its local and regional superiority. Therefore, even an equivalence in destructive power, even assured destruction for both sides is a revolution in NATO doctrine as we have known it. It is a fact that must be faced.

Kissinger went on to say, "the European allies should not keep asking us to multiply strategic assurances that we cannot possibly mean, or if we do mean, we should not want to execute because if we execute, we risk the destruction of civilization."[64] The speech encouraged the continued striving for unattainable superiority. Kissinger's fear of war grew with Soviet power. The real danger, however, was that a spark somewhere in the world would set off a reverberation throughout the defense systems of both superpowers. The Pershing IIs would add greatly to the speed of any reverberation.

Reagan
the Continuer

THE BOGEY

An ideologue now was in charge. It is hard to say whether we were more in danger than with a twice-born moral Christian, with a master intriguer, with a man who had to prove his courage, with a parsimonious general, or with a failed haberdasher who had to prove his worth. Reagan based his rapid expansion of defense expenditures firmly on the bogey, but he made no fundamental policy change. Carter had talked about deep cuts, but he had stepped up defense spending, had planned a protracted nuclear war, and had proposed the MX. Reagan only changed the rhetoric.

The Soviet strategic threat persisted, and the United States could not match it. The Congressional Budget Office (CBO) estimated that only 150 ICBM warheads of the total of 2,143 would survive a surprise Soviet attack, assuming that the United States did not launch on warning.[1] Since only the 1,650 Minuteman III warheads were highly accurate, the United States could not expect to eliminate most of the 1,398 Soviet ICBMs.[2] This disparity prompted the pressure for the MX program.

Secretary Caspar Weinberger pointed to Soviet defense spending, which, he said, amounted to 15 percent of the GNP, compared to the U.S. average of 5.9 percent in the 1970s. According to Weinberger, in 1980-81 Soviet expenditures on new strategic weapons were three times as great as U.S. expenditures; Soviet procurement of weapons for general purpose forces was 50 percent higher; and their R&D expenditures were twice as high. In 1981 the weapons procurement outlays of the Warsaw Pact nations were greater than those of NATO plus Japan. Between 1974 and 1982 the Warsaw Pact had produced 2,000 ICBMs compared to 350 for NATO; nearly 67,000 tanks and other armored vehicles versus 24,000 for NATO; and 6,900 tactical combat aircraft versus 5,700 for NATO. Only in general purpose naval warships did NATO outproduce the Warsaw Pact.[3] In the administration's view, the Soviet arms buildup had shifted the global military balance[4] and increased Soviet influence in many regions, including Afghanistan, South Yemen, and Ethiopia.[5]

The administration retained the doctrine that sufficient strategic strength had to survive a strike to threaten greater losses to the Soviets than they inflicted; and credibility required the capability of responding appropriately to a wide range of attacks.[6] The Defense Report for FY 1984 suggested how much superiority a credible deterrent required when it described the loss of deterrence power since the superiority of the early 1960s:

By the early 1960s, the U.S. had over 7,000 strategic nuclear weapons, most of which were carried by B-47s and the then new B-52s. The Soviet Union had fewer than 500 warheads. Throughout the 1960s, our nuclear posture presented the Soviet Union with a compelling deterrent if it considered launching a nuclear strike against the United States: because of the relatively small number of weapons the Soviet Union possessed and their ineffectiveness against any U.S. strategic forces, such an attack was impossible to execute successfully. If the Soviet planner targeted our missile silos and alert bomber bases with the systems he then possessed, he found that he would deplete his nuclear arsenal while not significantly reducing U.S. retaliatory forces. In other words, his ability to limit the certain massive retaliatory destruction of his own forces and assets was rather small.

The report continued with a regret about U.S. policy in the 1970s:

The Soviets expanded their land-based missile force and hardened their protective silos, and continued the improvement of their defense against air attack. At the same time, the United States made a choice to restrict its improvements to the yield and accuracy of its own missile forces so as not to threaten the Soviet Union with a sudden, disarming first strike. The net result of this was to allow the Soviet Union a "sanctuary" for its ICBM force, since U.S. forces by now could not attack them effectively. The Soviets, however, did not follow our self-imposed restraint. They developed a new generation of ICBMs specifically designed to destroy U.S. missile silos, which were hardened far less than Soviet silos, and the B-52 bases.[7]

Moscow probably did not regard the deployment of the Minuteman IIIs or the plans for the Mark 12A warheads with the equanimity suggested by the report.

Repeating Wohlstetter's old argument, the Defense Report said that in 1967 the number of weapons had been one-third larger than in 1980, and that in 1960 the total number of megatons had been as much as four times as high as in 1980.[8] The implication was that the United States had disarmed in the face of a continued Soviet build-up. The report did not mention the enormous growth in our offensive power.

The administration also maintained that the Soviet forces as a whole had grown more than our own and that the Warsaw Pact's forces had grown faster than NATO's. But, as we will see, the administration's estimates were wrong.

THE SCOWCROFT COMMISSION

Much of the continuing debate on the MX centered on the multiple-protective-shelter (MPS) basing mode. Opponents said the Soviets could deploy warheads as rapidly as the United States could add shelters. Nevada and Utah complained that the basing mode required a great deal of land and water. Advocates argued that the MPS basing mode was the most practicable solution to the survivability problem for a land-based force, and, without it, the MX would be a first-strike, not a retaliatory weapon.

Unwilling to override the prospective host states' opposition, in October 1981 Reagan jettisoned the MPS basing mode. Instead, he proposed the temporary expedient of placing some missiles in super-hardened, existing silos. He envisioned a permanent system that would use one of three alternative basing modes: aircraft capable of cruising for several days and large enough to launch an MX while in flight, silos that were thousands of feet underground, and silos defended by ABM missiles. Among the many skeptics in Congress, Senate Armed Services Committee Chairman John Tower objected to placing lucrative targets in vulnerable fixed silos. Congress required the administration to produce an acceptable basing mode for the MX by July 1983.[9]

Reagan next planned 100 launch sites in a 14-mile line, or a "densepack." The theory was that the attacking missiles, which would have to come in quick succession, would destroy each other. But this proposal, too, did not get very far. To gain congressional support for the deployment of an MX force of some kind, Reagan appointed the Presidential Commission on Strategic Forces, with General Scowcroft as chairman, and which included White House staffer Thomas Reed, Secretary of State Alexander M. Haig, former

CIA Director Richard Helms, and nuclear strategists John M. Deutch, William J. Perry, R. James Woolsey, and Admiral Levering Smith. The advisers were former Defense Secretaries Brown, Laird, Rumsfeld, and Schlesinger; Kissinger; former CIA Director John McCone; and Carter's assistant, Lloyd Cutler.[10] The administration hoped that Congressman Les Aspin, who had a hand in drafting the report, would support an MX program and win over other advocates of the build-down proposal, including Senators William Cohen, Charles Percy, and Sam Nunn, and Congressman Albert Gore, Jr.[11]

The report opened with the usual litany, saying that the United States and the Soviet Union disagreed on history, the nature of society, the individual's place in it, and that life in the Soviet Union was empty. The commission inferred that the Soviet leaders sought the conquest of other nations:

large, centralized, autocratic systems that seek to achieve and maintain control over all aspects of the lives of many diverse peoples. We should, with calm persistence, limit the expansion of today's version of this sort of totalitarian state, the Soviet Union. We should persuade its leaders that they cannot successfully divert attention from internal problems by resorting to international blackmail, expansion, and militarism—rationalized by alleged threats posed by us or our allies.

The report continued,

Deterrence is central to the calm persistence we must demonstrate in order to reduce these risks. American strategic forces exist to deter attack on the United States or its allies—and the coercion that would be possible if the public or decision makers believed that the Soviets might be able to launch a successful attack. . . . The strategic forces that are necessary to support such a policy by their very existence help to convince the Soviet Union's leaders: that the West has the military strength and political will to resist aggression; and that, if they should ever choose to attack, they should have no doubt that we can and would respond until we have so damaged the power of the Soviet state that they will unmistakably be far worse than if they had never begun.[12]

The commission repeated the old refrain without presenting any more evidence. However, since superiority was no longer available, parity would have to do. Emphasizing the AR, the report said that the current situation was unstable because the Soviets could destroy the whole range of strategic targets in the United States but we could not destroy a similar range in the Soviet Union. According to the report, "Such a situation could tempt the Soviets, in a crisis, to feel they could successfully threaten or even undertake conventional or limited nuclear aggression in the hope that the United States would lack a fully effective response."[13] But the logic is amiss. The argument that the U.S. inability to match the Soviet counterforce capability creates instability is wrong. The contrary is correct. Equally matched forces consisting of MIRVed, accurate missiles are what produces a high PR in a crisis. Each side will fear the destruction of its own retaliatory forces, and it will recognize that the fear is mutual. This recognition may induce one side to take preemptive action. A preponderance of power on one side reduces the mutual fear and therefore the PR.

The commission reached the conclusion that Soviet preponderance was dangerous because it assumed that the Politburo was so driven by its ambition for world domination that it would attack U.S. forces, even at the risk of sea-based retaliation. Apparently some probability of a U.S. sea-based retaliation was an insufficient deterrent. The Soviets were so greedy for more influence and territory that only the certainty of retaliation would deter them. Such certainty required the United States to match or exceed the Soviet capability of destroying land-based forces. The commission feared that the Soviets would be greedy enough for more power that they would be willing to take some risk of nuclear retaliation as long as they believed that retaliation was less than certain, and would either attack or threaten to attack. We must be clear that it is the Soviet perception with which we are concerned, not the president's decision in a crisis. Many policymakers have been concerned that the president would not risk the destruction of our own cities. The president might be reluctant to order a retaliatory attack on Soviet cities. But we need not demand certain retaliation to a Soviet attack to deter one. We need only convince the Soviets that the probability of retaliation is sufficiently high that they take a considerable risk of destruction of their own cities by attacking the United States itself or a region of vital interest. How high must the Soviets estimate the probability of retaliation for them to be unwilling to risk it? Surely the commission did not mean that they had to believe it to be literally certain. Was a probability of five in ten chances too high a risk? What about two in ten?

The report groups together nuclear and conventional aggression. But in order to estimate the Soviet estimate of the probability of U.S. nuclear retaliation, we must make this distinction. Even if the U.S. forces had less offensive capability than the Soviet forces, the probability of U.S. retaliation to a nuclear attack, even a limited one, on its land-based forces would be too high to risk. The Soviet leaders would surely estimate it to exceed two out of ten chances. Would they be willing to take this high a risk to gain control of West Germany? Of part of the Middle East? The commission's assumption of a powerful Soviet expansionist drive is essential to the conclusion that the Soviet leaders would take such a risk. If one does not accept the assumption, then one is forced to conclude no.

The next question is whether the Soviet leaders would expect the United States to retaliate with nuclear weapons against a conventional attack on Western Europe or on some other region. Clearly, the Soviet leaders would assess the probability of nuclear retaliation to such aggression as lower than the probability of such retaliation to a nuclear attack. Would they assess the probability at a sufficiently low level to make it worth taking the risk? Perhaps, if they are very hungry for more power, as the commission assumes. But to evaluate the prospect of a Soviet conventional attack, even if one accepts the commission's dubious assumption, one must consider the conventional strength available to defend Western Europe and other regions. The Soviets are unlikely to attack NATO's forces. The cost of an invasion would be too high, even for a power-hungry ruling group.

As for other regions, the risks of an attack there would have to be evaluated in detail, which the present book does not do. However, to urge that the United States build a more powerful offensive capability to keep the Soviets from placing conventional forces either in Iran or in other Middle East countries when crises occur is to urge a policy of games of Chicken with nuclear forces. We would choose to risk nuclear war to prevent the Soviets from gaining influence in this or other regions. The commission does not advocate such games explicitly, but this is the clear implication of the recommended policy.

If the bogey is true, then by adding to the MX force we can gain more deterrence against both nuclear and conventional deliberate, planned attacks. But if it is not true, then adding to our offensive capability enhances only the PR. The United States will play games of Chicken with the Soviets in recurrent crises, and if the president has the superior forces, then he is less likely to swerve and the Soviet leader will be more likely to do so. Not only will we take a risk of annihilation in each confrontation, but we will also promote the PR by accelerating the nuclear arms race. The Soviets will not stand idly by while we add to the Trident IIs and the MXs. The additions to the MIRVed, accurate missiles on both sides will raise the PR in future crises to even higher levels than it would reach with the present forces.

The report recommended quickly shoring up deterrence against conventional or limited nuclear attacks with the MX. The commission agreed that the Midgetman missiles, which would enhance stability, were preferable. Smaller and mobile, they would be less attractive and less vulnerable targets.[14] But while we awaited the Midgetman, the MX would fill the gap. The commission dismissed the vulnerability objection to the MX with the judgment that the combination of ICBMs and bombers was survivable. To force Soviet planners to take account of the MX, the commission recommended the prompt deployment of 100 missiles in existing Titan and Minuteman silos. The report neglected the sea-based deterrent.

Thus, the bargaining between the administration and certain members of Congress produced a report that had something in it for everybody. The administration won support for the MX from Aspin and other members of Congress, who got the administration to agree to develop the Midgetman.

THE MX AND A SURVIVABLE SECOND-STRIKE CAPABILITY

Reluctant to say that the MX was a first-strike weapon, the administration emphasized the weapon's second-strike capability. Accordingly, Congress wanted to know how much 100 vulnerable MX missiles would add to a surviving deterrent. The Congressional Budget Office (CBO) made some estimates for 1990 that assumed, following U.S. policy, that the missiles would be launched only after an attack.[15] By that year, the administration planned to have replaced 100 Minuteman IIIs with an equal number of MX missiles and to have acquired 8 Trident Is, 4 Trident IIs, and 100 B-1Bs. The pre-attack inventory was expected to include 450 Minuteman IIs, 450 Minuteman IIIs, 100 MXs, 31 Poseidons, 8 Trident Is, 4 Trident IIs, and 357 bombers.[16] The administration's program would increase the number of surviving warheads from a 1983 level of 6,000 to 9,900; hard-target warheads from 1,400 to 3,900; and prompt hard-target warheads from 150 to 180, not including the Trident II warheads, and to 890, including these warheads.

A major strike having eliminated all but 10 percent of them, the MX missiles would contribute only 1 percent of the surviving warheads, 3 percent of the hard-target warheads, and 11 percent of the prompt, hard-target warheads, including those on Trident IIs.[17] Moreover, the surviving MX missiles plus the other weapons would be unable to retaliate against a large part of the Soviet arsenal. More offensive power would not deter a Soviet first strike.

The pro-MX case featured bargaining. But, in a vulnerable basing mode and not to be used in a first strike, it was not much of a bargaining chip. Moreover, with the Trident II coming, the cancellation of the MX was not worth a high price.

The rarely discussed but real argument was that the counterforce strategy needed the MX to regain some credibility. Moscow would have reason to fear a first strike, the United States having refused to commit itself to no first use. Moreover, the Soviets would expect a launch on warning of the MX missiles, which together with the Trident II missiles could destroy enough of the Soviet forces to deter a second strike. Finally, production did not have to stop after the 100 missiles were built. Thus, the MX would signal willingness to engage in a limited war.

We return to the major issue. By going ahead, we would be exchanging a reduction in the AR for a more than offsetting increase in the PR. In a crisis, the president may shoot first to prevent their destruction. One hundred MX missiles would make up 81 percent of the land-based offensive power, 68 percent of the total land-based and sea-based offensive power, excluding bombers and cruise missiles, and 74 percent of the prompt hard-target capability, including the Trident IIs. Moreover, aside from bargaining-chip considerations, the purpose of the MX is to strengthen the hard-target capability, which would be of little value after a massive Soviet launching. We can only conclude that the administration seeks to enhance either a first-strike capability or the capability of conducting limited warfare.

What about the bargaining-chip argument? The administration is unlikely to weigh this argument heavily, since it says that the program is necessary to counter the new Soviet strength. If the MX is needed, then it will not be sacrificed in bargaining.

THE SOVIET BUILDUP

Reagan argued that Soviet defense spending was growing too rapidly not to be feared. New sharply lower CIA estimates in 1983 did not quiet the administration's fears. Earlier, the CIA had estimated the rate of growth to be between 3 and 5 percent, but now the CIA said that between 1976 and 1981 the rate had been only about 2 percent or less. Richard F. Kaufman, assistant director of the Joint Economic Committee, believes that the low rate continued through at least 1982.[18]

Reagan's warning featured the Soviet stock of weapons. With the original estimates of rates of growth between 3 and 5 percent the CIA had served some explanations, including the spurt in NATO's effort, the cruise missile, the Trident II, the MX, the Chinese menace, and the momentum of Soviet weapons production. Before 1983 the agency had maintained that the fall in economic growth did not slow down the growth in weapons production[19] because no Soviet leaders would dare oppose the military, especially with a succession struggle going on. This explanation joined the old estimates in the relic heap. According to the new estimates, from 1977 through 1981 hardware procurement grew only slightly, if at all; only the spending for operations, maintenance, and personnel costs increased.

The Defense Report for 1984 ducked the problem raised by these bothersome new estimates. According to the report,

Despite their sluggish economic situation, and nationwide food shortages, the Soviets currently allocate an estimated 15% of their GNP to defense. If the annual growth rate of their economy slows, as expected, their defense allotment could reach as much as 20% in the not so distant future. The United States, on the other hand, annually spent an average of 5.9% of GNP on defense during the 1970s.[20]

Admitting the slowdown, the 1985 Defense Report warned against the earlier large accumulations and the continuing rapid growth of Soviet military research and development.[21]

START

Reagan had nowhere to begin in the Strategic Arms Reduction Talks (START), and the suggestions by the Committee on the Present Danger did not show the way. Thus, in 1979 Nitze advocated equal limits on offensive capabilities, provisions guarding against a significant advantage to the attacker, true reductions in armaments, and verifiability. Nitze attacked the SALT II agreement, which gave the Soviets 308 very large ICBMs and the United States none, for damaging crisis stability, that is, raising the PR. He expected the Soviets by the early 1980s to be able to destroy 90 percent of our ICBMs with only one-fifth to one-third of their ICBMs, leaving an inferior U.S. force. U.S. security demanded a force that would match Soviet power after a Soviet first strike and a retaliatory attack. Since both superpowers could not have the specified capability, Nitze could not say what agreement would meet the bill. He was tilting at windmills. If the Soviet force could destroy much of the U.S. arsenal in a first strike, the goal was impossible, with or without an agreement.[22]

Nitze blamed the Carter administration for conceding the throw-weight lead to the Soviet Union. He bemoaned the SALT II agreement for limiting the number of warheads per missile. Following suit, Weinberger speculated that, abrogating the agreement, the Soviets would put their extra throw-weight into more warheads; the United States would not have the throw-weight to do the same. But this discussion did not point to a negotiating position.

Obsessed with general, ideological issues, Reagan rode far above the details of launchers, warheads, and throw-weight. The issues were simple for him: the Soviets were ahead, they must not gain any advantage, and there should be large reductions in Soviet power. Also, like Carter, he wanted acclaim for a unique achievement.

Without White House leadership, the interdepartmental struggles raged more fiercely than ever. The Defense and State Departments were free to pursue immediate bureaucratic objectives. The civilians in the Defense Department guarded their weapons programs and sought to cut back Soviet power. These objectives, which could not be met by any attainable agreement, showed up the Defense Department's intention of blocking one. Naturally, the proposals collided with those of the State Department, whose business it was to negotiate agreements and whose success was calibrated by the number of signed agreements. Content was secondary. Good proposals were those that were acceptable to the Soviets.

The Soviets having as much to gain from a reduction in the PR, an agreement promoting this objective was within reach. But with none of the agencies interested, the goal had little hope, and efforts to gain bargaining advantages with weapons programs worked against it. Needless to say, the administration's attitude toward communism did not help.

Weinberger's lack of familiarity with the technicalities and Secretary Haig's preoccupation with other matters left the direction to junior bureaucrats. Richard Perle, assistant secretary of defense for international security policy, and Richard Burt, the State Department's director of the Bureau of Politico-Military Affairs, became the rival leaders. As Senator Jackson's assistant, Perle had acquired formidable expertise and a large number of contacts in the field. Burt's background included covering defense for the *New York Times*.

In the spring of 1982 Perle proposed limits of 4,000 warheads on straetgic missiles and of 2 million kilograms of throw-weight. The first ceiling would halve the number of warheads for both sides, and the second would force the Soviets to give up 60 percent of their throw-weight at the cost of only a slight reduction in the U.S. level.

In short, the United States was to ask the Soviets to eliminate much of their counterforce capability in exchange for modest cuts. Even his suggested warhead limit was biased, if less obviously, since the United States planned to replace the Poseidons with fewer Trident IIs, which carried fewer warheads, while the Soviets had been adding ICBMs carrying a large number of warheads. Perle opposed limiting cruise missiles. He was not ready to yield a technological lead. In addition, he wanted the limits separated to prevent the Soviets from trading bombers, where the United States had the advantage, for missiles.[23] A Perle-type agreement would have required the Soviets to dismantle most of their new ICBMs, and the MX and Trident II programs would have survived.[24] Obviously, a Soviet rejection would not have upset Perle.

Refusing to concede that our arsenal was far inferior, Burt said that the demand for throw-weight equality invited counter-demands for large sacrifices in SLBMs, bombers, and cruise missiles. He pointed out that throw-weight no longer mattered so much since the improvement in Soviet accuracy. A large blast radius became redundant when the warhead struck close to a silo. In any case, the error in verifying compliance with a throw-weight limit might be as high as 100 percent. Finally, Burt predicted a flat rejection of Perle's proposal.

Only verifiability and negotiability mattered. Burt proposed to limit the number of launchers, ICBM silos, and SLBM tubes.[25] His suggested limit of 1,200 launchers, or 47 percent below the SALT II level, would have required the Soviet Union to remove 1,100 of its missiles and the United States to remove 400. His other suggested ceilings were 5,000 for all strategic warheads and 2,500 for ICBM warheads. At this time the Soviet Union had 6,000 ICBM warheads and the United States had 2,150.[26] To obtain bargaining chips, Burt proposed cruise-missile restrictions modeled on those of the SALT II agreement.[27]

On May 9, 1982, Reagan announced the U.S. proposals. The number of ICBM and SLBM warheads was to be cut to 5,000; each country had about 7,500. The maximum for missiles was to be 850, down from 2,500 for the Soviet Union and from 1,700 for the United States. The subceiling for ICBM warheads was to be 2,500. Under congressional pressure and in return for support for the MX, in October 1983 the administration agreed to advance the build-down scheme as a separate proposal in the START negotiations. The discussion of the scheme is left to Chapter 8. Haig announced the administration's willingness to consider limits for cruise missiles and bombers and its intention to ask for equal limits in total throw-weight that would be below the present actual U.S. total.[28] However, the actual proposals covered neither bombers nor cruise missiles. Reagan correctly hesitated to raise the PR by limiting the number of these purely retaliatory weapons.[29] Unhampered by bureaucratic interests, the president opposed provisions that conflicted with the objective of reducing the PR.

Late in 1983 the Soviets carried out their threat to break off the START negotiations as the first Pershing IIs arrived in West Germany. In 1985 Mikhail Gorbachev became the new Soviet supreme leader, and the arms control talks started again.

THE DEFENSE BUDGETS

Despite Reagan's economy drive, the increase in constant-dollar federal expenditures from fiscal 1980 through fiscal 1985 amounted to 11.5 percent, of which defense accounted for 53 percent. Constant-dollar defense expenditures grew by 45 percent, or at an annual rate of 7.7 percent, which was much higher than the 1.5 percent rate of the preceding five years. In fiscal 1985 federal expenditures amounted to $925.5 billion, of which defense accounted for $272.0 billion, or 29.4 percent. Thus, these outlays grew from 5.3 percent of the GNP in fiscal 1980 to 7.0 percent in fiscal 1985.[30] Strategic forces still imposed no great economic burden. In fiscal 1985 strategic forces absorbed only 10.3 percent of total defense expenditures.[31]

Forty-four percent of the increase in real expenditures was for the purchase of equipment and weapons.[32] Breaking procurement down, about one-third of the total expenditures was for the strategic forces, the most expensive items being the MX missile, the B-1B bomber, and the Trident II. Other substantial items were the ballistic missile defense (BMD) program and the continental air defense program, which included new F-15 fighters and airborne warning and control (AWAC) aircraft for antibomber defenses. In addition, Pershing II missiles and GLCMs were to be produced for deployment in Western Europe. About 25 percent of the total procurement budget was for the navy's 600-ship program, a large part of which was to be spent on the carrier task forces.

Strategic Forces

Reagan went ahead with the B-1B, which Carter had canceled. Capable of a quick takeoff, the aircraft promised less vulnerability than the B-52 and it also promised a greater capability of penetrating

Soviet defenses. However, the B-52's chief function will be to carry ALCMs, which will be launched before the aircraft can be attacked. It will be unnecessary for the ALCM carrier to expose itself to attack. The B-1B's penetration advantage is both unnecessary and expensive. Moreover, the penetration capability, if it is of some value, of the coming, less vulnerable Stealth bomber will be much greater.

The MX program was grossly uneconomic. Thirty billion dollars is a high price for the counterforce capability of five surviving missiles carrying 50 warheads. The Trident II, which will be much more survivable, will match the MX in counterforce capability. The more fundamental objections, of course, are the impossibility of the counterforce strategy and the weapon's PR effect. Recently Reagan has agreed to limit the number of MXs to 50 instead of the planned 100. The improvements in the anti-bomber defenses are similarly a waste. It is the ICBMs that are dangerous, not the Soviet bombers.

STAR WARS

On March 23, 1983, in a televised address, the president dramatically offered the hope of a defensive shield:

Would it not be better to save lives than to avenge them? . . . What if free people could live secure in the knowledge that their security did not rest upon the threat of instant U.S. retaliation to deter a Soviet attack; that we could intercept and destroy strategic ballistic missiles before they reached our own soil or that of our allies?

However, even optimistic advocates refrain from offering the assurance of an effective, which is to say near-perfect, defense of cities. The destruction of even 90 percent of thousands of attacking warheads would save few lives.

The speech restarted the late-sixties' ABM debate and the more recent one about basing modes. The defense issue returned because of recent advances in the technology of laser and particle beams, which can travel at near the speed of light, possibly permitting the destruction of attacking missiles in the boost phase of a launch or in midcourse. Improvements in the collection, processing, and transmission of vast quantities of data at high speed, which may facilitate the prompt assessment of the dimensions of an attack, also have contributed. Moreover, available equipment now can track warheads accompanied by many decoys. Without such equipment, Nixon could not accept the Safeguard system. In addition, the development of infrared sensors has improved the prospects for intercepting warheads in midcourse.[33]

Strategists have proposed breaking the defense into three and possibly more layers. The first layer, consisting of X-ray or heat-seeking chemical lasers, would strike the attacking missiles during the three- to five-minute boost phase of ascent. The second layer is expected to attack the warheads in the 20- or 25-minute midcourse flight outside the atmosphere. The terminal layer is to strike the warheads in the one or two minutes after they reenter the atmosphere.[34] Since no single layer will be perfect, the hope lies in several successive layers. If 1,000 warheads are launched and each of three defense layers destroys 80 percent of the surviving warheads, then 80 will strike the United States. If two warheads are needed to destroy a single silo, then 1,000 warheads can destroy only 40 silos. This level of effectiveness is not adequate for city defense, but it may be for the defense of missiles.

A prominently mentioned first-layer defense utilizes space-based chemical lasers. To ensure constant protection, many orbiting platforms will be needed. Assuming a plausible boost-phase period and speed of response, 320 laser platforms will be required to strike the missiles. The system will require the enormous task of lifting into space the platforms and equipment and also 6,000 tons of fuel to power them.[35]

Formidable as the deployment and operating problems of such a system will be, the most discouraging aspect is its vulnerability. Conventionally armed, inexpensive space mines will be able to damage the weapons' delicate optical components. They will be vulnerable to destruction by nuclear bombs and by ground-based laser beams over great distances. In addition, pre-attack high-altitude nuclear bursts will be able to destroy the system's sensors and communications. Moreover, to thwart the defense the attack missiles can be hardened, and heat-emitting bright rockets can be used as decoys. Finally, the Soviets can offset the defensive system at low cost by increasing the number of missiles. A space-based laser defense system cannot meet the ultimate economic test. It would be cheaper for the Soviets to cancel its effectiveness than for the United States to protect the system. The fatal objection to the ABM system applies also to the proposed space-based laser weapons.

An alternative to the space-based system relies on nuclear-powered X-ray lasers rapidly launched into space on missiles. Deployed on ground-based missiles, the laser stations can be launched or "popped up" on warning of an attack. However, this type of system will not respond quickly enough to strike in the five-minute boost phase. For the system to pop up within a few seconds of the enemy launch, computers will have to make the decision. Since an X-ray laser cannot be fired more than once, the computers will have to assess the size and other dimensions of the attack to avoid deception. Moreover, the attacker can defeat the X-ray laser, which is effective only outside the atmosphere, by modifying the missiles so that they complete their boost phase within the atmosphere.[36]

Another alternative boost-phase intercept system would rely on ground-based lasers aimed at high-altitude, large relay mirrors, which reflect the beams to low-altitude mirrors orbiting the earth. These will in turn redirect the beams to the targets. However, the few large focusing mirrors in space will be vulnerable to attack. In addition, atmospheric turbulence will present a problem; clouds will absorb the laser energy.[37]

According to Drell, Farley, and Holloway, scientists have not developed a concept for attacking many thousands of warheads and decoys in midcourse. Such a system, which will need very complex software, will consist of space-based chemical lasers or pop-up, ground-based X-ray lasers and intelligence, communications, and surveillance satellites, which will be vulnerable to attack. Moreover, the warheads, which are harder targets than the skin of the missile in the boost phase, will require much more energy to destroy.[38] Thus, a practical midcourse defense layer appears to be out of reach.

The real issue is the desirability of a terminal defense layer. The proponents' case must be based on the comparison of the costs of such a defense with the cost to the enemy of firing more reentry vehicles (RVs). Technological advances now may require the attacker to double the number of RVs sacrificed for any given number of missile silos to be destroyed. Thus, the price to the Soviets of destroying an undefended silo in 1990 may be as low as one RV at the present rate of progress in accuracy. But the deployment of a terminal defense system is expected to raise the price to at least two RVs, and possibly more.[39] Although the Soviets may be able easily to jam the defense system's sensor and communications systems, they must sacrifice RVs for this purpose; the defense system will have raised the attack price. Various strategies may raise it further. A preferential system limits the defense to some fraction of the silos, but since the enemy does not know which ones, it must expend as many RVs as would be required if all of them were defended. However, the attacker may also vary its strategy, and additional RVs come cheaply. Unless the defense system can raise the attack price to, say, five RVs, it is uneconomic. Nor can proponents count on an arms control limitation to the number of RVs, since a BMD system entails canceling the ABM Treaty. Nevertheless, a terminal defense system utilizing interceptors and sensors may be practical

within the next two decades. The plans for a first layer defense relying on lasers to attack missiles immediately after launching still are a
science-fiction day dream, as are those for a midcourse defense. The
policy issue thus concerns a third layer defense.

Colin S. Gray, a consistent hawk, contends that a defense system
is essential for the United States to fulfill its commitment to contain
Soviet power throughout the world. The Strategic Defense Initiative
(SDI) is part of a continued effort to improve our war-fighting
capabilities, and a terminal point-defense system may compensate for
a deficient offensive capability. A strong defense of the offensive
capability is necessary, given the strategic value of a first strike and
the increasing hardness of Soviet targets.[40] Gray views point defenses
simply as another technology for enhancing the U.S. offensive capability and thus deterrence.[41] He hopes that technological advances
will permit the United States to regain strategic superiority, which
will give it "escalation dominance" in war-fighting and "the relative
freedom of political-military action which that condition implies."[42]
Since Gray appears to have some influence on policy, his writings
suggest that the Soviet defense establishment is not the only one that
needs to be deterred.

SDI opponents no longer deny the possibility of an effective
terminal defense system. In this debate, a BMD system is judged to
be effective if it raises the attack price of a missile silo more economically than the enemy can increase the number of attacking warheads.
The opponents do not raise the fundamental objection that a terminal
defense system will be useful only if the defenders can fight a nuclear
war. Thus, while McGeorge Bundy, Kennan, McNamara, and Gerard
Smith reject the fantasy of a nationwide defense, they grant the possibility of a partially effective local defense of missile fields.[43] Their
main objection to the more limited proposal is that its implementation would violate the ABM Treaty. This is also Drell, Farley, and
Holloway's main criticism.[44] However, the fate of the ABM Treaty
is not the ultimate desideratum. If a viable defense of missile bases
enhances our security, then we should scrap the treaty.

The critical test of any proposal is the effect of its implementation
on the PR. A quick judgment may be favorable. If survivability reduces the PR, then a BMD system may do the job. If a BMD system
causes the attacker to lose more RVs than it destroys, then it can
gain no advantage. Thus, it is possible that a BMD system on both
sides will reduce the PR. The president was on the right track when
he suggested that to enhance mutual safety the United States should
make a gift of its defense technology to the Soviets.

However, neither the United States nor the Soviet Union will develop a completely effective BMD system. Since a major attack will exhaust the defender's interceptors, the attacker may still gain an advantage. It may not destroy many silos in a first strike, but the defender's missile bases will be vulnerable to a second strike. Thus, unless the costs of defense are much lower than those of attack, the deployment of a BMD system will not change the PR, even if we should accept the president's suggestion of allowing the Soviets to share any defense technology that our scientists develop. The available evidence so far indicates that the cost advantage remains with the offense.

I have assumed that the two sides develop equally competent BMD systems, but the hope of defense advocates is that the United States gains in the nuclear race. They would hardly be enthusiastic about it if they thought that the Soviets would quickly catch up. Would we be better off with a counterforce capability enhanced by a superior BMD system? Not if we fear the PR more than the AR. In a crisis, we are as likely to take preemptive action as the Soviets, and a BMD system would add to the inducement.

Finally, one of the more likely outcomes of the development of a BMD system is that it will add to the attacker's advantage. Suppose both sides have a BMD system of moderate effectiveness. The attacker may be able to destroy enough of the enemy's silos to prevent effective retaliation against its own remaining and defended counterforce capability. A BMD system probably will provide only incomplete protection, in which case the attractiveness of a first strike may increase, and along with it the PR.

A defense system will merely add to the counterforce capability. Its defensive nature is only a detail. An MPS basing mode and accelerating the Trident II program would accomplish the same purpose. To be consistent, supporters of the Trident II should favor the proposal. On the other hand, the objections to the Trident II and to the MX plus deceptive basing mode apply equally to the BMD system. They are all parts of the fantasy of a protracted nuclear war.

CONCLUSION

Apart from its decision to proceed with the B1-B bomber and the naval program, the Reagan administration has continued its predecessor's policy, and, despite its strong ideological commitment, the purpose of the policy is no clearer. Rhetoric does not simplify the problem of designing a strategy of vast destruction in the face of a strong retaliatory capability.

The confusion showed up in the arms control proposals of the first term. The Defense Department and the State Department disagreed even about the appropriate unit for measuring arsenals. Because it feared the potential Soviet counterforce capability, the Defense Department wanted to demand a large cut in Soviet throw-weight. The State Department, which wanted an agreement and was skeptical of the importance of throw-weight, proposed a reduction in the number of launchers. It is true that a big missile can carry more warheads, but the United States retains the lead in accuracy. Moreover, how seriously can one take any argument about winning a nuclear war? The two departments were at loggerheads because no one knew how to win a nuclear war.

A policy for reducing the PR would be less confusing. But so little interest does the administration have in this goal that the State Department was willing to propose reducing the ceiling on the number of launchers.

Because the PR worried them, members of Congress advanced the build-down and the Midgetman proposals and opposed the MX program. Congress, however, could not negotiate an arms control agreement.

8
The Debate Goes On

This chapter reviews the discussion of five issues at the center of the debate in the last few years plus one book that takes positions on several policy questions and deserves special attention. First, the freeze proposal that the United States halt improvements in its arsenal on the condition that the Soviet Union does the same; second, the no-use proposal by the Roman Catholic bishops; third, the no-first-use proposal by McGeorge Bundy, George Kennan, Robert McNamara, and Gerard Smith; fourth, the build-down proposal by Senators Cohen, Nunn, and Gore and Congressman Norman Dicks; fifth, two proposals specifically designed to reduce the PR. This chapter also examines the book, *Living with Nuclear Weapons*, by the Harvard Nuclear Study Group. The review covers in concentrated form the issues discussed elsewhere in the present book.

THE FREEZE PROPOSAL

SALT II was dead, Reagan won the election handily, and liberals were on the run. This apparently hostile climate nurtured the nuclear freeze movement, which flourished, so that in May 1983 the House voted 278 to 149 in favor of a mutual and verifiable freeze. Among those crowding the bandwagon were repentant, former administration officials Jerome Wiesner, George Ball, Clark Clifford, William Colby, Averell Harriman, George Kennan, and Paul Warnke.[1] The freeze movement became the chief opposition to the nuclear defense policy.

If one person was the founder, she was Randall Forsberg, who had been on the staff of the Stockholm International Peace Research

Institute (SIPRI). In 1974 she took up graduate studies in political science at MIT and she then founded the Institute of Defense and Disarmament Studies, of which she is the director.

The first paragraph of the campaign's central document, "Call to Halt the Nuclear Arms Race," which Forsberg drafted, called for a mutual and verifiable freeze on the testing, production, and deployment of nuclear weapons. It declared that since improvements in counterforce capability are dangerous, the governments should agree not to develop or deploy new weapons. A freeze would also stop the growth of the arsenals, the verifiable agreement would preserve the current nuclear parity, and a treaty could come later. The freeze was a prelude to ending the threat of first use and the reduction or elimination of the arsenals.

Emphasizing the effect of new weapons on crisis stability, which is to say the PR, Forsberg said that the United States and the Soviet Union should stop producing new counterforce weapons,[2] which made leaders trigger-happy in a crisis, and which might induce them to adopt a peacetime launch-on-warning policy. According to Forsberg, neither country was ahead. The Soviet Union had more ICBMs, SLBMs, and more and larger ICBM warheads, but the United States led in total warheads. It had more SLBM warheads, bombers, and cruise missiles. Neither country could eliminate the other's retaliatory capability, and a freeze would prevent Reagan from acquiring a destabilizing advantage in counterforce capability.[3] At the time, a freeze would have prohibited the deployment of the Pershing II missiles and the GLCMs, as well as of the MX. It should be noted that a freeze would permit the production of fissionable and other materials to replace the present arsenals.

Forsberg said nothing to challenge the bogey, but her argument suggested that the PR exceeded the AR. She might have said that even if the bogey were true, the United States had the weapons to deter a deliberate attack. However, she probably should not have ducked the issue of the hawks' central assumption that with superiority the Soviets would risk retaliation. Refusal to confront the bogey invited the criticism that a freeze would leave the United States vulnerable to a strike. Forsberg's arguable reply that the two arsenals were at parity created a false issue. The important and more relevant consideration was that the PR was the major risk by far. The freeze proponents had a stronger position than they knew. Opponents of a freeze also relied on the bargaining-chip argument. A freeze would require the United States to abandon the MX program without requiring a matching concession. Again, however, the freeze would achieve the primary goal of reducing the PR. We did not need to insist on Soviet concessions to reduce this risk. The freeze supporters could go further and say that a *unilateral* freeze would reduce the risk, since as long as the United States retained a minimum deterrent there was no danger of a deliberate attack. The bargain-chip argument was valid only if the AR exceeded the PR.

A detailed set of limitations would serve the goal of reducing the PR better than an overall freeze. A dramatically simple proposal like the freeze may win more support than a list of forgettable items, each with its own set of supporters, and we could move on from a freeze to a more sophisticated proposal. However, even a freeze is not simple to negotiate. Nor is a freeze obviously superior to adopting SALT II and continuing to negotiate further arms reductions. In any case, we cannot accommodate objectives to political realities without knowing the objectives.

Accepting the goal of reducing the PR, reductions of the MIRVed, accurate, hard-target capability are to be preferred to an overall freeze. The MX and Trident programs should be canceled, the Pershing IIs and the TNW should be withdrawn, and the SSBNs should be prohibited from approaching within some specified distance of the capitals of the two superpowers. Certain additions would be welcome. Crisis stability would be improved by additional bombers, cruise missiles, and Poseidons.

The movement did not advocate the politically unacceptable goal of a unilateral freeze, which may be the only road to a safer world. Moreover, since the Soviets have said that they would agree to a mutual freeze, they may respond favorably to U.S. unilateral action. Negotiating problems must not stand in the way of reducing the PR, which unilateral action will achieve. A U.S. halt to augmenting the arsenal would improve stability, whether or not the Soviets do the same. Moreover, in the past the process of bargaining has added to the PR by inducing enhancements of the arsenals.

The agreement relating to medium- and short-range missiles indicates that the Soviets are keenly aware of the PR. They will give up their SS-20s and SS-11s in Europe in exchange for the removal of the Pershing IIs, which can strike their missile bases with little advance warning. The SDI remains an obstacle to negotiating major reductions in the ICBM arsenals, but the prospects even in this area are promising.

To avoid antagonizing the right, the freeze movement did not deny the bogey and its companion, the goal of deterrence. But deterrence did not demand the dangerous counterforce capability already acquired. The capability may add to certainty, but even the hawks' imagined contingencies, with their stress on the PR, do not require a certain deterrent. The search for a certain deterrent only adds to the already high PR. Those who fear the bogey would gain the deterrence they seek from strong conventional forces, which are not backed by a powerful counterforce capability. They need not support a high-risk policy. The Red army cannot be certain of an easy victory even against NATO's present conventional forces. Those who believe additional security is needed can call for stronger conventional forces. Moreover, the Soviets are unlikely to make large sacrifices for control of Western Europe. The additional certainty from deploying TNW is not worth the resulting high PR. In a crisis originating in the Middle East the mere presence of TNW along the East-West border may ignite a nuclear war. Whether or not the Soviets offer a compensating reduction in their arsenal, the TNW should be removed.

THE NO-USE PLEDGE

On May 3, 1983, the U.S. Roman Catholic bishops issued a letter urging the United States to maintain deterrence with its nuclear weapons but to vow never to fire them.[4] This hat trick demands close scrutiny.

In a statement that tried to cover all the possibilities, the bishops flatly rejected the use of nuclear weapons. The proposed pledge would rule out attacks on cities, retaliatory action against cities, and the initiation of limited nuclear warfare.[5] Absolutely rejecting first use, the letter said that firing a large number of TNW in Western Europe would cause mass slaughter. Concerning strategic warfare, the bishops challenged the underlying theory. They doubted that the leaders could assess the damage, limit the exchanges, maintain "discriminate targeting," avoid computer errors, and prevent many casualties. They raised questions about the relationship between deterrence, targeting plans, and the required nuclear capability. With 40,000 military targets in the Soviet Union, including 60 in Moscow, limiting an attack to military targets would not avoid killing masses of people. A precise war-fighting strategy that avoided mass slaughter was impossible. The bishops also pointed out that the strategy undermined stability by threatening the other country's retaliatory forces.[6] Concerning the arsenal, the bishops advocated bilateral, verifiable agreements to halt the testing, production, and deployment of new nuclear weapons; deep cuts in the arsenals, especially in the number of destabilizing weapons; the removal of short-range nuclear weapons that threaten crisis stability; removal of nuclear weapons from areas where they were likely to be overrun in the early stages of war; strengthening the command and control over nuclear weapons. The bishops emphasized cuts in the arsenal that would reduce the PR.

Making a bold face about combining deterrence with a no-use pledge, the bishops did not admit a dilemma, to say nothing of trying to resolve it. My guess is that without saying so, they expected the Soviets to assume that in a crisis the United States would not honor the pledge. Otherwise, the arsenal would not achieve the objective of deterrence. But this game becomes tricky. Just as the Soviets may not have faith in the pledge, the United States may not keep it. The pledge alone will not make the world safer. As long as the two sides deploy nuclear weapons, they will plan to use them. Silos have to be constructed, crews must be trained, commanders must have instructions. Granted, some decisions may be left to the last minute. Thus, the authority of submarine commanders to fire SLBMs after the breakdown of communications with the NCA remains in question. Generally, however, it is difficult to maintain deterrence and avoid planning for war.

The call for a no-first-use policy is open to the same objection. A declaration by both sides, which governed their defense planning, would reduce the PR; in a crisis, war would not be set off by the distribution of warheads to field units. But such a policy would remove part of the deterrence.

A PR-reducing policy would not require verifiability or strictly bilateral changes, and it would not call for cuts in the number of bombers and of cruise missiles. The counterforce capability and the TNW would be the focus. Because the bishops did not clearly recognize what the primary goal required, they went off on the wrong track and insisted on balanced and verifiable arms reductions. Another reason they failed to urge unilateral restraint was their acceptance of the bogey. Perhaps, as Roman Catholic bishops, they agreed that the godless Soviet rulers were a menace. Once they accepted the bogey, it was difficult to reject entirely the defense policy that was based on it and that logically inferred a high AR. Nevertheless, the special attention they gave to the danger posed by the counterforce weapons implied that the PR was the major risk. But if it was the PR, not the AR, that was to be feared most, then the bishops should have proposed the withdrawal of the dangerous weapons, regardless of what the Soviets did.

The bishops, like most participants in the debate, were trapped by the deterrence argument. Agreeing with the defense policy's fundamental rationale, they could not advocate even limited unilateral disarmament. The plea for a no-use pledge was a desperate attempt to reconcile a policy of deterrence with the abhorrence of nuclear war. Unfortunately, this meant that the goal of deterrence (reducing the AR) took precedence over that of reducing the PR. The pledge alone does nothing for the PR, for, with powerful offensive capabilities at the ready, crises remain dangerous. True, if the pledge were to produce changes in war plans, it would reduce the risks. To reduce the PR, NATO should cancel its plans to distribute warheads to field units during a crisis. But NATO may as well withdraw the TNW. The bishops should have called for the withdrawal of the TNW if they were serious about the pledge.

But the bishops could not ask for the withdrawal of the TNW while insisting that they served deterrence. They failed because they did not choose which risk to minimize. The dilemma was unnecessary. When one recognizes the need to assess the risks before choosing weapons, the dilemma vanishes. Unless one decides that the Soviets are not obsessed with imperial goals, the inevitable conclusion is that policy should be directed at reducing the PR.

The opposition to the no-use proposal came mainly from hawks. Now a senior fellow at the Hoover Institution, Wohlstetter returned to the familiar specter of a small nuclear attack against isolated military targets in the United States.[7] Still pressing for a high-risk policy to deter what was a mere possibility, he urged a stronger counterforce capability to fight a limited nuclear war. Wohlstetter argued that a limited retaliation need not provoke escalation and would be less dangerous than retaliation against cities. Only the powerful offensive capability required to respond proportionately would ensure effective deterrence. This argument for enhancing the hard-target capability has been remarkably persistent over the years, despite the prospect of continuing superpower competition and a mounting PR. The bogey still lively in his mind, Wohlstetter refused to confront the PR issue. Since those who worried more about the PR did not deny the bogey, the head-on confrontation needed to resolve the issue failed to take place. It is interesting that Wohlstetter took their letter to be nothing more than an expression of fear of the MX.

One could hardly blame Wohlstetter for repeating his decade-old argument that the United States had disarmed unilaterally, which the Defense Department repeated. Kennedy's and Nixon's enormous enhancements again became unilateral disarmament. He said that in

1960 the arsenal's megatonnage had been four times higher than in 1980. The distorted representation of the change in offensive capability did not restrain Wohlstetter's attack on the bishops.[8]

THE NO-FIRST-USE PLEDGE

If we try to identify the greatest single source of danger, then the U.S. guarantee of a nuclear response to a conventional attack on Western Europe would be near, if not at, the top of the list. To implement this threat, TNW are deployed in vulnerable positions close to the East-West border. The game of Chicken is likely to begin early in a crisis with preparations for nuclear battle. As in the past, the United States may heat up minor issues into a major confrontation to shore up the credibility of its commitment. Concerned about the danger, early in 1982 McGeorge Bundy, George Kennan, Robert McNamara, and Gerard Smith recommended that the United States pledge itself to no first use. According to the authors, a limited nuclear war will not remain limited. Even TNW will kill many civilians, and their use will lead to more devastating exchanges.[9]

Proposing a conventional defense, the authors asserted that Soviet conventional strength had been exaggerated. The new anti-tank guided missiles reduced Soviet tank superiority, and the Warsaw Pact's non-Soviet troops were unreliable. The cost of a strong conventional defense was less than NATO members claimed. Further, the countries could manage more than the annual 3 percent real increase in defense expenditures, which they had set as a goal. It would be a small price to pay for the added safety of no first use.[10]

The authors suggested that under a no-first-use policy, we would need only a capability for retaliation, not for winning a nuclear war. No current or prospective Soviet "superiority" would tempt Moscow to risk launching its missiles,[11] and survivable, second-strike forces would ensure security. They did not advocate unilateral reductions to some "minimum" force, but they expected a no-first-use policy to reduce the requirements substantially, and U.S. political leaders would recognize the new reality.

The authors also said that the risk of conventional Soviet aggression in Europe never had been as great as the "prophets of doom" claimed. But who, if not they, were the prophets? The authors also said that the Allied effort over the past 20 years had reduced whatever threat there was, and additional effort under a no-first-use policy would reduce it even further.[12]

Four prominent West Germans—Karl Kaiser, Georg Leber, Alois Mertes, and Franz-Josef Schulze—immediately responded, arguing that no first use would invite aggression. The Soviets could cross the Elbe without fear of immediate nuclear retaliation against their homeland. While stronger conventional forces might do, only the nuclear threat was dependable.[13] The disagreement came down to the ranking of the risks. The Bundy group's chief fear was that nuclear warfare could not be kept limited, while the Kaiser group's was that a conventional defense would fail to deter a Soviet attack. Neither group was primarily concerned with the PR.

Kaiser and his associates said that the Bundy group exaggerated the danger of uncontrolled escalation; only after the conventional forces failed to hold the Soviets back would NATO fire its nuclear weapons, and then only a few small weapons, "perhaps even only a warning shot."[14] Both sides would take precautions against uncontrolled escalation.

According to the Kaiser group, no first use canceled the nuclear guarantee, which then only a Soviet nuclear attack would invoke. Since the pledge would be binding even after the destruction of NATO's armies, the advocates would choose the surrender of Western Europe over firing the TNW. Moreover, not only would the pledge cancel deterrence, but it would add to Moscow's conventional superiority, for only the threat of a nuclear counterattack would prevent the Soviets from concentrating their troops at selected invasion points. Protected by a no-first-use pledge, the Soviets would not have to disperse their forces, and NATO would need larger combat forces than it now has.

To acquire an adequate conventional defense the United States and the United Kingsom would have to introduce the draft, and other countries would have to extend their period of military service.[15] The cost would be enormous, and the West may not be prepared to accept new, higher defense burdens. In addition, Western Europe would suffer from Soviet political blackmail. Finally, exposed areas, such as northern Norway, Thrace, and West Berlin, would be threatened. In short, these authors feared a deliberate Soviet attack.

Not having confronted the bogey, the Bundy group did not deal with this issue. The members simply disagreed with Kaiser and company about the possibility of adequate conventional protection.

The Bundy group probably is right. NATO either already has adequate conventional forces or they are within reach. Moreover,

Kaiser and his associates underestimated the risks of a first-use policy, implemented with TNW in forward positions. The Bundy group, whose greatest fear was escalation, also underestimated the PR associated with a no-first-use pledge. They did not neglect the PR entirely, for they asserted that no first use created a wide and strong firebreak between nuclear and conventional warfare. They counted on the clear physical evidence of nuclear warfare to define the beginning of such warfare and on fear. But, even these barriers are likely to be broken when TNW are strung out along the border and first use yields immediate military advantages. The pledge alone is no guarantee of no first use.

The West Germans have insisted on maximizing deterrence by placing TNW in forward positions. They recognized early that the most effective deterrent against any kind of aggression was a high risk of nuclear war. Deterrence required the Soviets to pay a high price for an attack, as Schelling would agree. Schelling advised a threatened army to commit itself in advance to a particular position and then to make it difficult to withdraw. He called for "the burning of bridges behind oneself to persuade an adversary that one cannot be induced to retreat."[16] The forward strategy conformed to Schelling's principles. But Schelling's strategy was designed only to minimize the AR. NATO accepted this advice and thus the bad bargain of exchanging a small AR for a large PR.

The Bundy group implicitly assigned the higher priority to the PR, but it expected too much from the pledge. Instead of advocating the withdrawal of the TNW and of counterforce weapons, the authors predicted that with a no-first-use policy the governments will decide that war-fighting weapons are unnecessary. Perhaps, but the Bundy group would have done better to take a position. The authors failed to investigate the PR effect of a promise not coupled with a specific arms policy. Promises alone are worthless. After all, the Soviets have promised no first use. Can one believe them when they add SS-18s and SS-20s to their arsenal? When two men hold guns to each other's head, of what use is a promise not to shoot first? Not enough to put one's gun down.

Some of the authors of the original article later went beyond advocating the pledge. In February 1983, in a letter to the Senate and House Budget Committees, Bundy and McNamara, joined by Cyrus Vance and Admiral Zumwalt, said that a protracted nuclear war could achieve no meaningful goal, and the MX program should be canceled.[17] Further, the MX was an extravagance; other weapons could do the same job. Since they agreed that the Soviet Union's large and increasing defense expenditures were a threat, they did not oppose increases in U.S. defense expenditures.[18] The letter did not urge reducing the PR, and the authors' support of the Trident II was inconsistent with this goal. Moreover, for budgetary reasons, the authors opposed increasing stocks of ammunition for ground warfare, which reduce the PR.

It took some time for them to come around to it, but more recently, Bundy, Kennan, McNamara, and Smith, joined by Morton H. Halperin, William W. Kaufmann, Madalene O'Donnell, Leon V. Sigal, Richard H. Ullman, and Paul C. Warnke, discovered the importance of the PR. The authors now urged that the United States base its military plans, training programs, defense budgets, weapons deployment, and arms negotiations on the assumption that it will not initiate the use of nuclear weapons.[19] NATO would pull back its vulnerable, forward-based nuclear weapons and facilitate reductions in the number of weapons in Western Europe. Short-range nuclear artillery shells, atomic demolition munitions, and other weapons intended to be used early would be withdrawn and their storage facilities secured against conventional attacks. NATO would also halt programs to modernize nuclear artillery shells and other early-use weapons. The withdrawal of the tactical weapons would reduce the PR. The artillery would be moved to less vulnerable locations. The nuclear shells were never actually deployed in forward positions; only the artillery with which to fire the shells have been located close to the East-West border. The shells have been in ammunition depots well behind the lines. In a crisis, it will now be necessary to bring forward the artillery, as well as the shells, if they are to be used.

The proposed pledge covered the use of strategic as well as tactical weapons. Vulnerable systems, such as the MX, would not be deployed. It would also eliminate the need for the capability to destroy large numbers of hard targets, including the Trident II.[20]

THE BUILD-DOWN PROPOSAL

Congressional supporters of arms control were dubious about a freeze. Aspin only supported it because he was unhappy with the Reagan proposals; he wanted to keep the issues alive. Gore wanted the Midgetman, which a freeze would prohibit. In this setting Senators Cohen, Nunn, and Percy teamed up with Gore, Aspin, and Congressman Norman Dicks to press for the build-down proposal as part of the U.S. START position. In exchange for the group's promise to support the MX, the administration agreed to incorporate the build-down proposal.

The proposal would discourage the deployment of MIRVed ICBMs by requiring the retirement of two warheads for each new one deployed on such missiles. To reduce the PR further by promoting survivability, the proposal favored SLBMs against ICBMs. Three retirements would be required for each two new warheads deployed on MIRVed SLBMs. The exchange ratio for new single-warhead ballistic missiles would be one for one. The exchange did not have to occur within any one system. In addition, each country would agree to reduce its arsenal of ballistic missile warheads by a minimum of 5 percent per year. If larger reductions were made to conform to the build-down ratios, these would take precedence. Both sides would be required to come down to the plateau of 5,000 ballistic missile warheads. When this was achieved, each side would remain at this level; one new warhead would require the withdrawal of one old one.[21]

The administration agreed to the application of the build-down concept to the number of bombers and to a limitation on the number of ALCMs. Finally, there would be some formula based on potential destructive capacity for balancing reductions in missile throw-weight against reductions in bomber carrying capacity.[22]

The goal was to reduce the PR by inducing the replacement of MIRVed ICBMs with single-warhead missiles. The Midgetman, a single-warhead mobile missile, proposed by Gore, was regarded as a less attractive target than a MIRVed ICBM, and many small missiles moving about would be hard to target. But, as William Kaufmann pointed out, the survivability of even these missiles was dubious. An airburst nuclear weapon, which covers many square miles with overpressures of up to 150 pounds per square inch (psi), can destroy mobile, small ICBMs (SICBMs) by blanketing an area; hits at individual missiles would be unnecessary. Unlike fixed silos, which are hardened up to several hundred psi, the soft targets presented by mobile launchers will be easy to destroy. The SICBMs will be vulnerable unless their transporters are both fast and hardened, or unless they move about regularly in a very large area. Their ICBM throw-weights would enable the Soviets to destroy with a barrage attack the SICBMs hardened to withstand 50 psi and distributed over a wide area. Thus, the SICBM does not offer the survivability that its proponents have hoped for.[23]

If SICBMs roam a very large area, they will be less vulnerable. Kaufmann estimated that with a 20-minute warning of an attack, and transporters, hardened to 20 psi and operating over an area of 30,788 square miles, the Soviets would need 5,110 weapons, each with a yield of .4 mt. to destroy the SICBMs in that area. Cutting the area by half would reduce the required number of weapons by the same proportion.[24] Thus, as the area declines, the SICBMs become more vulnerable. But the public might not relish the prospect of cars hitting transporters on the public highways, and it would be virtually impossible to assemble the required large tracts to keep the SICBMs off the highways. To understand how large an area 15,000 square miles is, we can compare it with the area of Massachusetts, which is 8,257 square miles. In addition, to hire the number of crews necessary to keep 1,000 SICBMs on the move all the time would be expensive. The task might be made somewhat easier by arms control agreements that kept the number of Soviet warheads below the number needed to destroy the SICBMs.

Moreover, if the SICBM is as accurate as the MX, it may not significantly reduce the U.S. incentive to shoot first. Since the proposal calls for the withdrawal of a single warhead for each SICBM deployed, a ten-warhead MX would be the equivalent of ten SICBMs. If these SICBMs have the same counterforce capability as a single MX and are as vulnerable, the incentive for a U.S. first strike will not be affected. Thus, it is not certain that replacing MIRVed ICBMs with single-warhead missiles will reduce the PR.

THE PREEMPTION RISK

In recent years other authors, including proponents of the counterforce strategy, have come around to the position that a greater effort must be made to enhance crisis stability or reduce the PR. Schelling, who originally supplied the theory underlying the counterforce strategy, recently proposed measures to improve crisis confidence. His concern was that misinformation about the potential enemy's intentions and actions might frighten the leaders of either side into ordering an attack.[25] The confusion in a crisis or in an actual war involving one of the superpowers might pose a threat to the other. Schelling's examples include a Soviet preemptive attack on the nuclear forces of France or the United Kingdom, a U.S. invasion of Cuba, an airlift of U.S. troops to the Middle East, an airlift of Soviet troops to the same region, the use of nuclear weapons in another third area, or undersea warfare between the superpowers.[26] Either superpower might infer preparations for a strategic attack from signals transmitted by an enemy command center, and it might launch a preemptive attack. Good information would reduce the danger.

The superpowers' current reconnaissance and surveillance capability can detect certain types of preparations promptly and sufficiently reliably for the leaders not to be misled by rumors. Most notably these include massive movements of population, which would be a most frightening danger signal. But some kinds of preparations will escape detection. Schelling suggested that each superpower would wish to know with certainty the whereabouts of the potential enemy's civilian and military leaders. He also suggested the exchange of hostages; each side would transport some of its own people rapidly to locations in the other's country. Finally, he suggested that the superpowers establish facilities in a neutral country for urgent negotiations in a crisis.[27]

Such measures should reduce the PR arising from misinformation during a crisis when numerous messages are flooding the intelligence networks. The United States and the Soviet Union should not object to making arrangements for reducing this significant source of PR.

However, erroneous rumors and the misinterpretation of signals are not the only PR sources. Bargaining threats to fire nuclear weapons are another source. Schelling's early work proposed the use of such threats. On the other hand, as he recently pointed out, the facilities for improving information to reduce the risk arising from error can also be used to ensure the accurate transmission of threats.[28] Thus, if Moscow wants to threaten Washington, the leaders can send a signal by placing themselves and their families in hardened shelters.

Schelling's proposals would reduce the PR due to misinformation, but the remaining PR is not negligible. It was not misinformation that brought us close to war in the Berlin and Cuban crises. On the U.S. side, the determination to show resolve was the biggest component of the risk. In the Berlin crises the Soviet Union was trying to protect its hold on Eastern Europe, and in the Cuban crisis it was seeking to enhance its offensive capability. Any further reduction in the PR can come only from the removal of accurate MIRVs, which give the attacker an advantage. Indeed, improvement in the accuracy of information without any change in the offensive capability may increase the overall PR. Any signal of a threatening move, which earlier might be dismissed as false unless corroborated by other information sources, might trigger an attack. And it is not obvious that an improvement in information would encourage the superpowers to avoid making bargaining threats.

Both sides have moved to increase their counterforce capability, despite the greater awareness of the effect on the PR. Harold A. Feiveson and John Duffield have pointed out that the navy's Improved Accuracy Program is expected to result in a CEP of 200 meters or less for the Trident I and one of about 120 meters for the

Trident II.[29] The Global Positioning System will increase the accuracy of the Trident I by a factor of four, which would give it a single shot kill probability of 86 percent against hardened targets.[30] Soviet SLBMs can be expected to achieve similar accuracies. According to Feiveson and Duffield, a sea-based counterforce threat may lead to dangerous defensive policies, including launch-on-warning, delegation of launch decisions to many commanders, and reliance on preprogrammed routines.[31]

Therefore, the authors propose a ban on the deployment and flight-testing of new SLBMs and limitations on the flight-testing of existing SLBMs. An arms limitation agreement containing such provisions would place severe limits on the development of a sea-based first-strike capability without diminishing the survivability of the weapons.[32] They also accept the proposal of banning the approach of submarines within a specified distance of the coasts of the two superpowers.[33]

The adoption of these proposals would reduce the PR considerably.

THE HARVARD NUCLEAR STUDY GROUP

I have suggested that the influence of strategists has contributed to increasing the PR. Because their strategy model assumed a high AR, they have proposed additions to the counterforce capability that raised the PR. This can be seen in the book, *Living with Nuclear Weapons*,[34] which expressed the views of the Harvard University Nuclear Study Group, consisting of Albert Carnesale, dean of the Kennedy School of Government and a member of the U.S. SALT I delegation; Paul Doty, director of the Center for Science and International Affairs and a member of the Science Advisory Committee in the Kennedy and Johnson administrations; Stanley Hoffmann, chairman of the Center for European Studies and author of numerous books and articles on foreign affairs; Samuel P. Huntington, director of the Center for International Affairs and a member of the NSC staff in the Carter administration; Joseph S. Nye, Jr., professor of government and deputy to the undersecretary of state for security assistance in the Carter administration; and Scott D. Sagan, graduate student and staff director for the project. The group took a middle-ground position and could not make up its mind about the MX.

The book began by assuming a high AR. The Soviet bogey never dies. The authors repeated the standard recitation about the tsars, the Eastern European acquisitions, and the growth of a military presence in other areas. The book did not consider recent developments in evaluating the seriousness of the threat, but relied on old materials. The authors dredged up the Kennan argument that the Soviets "cultivate and maintain armed forces on a scale far greater than any visible threat to their security would seem to warrant."[35] They went so far as to say that the Soviet leaders act on long-term plans for world hegemony. Thus, the authors based their support of the high-risk U.S. policy on a boiler-plate statement of the central premise of Soviet expansionism.

The bogey was real enough for the authors to advocate reducing the AR at the cost of raising the PR. They dismissed the possibility of a surprise all-out attack on the United States, but they agreed with the administration that the United States needed a more powerful arsenal to deter a deliberate, selective attack on the vulnerable part of the arsenal. Their central argument was that the deterrent against a limited Soviet attack was of dubious credibility,[36] implying that unless the United States added to its counterforce capability, the probability of a limited Soviet attack was high. Despite the importance of this argument, which continues to justify enhancements, the authors failed to develop it. They only supported the assertion of a high AR with the standard historical argument. Trapped by the possibility argument, they did not specify the Soviet gains that would warrant the deliberate initiation of a nuclear war. The mere possibility of a Soviet attack warranted a high-risk U.S. policy. Although the opposition to the MX and the Trident II has focused on their effect on crisis stability, the authors did not investigate this question. Nor did they evaluate the relative magnitudes of the AR and the PR; they merely asserted that the AR was high.

The Harvard group said that withdrawal of the nuclear umbrella would raise the risk of aggression against Western Europe without indicating whether the probability was high.[37] The authors neglected to mention that the withdrawal would also raise the risk of an attack by Albania. Apparently, the probability of a Soviet attack is high enough to warrant a high-risk policy. Concerning conventional forces, only a single inconclusive paragraph was devoted to comparing the opposing strengths.

The Harvard group admitted the importance of enhancing crisis stability (reducing the PR), but it immediately warned that this goal conflicted with credible deterrence (reducing the AR). According to the group, crisis stability demanded an invulnerable arsenal consisting of inaccurate, slow missiles. Such a purely retaliatory arsenal would reduce mutual fears of preemption. Nevertheless, the authors advocated a counterforce capability to maintain a credible deterrent.[38] They even urged the continued deployment of the TNW for this reason. As they saw it, the TNW added to the credibility of the ultimate deterrent.[39] The Harvard group ignored the relative magnitudes of the PR and the AR despite their seven war scenarios, which suggested that while a bolt-from-the-blue massive attack or a deliberate limited attack was improbable in a crisis, a preemptive attack was not improbable.[40] Evidently, the authors forgot the scenarios at the front of the book when they reached the policy section. They needed only to take the argument one step further and compare the PR and the AR to come to the opposite conclusion.

The authors lacked enough confidence in the deterrence argument to endorse the strategic guarantee of Western Europe's integrity entirely on this basis. They also grasped the thin reed of the perceptions argument: the nuclear umbrella maintained U.S. political influence as well as deterred an attack. The Pershing IIs paid political dividends.[41]

The book reported that the group split over the MX. The pro-MXers valued deterrence above all, and for good measure they threw in the bargaining-chip argument.[42] The anti-MXers did not also oppose the Trident II. The survivability of the SLBM apparently offset the danger from its hard-target capability.

Its primary objective being deterrence, the study group rejected the no-first-use proposal. The authors lacked confidence in the strength of NATO's conventional forces.[43]

As much enthralled by the Soviet bogey as other policymakers, the group supported the main features of the national defense policy. The goal of reducing the AR prevailed when it came to endorsing the TNW, the Pershing II, and the Trident II.

9

Where to from Here?

THE SOVIET THREAT

Following its predecessors in choosing to minimize the AR, the administration keeps raising the already high PR by deploying the MX and the Trident II. It does not recognize the tradeoff between the AR and the PR and that the PR is the greater risk. This book has argued that the combination of a high PR and a low AR demands a policy of reducing the PR, even at the cost of raising the AR.

We owe the persistence of the dangerous policy to the stubborn Soviet bogey. The Soviet leaders do not plan to seize Western Europe. To infer such an ambition from their occupation of Eastern Europe four decades ago or from the Berlin crises is paranoia. The Soviets may sing revolutionary songs, but they do not commit their own forces in any wars, except the one in Afghanistan, and this single case does not portend an attack on the West. In other countries the Soviet Union only assisted local, powerful groups. Although many agree that the AR is small, they accept the objective of deterrence. Deterrence has become the slogan that unites all sides. But, unless the AR is high, there is no need for a policy that entails a high PR. Further, "deterrence" frequently is interpreted to refer to discouraging the enemy from launching its weapons during a crisis provoked by a revolution or other event, not instigated by the Kremlin. But increases in the counterforce capability enhance this danger. The mutual fear that the enemy will shoot first or has already fired its weapons will provoke an attack. In other words, it is the PR that is to be feared in crises of this kind.

New estimates indicate that the Soviets have slowed their defense buildup or that they never spent as much as we feared. Moreover, the two-sided relationship frustrates attempts to read Moscow's intentions, and even a rapid buildup may signal only an attempt to catch up. What is more, even if the Soviet buildup seems out of proportion to prior U.S. increases, Moscow may only be anticipating further U.S. accumulation. After all, being ahead has never reassured U.S. hawks, who have judged the race by the rates of increase, not by the current stockpiles. An effort to catch up made the Soviets the winner.

Nevertheless, we cannot be certain that the hawks are crazy and that the Soviets want nothing but peace: the AR may exceed zero. Moscow's dreams may be grander than its achievements, perhaps because of the threat of U.S. missiles. The large forces that Moscow keeps in Eastern Europe to suppress revolts and to prevent Western intervention may also be used to invade Western Europe when hostilities break out elsewhere, and we cannot rule out completely the possibility of Soviet expansionism. Unable to await certain proof, policymakers need guidelines based on an evaluation of the risks entailed by each choice. Since the AR may exceed zero, the United States should continue to support NATO. However, the United States should promise only to join a conventional defense against a conventional attack. The nuclear guarantee should be limited to retaliation against a nuclear attack.

The balance of power is not so fragile that the United States must defend all friendly governments. The North Vietnamese victory, which imposed a burden of assistance on Moscow, had no significant effect on the global balance. Moreover, communist governments trade with the United States. In Angola a U.S. company continues to produce oil. Communist victories will not cut off essential supplies to the United States.

The incredibility of the nuclear threat led the United States into Vietnam. The need to demonstrate national resolve may again drag us into a costly, local war. Much worse, continued implementation of Flexible Response entails a high PR. Small issues will be magnified, and future leaders may feel compelled to exacerbate crises for the sake of establishing the credibility of the nuclear threat.

THE PREEMPTION RISK

Whatever the origin of a crisis, one side may attempt a preemptive strike. If the issue is unimportant to one, then it may also be unimportant to the other; both sides will recognize the symmetry, and, because each episode is a subgame in a long struggle, neither may concede. Both sides may seek credibility by taking risks. One of them may take the risk of firing a demonstration shot, the other may respond by escalating to two such shots, and so on. The fear of preemption when both sides are preparing for war also may bring one on. With communications systems always tuned into each other, during a crisis either side may misinterpret signals. Preparations for retaliation will be indistinguishable from offensive preparations.

The danger has grown with the counterforce capability. Superpower crises will recur, and over an extended period the risk of nuclear war is high. The goal of reducing the PR should guide the choice of weapons. The United States should not deploy the MX and the Trident II, and the agreement calling for the withdrawal of the Pershing IIs should be implemented. The TNW should also be withdrawn or at least relocated in a less vulnerable position. Unless the MX is deployed in a secure basing mode, its retaliatory power will not provide a significant deterrent to a limited or all-out attack. One hundred MX missiles can be destroyed by only 20 SS-18 missiles. A better deterrent case can be made for the Trident II. But this weapon, as well as the MX, raises the PR. We already have a large survivable retaliatory capability in the Poseidons, which reduce the AR as well as the PR. Adding the Trident II does not strengthen U.S. retaliatory power significantly, and if more retaliatory power is desired, then we can always acquire more Poseidons. The Trident II will increase the U.S. incentive to strike first. Unless both sides have survivable arsenals, the Trident II will increase the PR. These considerations also apply to a survivable basing mode for the MX and to an effective BMD system.

National security requires a survivable counterforce system only if a deliberate Soviet attack is probable without it. The counterforce analysis without the bogey leads to the conclusion that either side may attack first and therefore that both parties should have survivable counterforce weapons. The counterforce theory thus breaks down without the bogey. If both sides have secure counterforce capabilities, neither side has one. They cancel each other. We are left with only city-strike forces.

Adding the bogey does not greatly help the case for a survivable counterforce capability, since in a crisis the chief danger is of a preemptive strike. However ambitious the Soviets are, they would have to be insane to risk nuclear war. Superiority can assure Moscow neither that the United States will refrain from retaliation, nor that threats will force major concessions, as long as the United States maintains a survivable city-strike deterrent.

Armed as the Soviets are, we need retaliatory nuclear weapons. The Poseidons, which are highly survivable and useful only for retaliation, should be retained. As long as their warheads remain inaccurate, they cannot threaten the Soviet nuclear forces. Under war conditions communications will be unreliable, but the likelihood of the NCA maintaining control over the land-based force also is slim. The choice of weapons should not depend on the expected state of wartime communications.

The Minuteman IIIs, which no longer threaten the survival of the Soviet retaliatory forces, may be retained to supplement the sea-based force. Their vulnerability should not be a concern as long as there are SLBMs, aircraft, and cruise missiles for retaliation.

The accurate Pershing IIs, which may trigger a Soviet preemptive attack, are particularly dangerous. The Soviets have the same fear of the Pershing IIs as we had of the prospect of nearby Soviet missiles during the Cuban missile crisis. These weapons should be withdrawn, as called for by the recent agreement.

NATO should also withdraw the TNW deployed in West Germany. Unless this is done, small clashes along the East-West border may quickly erupt into nuclear warfare. Moreover, war preparations will entail equipping artillery units with warheads, and, once hostilities begin, they are likely to attract preemptive attacks. At the very least, the TNW should be moved well back of the East-West border.

Reducing the PR is the main argument usually advanced for substituting the mobile, single-warhead SICBM or Midgetman for the MX. But such a shift will not eliminate the preemption incentive. The PR will be reduced only if both sides abandon MIRVed, heavy weapons and shift to SICBMs in hardened, fixed silos. Unless all these conditions are met, the build-down proposal is unlikely to reduce the risk.

I have left cruise missiles to the last. There should be no limit to the number of cruise missiles, nor to their range. Owing to their slowness, they are useful only as retaliatory weapons. It is unfortunate that the recent agreement calls for their withdrawal from West Germany.

REDUCE RIVALRY

The counterforce strategy, with its threat of a deliberate, slow nuclear war, has been more attractive than incredible Massive Retaliation. But the counterforce strategy has increased the PR by encouraging the search for superiority. The strategy assumes that the more powerful arsenal will win a nuclear war. The expectation of a victory after dozens or hundreds of missiles have been fired is astonishing, and the belief that a nuclear war can be carried out in some coherent, organized manner is even more ludicrous. Nevertheless, these beliefs dominate the current policy.

Supporters of the policy who reject the possibility of victory in a nuclear war argue that the bargaining takes the form of the arms control negotiations plus an arms race; that no one really believes that a war will be fought. The real struggle is for political power, which goes to the side with the most powerful arsenal. In confrontations, the one with the most powerful arsenal will prevail without war. Whatever the effect is of apparent military power in the struggle for political power, the game has become too dangerous for the prize. It is extremely optimistic to expect confrontations to be settled without war when both sides have powerful counterforce weapons threatening each other. In any case, the argument concerning political influence is relevant to the defense policy only when conventional wars are expected. It hardly justifies raising the risk of a nuclear war.

Nor does the political argument justify dismissing the military theory. If a confrontation does boil over, the counterforce strategy will become the plan of action. The rivalry will have real consequences in a crisis. Moreover, the prospect of such a crisis justifies the current planning and policy.

Ultimately, the problem comes down to the incompatibility of the goals of winning and of reducing the risk of a nuclear war. A strategy for victory prescribes a superior arsenal. Since the Soviets are not ready to concede, the result is rivalry and increases in the PR. If the principal goal is to minimize the risk, then we must discard the counterforce strategy and the goal of victory.

THE COST OF CONVENTIONAL DEFENSE

NATO policymakers may not agree that the Soviet threat is a bogey. Assuming that the threat is real, the sensible alternative to a nuclear defense policy is a conventional-force policy, which may be more expensive. With government receipts over 30 percent of the GNP, political leaders may oppose additional taxes. European governments probably cannot increase income tax rates and maintain the same progressivity. Further increases in the personal income tax rates in the upper range may be politically impossible. Higher sales or value-added taxes may be needed to pay for stronger conventional forces. Perhaps the greatest Soviet advantage is the concealed, high consumption tax. Despite egalitarian political ideals, most of NATO's members already collect a substantial proportion of their revenues from such taxes, and the goal of minimizing the risk of nuclear war merits increases.

The objection to increases in taxes that they damage work and investment incentives applies only to the highly progressive personal income tax. Increases in general sales or excise taxes or in the value-added tax will not reduce total output. The United States, which has no federal general sales tax or value-added tax, may have to impose one. It makes no more sense to attack increases in the purchase of public services than it does to attack an increase in expenditures for entertainment, food, or transportation. Whether the services are provided out of public funds or private funds makes no difference.

The dependence on progressive income taxes has restricted defense expenditures excessively. The resistance to increases in tax rates has led to a highly risky defense policy. Political leaders have found it easier to cut defense expenditures than to raise taxes, and they have been unable to reduce other public expenditures sufficiently to permit expanding the conventional forces significantly. The restraint on defense expenditures should be no tighter than on any private expenditures, but high marginal tax rates have prevented them from being raised further. The recent reductions in personal income tax rates in this country testify to the problem. A shift to indirect taxes will permit public expenditures, including those for defense, to grow more readily.

MINIMIZING THE RISK OF NUCLEAR WAR

To minimize the risks of nuclear war, the United States should stop acquiring destabilizing weapons and divest itself of those it has. The reply is that the Soviets, expecting the United States not to respond, may threaten cities or even begin to inflict destruction. However, it is impossible completely to eliminate the risk. We must choose which risk to reduce. Even an MX force cannot preclude the threat. The policy of minimum deterrence has the advantage of reducing the major risk, and thus the total risk of nuclear war.

Box 9.1 sets out the premises for the policy advocated here. I assume that Soviet intentions are unknown (premise 1). There will be confrontations and thus some risk of war (premise 2). But the PR is the major risk, not the AR (premise 3). The major policy goal should be to reduce the risk of nuclear war (premise 4).

Since we do not know if the Soviets have aggressive intentions toward Western Europe, it is necessary to provide for its defense. However, since the major risk of nuclear war is the PR, the United States should withdraw its nuclear guarantee of Western Europe's security (policy 1). The United States should agree to cooperate with the

---

Box 9.1
An Alternative Defense Policy

The Premises
1. Soviet intentions are unknown.
2. Confrontations with the Soviet Union will result in some risk of war.
3. The preemption risk exceeds the aggression risk.
4. The major policy goal should be to minimize the risk of nuclear war.
5. The highest priority should be given to reducing the preemption risk.

The Policy
1. Withdraw the nuclear guarantee against a Soviet invasion of Western Europe.
2. Build a strong conventional force.
3. Retain the Poseidons.
4. Retain the B-52s and expand the number of cruise missiles.
5. Withdraw the Pershing IIs and the TNW. Cancel the MX and Trident II programs.

The Consequence
1. Reduce the preemption risk and the risk of nuclear war.

Western European powers to strengthen NATO's conventional forces (policy 2). To retain deterrence and increase stability, the present SLBMs should be retained (policy 3). The B-52s should also be retained, and the number of cruise missiles, including ALCMs, GLCMs, and SLCMs, should be increased (policy 4). We should withdraw the Pershing IIs from Western Europe and not proceed with the MX or the Trident II (policy 5). We can expect to reduce the PR and thus the risk of nuclear war (consequence 1).

The Soviets will continue to uphold revolutionary causes in the Third World, in opposition to U.S.-supported right-wing groups. Such conflicts do not herald a confrontation for world control, but they may ignite a nuclear war. This is the danger that the defense policy should be designed to minimize.

Many who fear a Soviet drive for world power disagree with this book's policy recommendations. Many will think that it is overly optimistic to expect the Soviets not to risk a major war if we dismantle our counterforce weapons. But even pessimists may agree that great Soviet ambitions can be restrained by a less dangerous policy than the present one. Indeed, as we have seen, part of the case for the nuclear defense policy rests on economic arguments. What an adequate conventional defense will require is one of the issues. What is often omitted from the hawks' case is that effective deterrence does not require the assurance of an ultimate Soviet defeat. Despite any expectations of ultimate victory, an expansionist Soviet Union will not risk large losses, and the conclusion that the Soviet conventional forces can defeat NATO is not shared by all military analysts. We can conclude that the Soviets cannot expect an easy victory. In any case, fearful hawks can press for the expansion of NATO's conventional forces. The Soviets cannot be so much stronger that any conventional defense within the West's means is impossible.

As this is being written, the chances of our survival appear to be improving. Under the recent agreement to eliminate the IRBMs in Europe, the Soviets will withdraw the SS-20s, and in exchange, the United States will withdraw the Pershing IIs from Western Europe. This agreement will remove one of the major sources of the PR in any crisis. The opposition fears that Western Europe will fall under Soviet domination; Moscow's conventional power will decide issues in conflicts centered in Western Europe and also possibly in other areas. Opponents of the agreement fear an invasion of Western Europe when the Soviets no longer risk strategic retaliation. Thus, the old issues persist. Every step of the way we must assess the PR and the AR and make our decisions accordingly. The administration now apparently believes that the PR exceeds the AR. It must be supported in this assessment and in reaching the appropriate agreement. The administration's success in negotiating the removal of the IRBMs from Europe is an historic accomplishment.

The United States also has agreed to remove its GLCMs from West Germany. As this book has argued, these purely retaliatory weapons reduce the PR. However, the United States probably had to make this unfortunate concession to reach an agreement.

Although the SS-20s do not threaten the U.S. retaliatory capability, their elimination also will reduce the PR. Some war scenarios depict the escalation of conventional war to strategic warfare; exchanges between intermediate-range weapons are expected at an intermediate stage. Strategists have advocated the deployment of IRBMs to enhance deterrence because an IRBM threat is more credible than a suicidal ICBM threat. To the degree that the deployment of IRBMs increases the probability of a crisis setting off a nuclear war, their removal reduces the PR. Therefore, the removal of the SS-20s as part of a package that includes removal of the Pershing IIs contributes to lowering the PR.

Arms control negotiations aimed at reducing the PR will seek the removal of Soviet SS-18s and SS-9s in exchange for the cancellation of the MX and Trident II programs. Once the Pershing IIs are removed, these will be the chief sources of danger. Insistence on the SDI program should not block further agreements. Any defense system that is developed will protect only missile bases, which is equivalent to adding to the offensive capability. The installation of missile defenses will accelerate the arms race. If the Soviets cannot develop their own defense system, they will deploy more ICBMs to offset the enhanced U.S. offensive capability. The United States should not deploy a defense system that would increase the risk of war.

Notes

CHAPTER 1

1. The Harvard Nuclear Study Group, *Living with Nuclear Weapons* (New York: Bantam Books, 1983), pp. 47-60; Michael Nacht, *The Age of Vulnerability: Threats to the Nuclear Stalemate* (Washington, DC: The Brookings Institution, 1985), pp. 104-6; Lawrence Freedman, *The Evolution of Nuclear Strategy* (New York: St. Martin's Press, 1983), pp. 180-81, 216-17.

2. Thomas C. Schelling, *Arms and Influence* (New Haven, CT: Yale University Press, 1966), pp. 92-125.

CHAPTER 2

1. Robert J. Donovan, *Conflict and Crisis: The Presidency of Harry S. Truman, 1945-48* (New York: W. W. Norton, 1977), p. 35.

2. Walter Millis, *The Forrestal Diaries* (New York: Viking Press, 1951), pp. 48-51.

3. Donovan, *Conflict and Crisis*, pp. 41-42.

4. Charles L. Mee, Jr., *The Marshall Plan: The Launching of the Pax Americana* (New York: Simon & Schuster, 1984), pp. 26-30.

5. Donovan, *Conflict and Crisis*, p. 96.

6. Ibid., p. 84.

7. George F. Kennan, *Memoirs: 1925-1950* (Boston: Little, Brown, 1967), p. 284.

8. Ibid., pp. 290-91.

9. Kennan, *Memoirs: 1925-1950*, pp. 546-59; "X," "Sources of Soviet Conduct," *Foreign Affairs* (July 1947):566-82.

10. Walter Lippmann, *The Cold War: A Study in US Foreign Policy* (New York: Harper & Bros., 1947), pp. 30-31.

11. George F. Kennan, *Memoirs: 1950-1963* (Boston: Little, Brown, 1972), pp. 238-54.

12. Donovan, *Conflict and Crisis*, p. 40; Omar N. Bradley and Clay Blair, *A

General's Life: An Autobiography (New York: Simon & Schuster, 1983), p. 470.

13. Millis, *The Forrestal Diaries*, pp. 48-51.

14. Ibid., pp. 72-73.

15. Ibid., pp. 247-49.

16. Donovan, *Conflict and Crisis*, p. 187.

17. Harry S. Truman, *Memoirs by Harry S. Truman*, vol. 2, *Years of Trial and Hope* (Garden City, NY: Doubleday, 1956), p. 103.

18. Dean Acheson, *Present at the Creation: My Years in the State Department* (New York: W. W. Norton, 1969), p. 195.

19. Ibid., p. 219.

20. Ibid.

21. Ibid., p. 221.

22. Charles E. Bohlen, *Witness to History, 1919-1969* (New York: W. W. Norton, 1973), p. 261; Mee, *The Marshall Plan*, p. 48.

23. Acheson, *Present at the Creation*, pp. 222-25.

24. Mee, *The Marshall Plan*, p. 211.

25. Ibid., pp. 243-45.

26. Ronald Steel, *Walter Lippmann and the American Century* (Boston: Little, Brown, 1980), p. 451.

27. Donovan, *Conflict and Crisis*, pp. 363-65.

28. Ibid., p. 367.

29. Kennan, *Memoirs: 1925-1950*, pp. 419-25; Louis J. Halle, *The Cold War as History* (New York: Harper Torchbooks, 1967), pp. 163-67; Charles E. Bohlen, *Witness to History*, pp. 274-77.

30. Matthew A. Evangelista, "Stalin's Postwar Army Reappraised," *International Security* 7, 3 (Winter 1982/83):110-38, esp. pp. 112-13.

31. Ibid., p. 116-17.

32. Stephen E. Ambrose, *Eisenhower*, vol. 1, *Soldier, General of the Army, President-elect, 1890-1952* (New York: Simon & Schuster, 1983), p. 449.

33. Ibid., pp. 114-15.

34. Ibid., p. 110.

35. Ibid., p. 115.

36. B. H. Liddell Hart, *Deterrence or Defense: A Fresh Look at the West's Military Position* (New York: Praeger, 1960), pp. 134-35.

37. Timothy W. Stanley, *NATO in Transition: The Future of the Atlantic Alliance* (New York: Praeger, 1965), p. 270.

38. Thomas W. Wolfe, *Soviet Power and Europe 1945-1970* (Baltimore, MD: Johns Hopkins University Press, 1970), p. 10, notes 3-6.

39. Evangelista, "Stalin's Postwar Army Reappraised," pp. 118-19.

40. Mee, *The Marshall Plan*, p. 57.

41. Evangelista, "Stalin's Postwar Army Reappraised," p. 121.

42. Ibid., pp. 123-24.

43. Ibid., pp. 125-31.

44. Ibid., pp. 132-33. Evangelista cited Joint Intelligence Staff, "Soviet Capabilities," November 9, 1945, Appendix C.

45. Ibid., pp. 132-33. Evangelista cited ORE 58-48, October 27, 1948, p. 39; ORE 46-49, "The Possibility of Direct Soviet Military Action during 1949," May 3, 1949, p. 1.

46. Gregg Herken, *The Winning Weapon: The Atom Bomb in the Cold War, 1945-50* (New York: Knopf, 1980), p. 138.

47. Evangelista, "Stalin's Postwar Army Reappraised," p. 133. Citation is letter dated February 1, 1947, p. 3.

48. Ibid. Evangelista cited CIA National Intelligence Estimate, NIE-3, "Soviet Capabilities and Intentions," November 15, 1950, pp. 1-2, 66.

49. The discussion of the changes in the military forces and in expenditures and taxes is based on *National Defense Budget Estimates for FY 1984*, Office of the Assistant Secretary of Defense (Comptroller), March 1983, pp. 91-96, and on Joseph A. Pechman, *Federal Tax Policy* (Washington, DC: Brookings Institution, 1966), pp. 244-45.

50. Warner R. Schilling, "The Politics of National Defense: Fiscal 1950," in Warner R. Schilling, Paul Y. Hammond, and Glenn H. Snyder, *Strategy, Politics, and Defense Budgets* (New York: Columbia University Press, 1968), pp. 126-27.

51. Ibid., pp. 139-40.

52. Paul Y. Hammond, "NSC: Prologue to Rearmament," in Schilling, Hammond, and Snyder, *Strategy, Politics, and Defense Budgets*, p. 328.

53. Schilling, "The Politics of National Defense: Fiscal 1950," pp. 101-3.

54. Samuel P. Huntington, *The Common Defense: Strategic Programs in National Politics* (New York: Columbia University Press, 1961), p. 46.

55. Omar N. Bradley and Clay Blair, *A General's Life*, p. 487. See also pp. 473-74, 488.

56. Seyom Brown, *The Faces of Power: Constancy and Change in United States Foreign Policy from Truman to Johnson* (New York: Columbia University Press, 1968), pp. 50-51.

57. Schilling, "The Politics of National Defense: Fiscal 1950," pp. 41-47.

58. Hammond, "NSC: Prologue to Rearmament," p. 306.

59. Huntington, *The Common Defense*, p. 54.

60. Robert Osgood, *NATO: The Entangling Alliance* (Chicago: University of Chicago Press, 1962), pp. 66-68.

61. Huntington, *The Common Defense*, p. 63.

62. Steven L. Rearden, *The Evolution of American Strategic Doctrine: Paul H. Nitze and the Soviet Challenge* (Johns Hopkins Foreign Policy Institute, School of Advanced International Studies. Boulder, CO: Westview Press, 1984), p. 9.

63. Ibid., pp. 20-21.

64. Ibid., 22-24.

65. Walter LaFeber, *America, Russia, and the Cold War, 1945-75*, 3rd ed. (New York: Wiley, 1976), p. 84.

66. Thomas B. Cochran, William M. Arkin, Milton M. Hoenig, *Nuclear Weapons Handbook*, vol. 1, *U.S. Nuclear Forces and Capabilities* (Cambridge, MA: Ballinger, 1984), p. 6.

67. David A. Rosenberg, "The Origins of Overkill: Nuclear Weapons and American Strategy, 1945-1960," *International Security* 7, 4 (Spring 1983):3-71, esp. p. 13.

68. Ibid., pp. 15-16.

69. Rearden, *The Evolution of American Strategic Doctrine*, p. 10.

70. Rosenberg, "The Origins of Overkill," p. 16.

71. Ibid., p. 19.

72. Ibid., p. 21.

73. Ibid., p. 22.

74. Acheson, *Present at the Creation*, pp. 151-52.

75. John Lewis Gaddis, *The United States and the Origins of the Cold War,*

1941-1947 (New York: Columbia University Press, 1972), p. 332.

76. David E. Lilienthal, *The Journals of David E. Lilienthal: The Atomic Energy Years, 1945-1950* (New York, 1964), p. 30. Quoted by Gregg Herken, *The Winning Weapon,* p. 160.

77. Gaddis, *The United States and the Origins of the Cold War,* p. 334.

78. Ibid., p. 335.

79. J. C. R. Dow, *The Management of the British Economy, 1945-1960* (Cambridge: Cambridge University Press, 1970), pp. 17-18.

80. Ibid., pp. 37-38.

81. Ibid., p. 46.

82. Ibid., p. 55.

83. Ibid., p. 40.

84. Osgood, *NATO,* p. 82.

85. Ibid., p. 68.

86. Ibid., pp. 70, 83-84.

87. Ibid., p. 76.

88. Glenn H. Snyder, "The 'New Look' of 1953," in Schilling, Hammond, and Snyder, *Strategy, Politics, and Defense Budgets,* pp. 388-89.

89. Ibid., pp. 388-89.

90. Ibid., p. 67.

91. Ibid.

92. Stanley, *NATO in Transition,* p. 275.

CHAPTER 3

1. Dwight D. Eisenhower, *Waging Peace: The White House Years, 1956-61* (Garden City, NY: Doubleday, 1965), p. 127.

2. Ibid., p. 128.

3. Ibid., p. 380.

4. Ibid., p. 218.

5. John Foster Dulles, *War or Peace* (New York: Macmillan, 1950), p. 9. Cited by Townsend Hoopes, *The Devil and John Foster Dulles* (Boston: Little, Brown, 1973), p. 64.

6. John Foster Dulles, "A Policy of Boldness," *Life,* May 19, 1952, p. 146. Cited by Hoopes, *The Devil and John Foster Dulles,* pp. 126-28.

7. Hoopes, *The Devil and John Foster Dulles,* p. 128.

8. Ibid., p. 171.

9. Ibid.

10. Ibid.

11. Emmet John Hughes, *The Ordeal of Power: A Political Memoir of the Eisenhower Years* (New York: Atheneum, 1963), p. 105.

12. W. W. Rostow, *Europe After Stalin: Eisenhower's Three Decisions of March 11, 1953* (Austin, TX: University of Texas Press, 1982), p. 63.

13. Stephen E. Ambrose, *Eisenhower,* vol. 2, *The President* (New York: Simon & Schuster, 1984), p. 51.

14. Dwight D. Eisenhower, *The White House Years; Mandate for Change: 1953-1956* (Garden City, NY: Doubleday, 1963), p. 181.

15. Ambrose, *Eisenhower,* p. 179.

16. Ibid., p. 239.

17. Ibid.

18. Ibid., p. 503.

19. Ibid.

20. Ibid., p. 504.

21. Ibid., p. 517.

22. Ibid.

23. Ibid.

24. Seyom Brown, *The Faces of Power: Constancy and Change in United States Foreign Policy from Truman to Johnson* (New York: Columbia University Press, 1968), pp. 153-55.

25. Ambrose, *Eisenhower*, p. 518.

26. Discussion of defense budgets based on *National Defense Budget Estimates for FY 1984*, Office of Assistant Secretary of Defense (Comptroller), March 1983, pp. 61, 62, 91-96.

27. Glenn H. Snyder, "The 'New Look' of 1953," in Warner H. Schilling, Paul Y. Hammond, and Glenn H. Snyder, eds., *Strategy, Politics, and Defense Budgets* (New York: Columbia University Press, 1962), pp. 393-97.

28. Ambrose, *Eisenhower*, p. 224.

29. Ibid., p. 225.

30. Ibid., p. 223.

31. Ibid., p. 224.

32. Robert Osgood, *NATO: The Entangling Alliance* (Chicago: University of Chicago Press, 1962), pp. 106-7.

33. Alain C. Enthoven and K. Wayne Smith, *How Much Is Enough? Shaping the Defense Program, 1961-69* (New York: Harper & Row, 1971), pp. 124-25.

34. Maxwell D. Taylor, *The Uncertain Trumpet* (New York: Harper & Row, 1960), p. 61.

35. David A. Rosenberg, "The Origins of Overkill: Nuclear Weapons and American Strategy, 1945-60," *International Security* 8, 1 (Spring 1983):42.

36. Ambrose, *Eisenhower*, pp. 144-45.

37. Taylor, *The Uncertain Trumpet*, p. 38.

38. Glenn H. Snyder, "The 'New Look' of 1953," pp. 458-59.

39. Ambrose, *Eisenhower*, p. 225.

40. Samuel P. Huntington, *The Common Defense: Strategic Programs in National Politics* (New York: Columbia University Press, 1961), p. 94.

41. Ibid., p. 95.

42. Ibid., pp. 74-75.

43. Ibid., p. 80.

44. Rosenberg, "The Origins of Overkill," p. 42.

45. Ibid., p. 35.

46. Ibid., p. 66.

47. Ibid., p. 46.

48. Ibid., p. 32.

49. Ibid., p. 33.

50. Ibid., p. 34.

51. Ibid., p. 36.

52. Ibid., pp. 38-39.

53. Ibid., p. 56.

54. Ibid., p. 57.

55. Ibid., p. 58.

56. Ibid., p. 59.

57. Ibid., p. 65.

58. Ambrose, *Eisenhower*, p. 433.

59. Morton H. Halperin, *National Security Policy-Making: Analyses, Cases, and Proposals* (Lexington, MA: Lexington Books, 1975), pp. 105-9.

60. Fred Kaplan, *The Wizards of Armageddon: Strategists of the Nuclear Age* (New York: Simon & Schuster, 1983), pp. 136-41.

61. Ibid., pp. 128-29.

62. Halperin, *National Security Policy-Making*, p. 65, n.21. Halperin cited Joseph Kraft, "RAND: Arsenal for Ideas," *Harper's* 221 (July 1960):71-73.

63. Halperin, *National Security Policy-Making*, p. 78.

64. Ibid., p. 90.

65. Ibid., pp. 78-79.

66. Ibid., p. 89.

67. Ibid., p. 90.

68. Ibid.

69. Ibid., p. 65, n.21.

70. Ibid., p. 51.

71. Ibid., p. 54.

72. Ambrose, *Eisenhower*, p. 434.

73. John F. Kennedy, *John Fitzgerald Kennedy: A Compilation of Statements and Speeches Made During His Service in the United States Senate and House of Representatives*, 88th Congress, 2nd Session, Senate Document No. 79 (Washington, DC: Government Printing Office, 1964, August 14, 1958), pp. 705-15. Cited by Richard A. Aliano, *American Defense Policy from Eisenhower to Kennedy: The Politics of Changing Military Requirements, 1957-1961* (Athens, OH: Ohio University Press, 1975), p. 233.

74. Aliano, *American Defense Policy from Eisenhower to Kennedy*, p. 234.

75. Ibid., p. 235.

76. Ibid., p. 236.

77. Henry A. Kissinger, *Nuclear Weapons and Foreign Policy* (New York: Harper and Brothers, 1957).

78. Albert Wohlstetter, "The Delicate Balance of Terror," *Foreign Affairs* 37 (January 1959):209-34.

79. Rockefeller Brothers Fund, *Prospects for America: The Rockefeller Panel Reports*, Report II: "International Security: The Military Aspect" (Garden City: Doubleday, 1961), p. 146. Cited by Aliano, *American Defense Policy from Eisenhower to Kennedy*, pp. 191-92.

80. Ibid.

81. Walter Laqueur, *Europe Since Hitler: The Rebirth of Europe*, rev. ed. (New York: Penguin Books, 1983), p. 219.

82. Ibid., p. 253.

83. Ibid., p. 254.

84. Alfred Grosser, *The Western Alliance: European-American Relations Since 1945* (New York: Random House, Vintage, 1982), p. 164.

85. Ibid.

86. Wolfram F. Hanrieder, *West German Foreign Policy, 1949-1963: International Pressure and Domestic Response* (Stanford, CA; Stanford University Press, 1967), pp. 149-51.

87. Ibid., p. 166.

88. OECD, *Public Expenditure Trends* (Paris, June 1978), p. 14.

89. Osgood, *NATO: The Entangling Alliance*, p. 133.

90. F. W. Mulley, *The Politics of Western Defense* (New York: Praeger, 1962), p. 124.

91. Osgood, *NATO: The Entangling Alliance*, p. 131.

92. Hanrieder, *West German Foreign Policy, 1949-1963*, pp. 149-51.

CHAPTER 4

1. Theodore C. Sorensen, *Kennedy* (New York: Harper & Row, 1965), p. 579.

2. Ibid.

3. John F. Kennedy, *Strategy of Peace* (New York: Harper & Row, 1960), pp. 37-38.

4. Sorensen, *Kennedy*, p. 590.

5. Ibid., p. 276.

6. William W. Kaufmann, "The Requirements of Deterrence," in William W. Kaufmann, ed., *Military Policy and National Security* (Princeton, NJ: Princeton University Press, 1956), pp. 12-37.

7. Ibid., p. 16.

8. Ibid., p. 27.

9. Ibid., p. 29.

10. Ibid., p. 18.

11. Albert Wohlstetter, "The Delicate Balance of Terror," *Foreign Affairs* 37, 2 (January 1959):209-34. Reprinted in Henry A. Kissinger, ed., *Problems of National Strategy* (New York: Praeger, 1965), pp. 34-58.

12. Ibid., p. 34.

13. Ibid., p. 41.

14. Ibid.

15. Thomas C. Schelling, *The Strategy of Conflict* (Cambridge, MA: Harvard University Press, 1960).

16. William W. Kaufmann, *The McNamara Strategy* (New York: Harper & Row, 1964), p. 75.

17. "Remarks by Secretary McNamara, NATO Ministerial Meeting, 5 May 1962, Restricted Session." Quoted by David N. Schwartz, *NATO's Nuclear Dilemmas* (Washington, DC: Brookings Institution, 1983), p. 157. Schwartz notes that the speech was declassified on August 17, 1979.

18. Ibid., p. 158.

19. Ibid., p. 160.

20. Robert Osgood, "Stabilizing the military environment," *American Political Science Review* 55, 1 (March 1961). Cited by Lawrence Freedman, *The Evolution of Nuclear Strategy* (New York: St. Martin's Press, 1982), p. 241.

21. Henry S. Rowen, "The Evolution of Strategic Nuclear Doctrine," in Laurence Martin, ed., *Strategic Thought in the Nuclear Age* (Baltimore, MD: Johns Hopkins University Press, 1979), pp. 145-46.

22. Sorensen, *Kennedy*, pp. 687-88.

23. Freedman, *The Evolution of Nuclear Strategy*, p. 239.

24. Seyom Brown, *The Faces of Power: Constancy and Change in United States Foreign Policy from Truman to Johnson* (New York: Columbia University Press, 1968), p. 24.

25. Ibid., p. 245.

26. Ibid., p. 244.

27. Brown, *The Faces of Power*, p. 248.

28. Ibid., pp. 248-49.

29. Sorensen, *Kennedy*, p. 668.

30. Brown, *The Faces of Power*, p. 247.

31. Sorensen, *Kennedy*, p. 662.

32. Ibid.

33. Ibid., pp. 663-64.

34. Ibid.

35. Brown, *The Faces of Power*, p. 252.

36. Sorensen, *Kennedy*, pp. 665-67.

37. Fred Kaplan, *The Wizards of Armageddon* (New York: Simon & Schuster, 1983), p. 298.

38. Ibid., p. 299.

39. Ibid., pp. 300-1.

40. Gregg Herken, *Counsels of War* (New York: Knopf, 1985), p. 158.

41. Stephen E. Ambrose, *Eisenhower*, vol. 2, *The President* (New York: Simon & Schuster, 1984), p. 643.

42. Sorensen, *Kennedy*, pp. 762-64.

43. Ibid., p. 778.

44. Ibid., p. 764.

45. George F. Ball, *The Past Has Another Pattern: Memoirs* (New York: W. W. Norton, 1982), p. 295.

46. Michael Mandelbaum, *The Nuclear Question: The United States and Nuclear Weapons, 1946-1976* (Cambridge: Cambridge University Press, 1979), p. 136.

47. Ball, *The Past Has Another Pattern*, pp. 290-91.

48. Ibid., p. 291.

49. Ibid., p. 292.

50. *Setting National Priorities* (Washington, DC: Brookings Institution, 1974), p. 294.

51. David Holloway, *The Soviet Union and the Arms Race* (New Haven, CT: Yale University Press, 1983), p. 85. For the estimate of four ICBMs, Holloway cited Lawrence Freedman, *US Intelligence and the Soviet Strategic Threat* (London: Macmillan, 1977), p. 73.

52. Sorensen, *Kennedy*, p. 680.

53. Ibid., p. 446.

54. Richard D. Lawrence and Jeffrey Record, *United States Force Structure in NATO: An Alternative* (Washington, DC: Brookings Institution, 1974), p. 93.

55. Roswell Gilpatric, *Speech before Business Council, Hot Springs, Virginia, October 21, 1961*, Department of Defense, Office of Public Affairs, Release 1173-61, pp. 1-2. Cited by Harland B. Moulton, *From Superiority to Parity: The United States and the Strategic Arms Race, 1961-1971* (Westport, CT: Greenwood Press, 1973), p. 65.

56. Moulton, *From Superiority to Parity*, p. 27.

57. Holloway, *The Soviet Union and the Arms Race*, p. 58.

58. Fred Kaplan, *The Wizards of Armageddon*, pp. 271-74.

59. Sorensen, *Kennedy*, p. 686; William Kaufmann, *The McNamara Strategy* (New York: Harper & Row, 1964), p. 69.

60. John Lewis Gaddis, *Strategies of Containment: A Critical Appraisal of Post-*

war American National Security Policy (New York: Oxford University Press, 1982), p. 220.

61. Ibid., p. 221n.

62. Kaufmann, *The McNamara Strategy*, p. 88.

63. Robert S. McNamara, "Defense Arrangements of the North Atlantic Community," Department of State Bulletin 47, July 9, 1962, pp. 67-68. Cited by Freedman, *The Evolution of Nuclear Strategy*, p. 235.

64. Gaddis, *Strategies of Containment*, p. 219.

65. Ibid., p. 218.

66. Kaufmann, *The McNamara Strategy*, p. 137; Moulton, *From Superiority to Parity*, p. 56.

67. For example, Lawrence Freedman, *The Evolution of Nuclear Strategy*, pp. 245-50.

68. Alain C. Enthoven and K. Wayne Smith, *How Much Is Enough? Shaping the Defense Program 1961-69* (New York: Harper & Row, 1971), pp. 140-49.

69. Arthur Schlesinger, Jr., *A Thousand Days: John F. Kennedy in the White House* (New York: Fawcett Premier, 1965), pp. 461-62.

70. Sorensen, *Kennedy*, p. 686.

71. *US News and World Report.* Reprinted in *Congressional Record*, April 7, 1965 S-7271. Cited by Lawrence W. Martin, "Military Issues: Strategic Parity and Its Implications," in Robert E. Osgood, ed., *Retreat from Empire? The First Nixon Administration* (Baltimore: Johns Hopkins University Press, 1973), p. 140.

72. Robert S. McNamara, *The Essence of Security: Reflections in Office* (New York: Harper & Row, 1968), pp. 57-60.

73. Lauren H. Holland and Robert A. Hoover, *The MX Decision: A New Direction in US Weapons Procurement Policy?* (Boulder, CO: Westview Press, 1985), p. 46.

74. Ibid., pp. 125-26.

75. Kaplan, *The Wizards of Armageddon*, pp. 363-64.

76. Ronald L. Tammen, *MIRV and the Arms Race: An Interpretation of Defense Strategy* (New York: Praeger, 1973), p. 65.

77. Ibid., p. 78.

78. Ibid., p. 117.

79. Ibid., pp. 120-21.

80. Ibid., p. 121.

81. Ibid., p. 99.

82. Ibid., p. 121.

83. Ibid., p. 104.

84. Ibid., p. 105.

85. Ibid., p. 72.

86. James L. Richardson, *Germany and the Atlantic Alliance: The Interaction of Strategy and Politics* (Cambridge, MA: Harvard Univ. Press, 1966), pp. 76-78.

87. Helmut Schmidt, *Defense or Retaliation: A German Contribution to the Consideration of NATO's Strategic Problem* (Edinburgh: Oliver and Boyd, 1962).

88. Richardson, *Germany and the Atlantic Alliance*, p. 78.

89. Schmidt, *Defense or Retaliation*, pp. 185-87.

90. Enthoven and Smith, *How Much Is Enough?* p. 126.

91. Schmidt, *Defense or Retaliation*, p. 187.

92. Ibid., p. 95.

93. Kaufmann, *The McNamara Strategy*, p. 106.

94. T. W. Stanley, *NATO in Transition: The Future of the Atlantic Alliance* (New York: Praeger, 1965), pp. 280-81. Stanley cited Pierre Messner, "The French Military Establishment of Tomorrow," *Orbis*, Summer 1962, pp. 207-9; F. O. Miksche, "Economic, Technological, and Political Aspects of the European Shield," *NATO's Fifteen Nations*, December 1962-January 1963, pp. 38-43; and Secretary McNamara Statement, February 6, 1963.

95. This section is based on Paul Bracken, *The Command and Control of Nuclear Forces* (New Haven, CT: Yale University Press, 1983).

96. Ibid., pp. 10-13.

97. Ibid., p. 13.

98. Ibid.

99. Ibid., p. 14.

100. Ibid., pp. 26, 28.

101. Ibid., p. 35.

102. Ibid., p. 43.

103. Ibid., p. 60.

CHAPTER 5

1. For example, John Lewis Gaddis, *Strategies of Containment: A Critical Appraisal of Postwar National Security Policy* (New York: Oxford University Press, 1982), pp. 279-80.

2. Henry Kissinger, "A New Approach to Arms Control," *Time*, March 21, 1983. Reprinted in Henry Kissinger, *Observations: Selected Speeches and Essays, 1982-1984* (Boston: Little, Brown, 1985), p. 156.

3. Barry M. Blechman, Edward M. Gramlich, and Robert W. Hartman, *Setting National Priorities: The 1975 Budget* (Washington, DC: The Brookings Institution, 1974), p. 65.

4. John M. Collins, *U.S.-Soviet Military Balance: Concepts and Capabilities, 1960-1980* (New York: McGraw-Hill, 1980), p. 443.

5. Richard Nixon, *The Real War* (New York: Warner, 1981), p. 23.

6. Henry A. Kissinger, *Nuclear Weapons and Foreign Policy* (New York: Harper Brothers Doubleday Anchor, 1958), pp. 3-4.

7. Ibid., pp. 43-60.

8. Ibid., pp. 6-8.

9. Writings published in the 1960s and since do not suggest any evidence of planning for a massive invasion of Western Europe. These studies include Adam B. Ulam, *The Rivals: America and Russia Since World War II* (New York: Penguin, 1971); Thomas W. Wolfe, *Soviet Power and Europe, 1945-1970* (Baltimore: Johns Hopkins Press, 1970); Joseph L. Nogee and Robert H. Donaldson, *Soviet Foreign Policy Since World War II* (New York: Pergamon, 1981); David Holloway, *The Soviet Union and the Arms Race* (New Haven, CT: Yale University Press, 1983); Robin Edmonds, *Soviet Foreign Policy: The Brezhnev Years* (Oxford: Oxford University Press, 1983); Marshall D. Shulman, "Relations with the Soviet Union," in Kermit Gordon, ed., *Agenda for the Nation: Papers on Domestic and Foreign Policy Issues* (Washington, DC: Brookings Institution, 1968), pp. 373-406.

10. Henry Kissinger, *Years of Upheaval* (Boston: Little, Brown, 1982), p. 263.

11. Henry Kissinger, *White House Years* (Boston: Little, Brown, 1979), p. 217.
12. Ibid., p. 216.
13. Kissinger, *Years of Upheaval*, p. 979.
14. Ibid., pp. 979-80.
15. Ibid., p. 1003.
16. Ibid., pp. 980-81.
17. Ibid., p. 1003.
18. James W. Canan, *The Superwarriors* (New York: Weybright and Talley, 1975), pp. 150-51.
19. Kissinger, *Years of Upheaval*, p. 1003.
20. Ibid., pp. 980-81.
21. Ibid., p. 1009.
22. Kissinger, *White House Years*, p. 128.
23. Kissinger, *Years of Upheaval*, p. 257.
24. Ibid., p. 259.
25. Ibid., p. 261.
26. *US Foreign Policy for the 1970s: Shaping a Durable Peace, a Report to the Congress by Richard Nixon*, May 3, 1973, pp. 178-86. Extract reprinted in Robert J. Pranger and Roger P. Labrie, eds., *Nuclear Strategy and National Security: Points of View* (Washington, DC: American Enterprise Institute for Public Policy Research, 1977), pp. 21-23.
27. *World Armaments and Disarmament: SIPRI Yearbook 1968/69* (Stockholm International Peace Research Institute, Sweden, 1970), pp. 32-33. To be cited hereafter as *SIPRI Yearbook*.
28. James R. Schlesinger, *Annual Defense Department Report, FY 1975* (Washington, DC, March 4, 1974), pp. 25-45. Extract reprinted in Pranger and Labrie, *Nuclear Strategy and National Security*, p. 97.
29. *SIPRI Yearbook 1975*, pp. 39-40.
30. Fred Charles Iklé, "Can Nuclear Deterrence Last Out the Century?" *Foreign Affairs* 51, 2 (January 1973):267-85. Reprinted in Robert J. Pranger and Roger P. Labrie, eds., *Nuclear Strategy and National Security*, pp. 57-74.
31. William R. Van Cleave and Roger W. Barnett, "Strategic Adaptability," *Orbis* 18, 3 (Fall 1974):655-76. Reprinted in Pranger and Labrie, *Nuclear Strategy and National Security*, pp. 203-23.
32. Paul Bracken, *The Command and Control of Nuclear Forces* (New Haven, CT: Yale University Press, 1983), pp. 179-237.
33. John D. Steinbrunner and Thomas M. Garwin, "Strategic Vulnerability: The Balance between Prudence and Paranoia," *International Security* 1, 1 (Summer 1976):138-70. Reprinted in Pranger and Labrie, *Nuclear Strategy and National Security*, pp. 247-78, esp. pp. 252-57.
34. Samuel P. Huntington, "Renewed Hostility," in Joseph S. Nye, Jr., ed., *The Making of America's Soviet Policy* (New Haven, CT: Yale University Press, 1984), p. 273.
35. Albert Wohlstetter, "Is There a Strategic Arms Race?" *Foreign Policy* 15 (Summer 1974):3-20; and "Rivals But No 'Race'," *Foreign Policy* 16 (Fall 1974):48-81.
36. Wohlstetter, "Is There a Strategic Arms Race?" pp. 5-6.
37. Wohlstetter, "Rivals But No 'Race'," p. 59.
38. Ibid., p. 64.
39. Ibid., p. 66.

40. Lawrence J. Korb, *The Fall and Rise of the Pentagon: American Defense Policy in the 1970s* (Westport, CT: Greenwood, 1979), p. 145.

41. Franklyn D. Holzman, "Is There a Soviet-U.S. Military Spending Gap?" *Challenge* 23, 4 (September/October 1980):3-9, esp. 6-7.

42. Ibid., pp. 8-9.

43. Gerard Smith, *Doubletalk: The Story of the First Strategic Arms Limitation Talks* (Garden City, NY: Doubleday, 1980), p. 177.

44. Kissinger, *White House Years*, p. 149.

45. Smith, *Doubletalk*, p. 175.

46. John Newhouse, *Cold Dawn: The Story of Salt* (New York: Holt, Rinehart and Winston, 1973), p. 156.

47. Kissinger, *White House Years*, p. 206.

48. Ibid., pp. 539-40.

49. John Collins, *U.S.-Soviet Military Balance: Concepts and Capabilities, 1960-1980* (New York: McGraw-Hill, 1980), pp. 163, 463.

50. Smith, *Doubletalk*, p. 162.

51. Kissinger, *White House Years*, p. 211.

52. Ibid., p. 541.

53. Smith, *Doubletalk*, pp. 160-61.

54. Newhouse, *Cold Dawn*, pp. 162, 178.

55. Smith, *Doubletalk*, p. 169.

56. Ibid., p. 170.

57. Ibid., p. 172.

58. Ibid., p. 173.

59. Ibid., pp. 162-63.

60. John Edwards, *Superweapon: The Making of MX* (New York: Norton, 1982), p. 67.

61. Henry Kissinger, "A New Approach to Arms Control," *Time*, March 21, 1983. Reprinted in Henry Kissinger, *Observations: Selected Speeches and Essays, 1982-1984* (Boston: Little, Brown, 1985), pp. 153-63, esp. 156.

62. Thomas C. Schelling, *The Strategy of Conflict* (Cambridge, MA: Harvard University Press, 1981), pp. 199-200.

63. The description of the events is drawn from Barry M. Blechman and Douglas M. Hart, "The Political Utility of Nuclear Weapons: The 1973 Middle East Crisis," *International Security* 7, 1 (Summer 1982):132-56.

CHAPTER 6

1. Raymond L. Garthoff, *Détente and Confrontation: American-Soviet Relations from Nixon to Reagan* (Washington, DC: Brookings Institution, 1985), p. 798.

2. Zbigniew Brzezinski, *Power and Principle: Memoirs of the National Security Adviser, 1977-1981* (New York: Farrar, Straus, Giroux, 1983), p. 49.

3. John Edwards, *Superweapon: The Making of MX* (New York: W. W. Norton 1982), p. 197.

4. Cyrus Vance, *Hard Choices: Critical Years in America's Foreign Policy* (New York: Simon & Schuster, 1983), p. 138.

5. Jimmy Carter, *Keeping Faith: Memoirs of a President* (New York: Bantam Books, 1982), pp. 219, 241.

6. Zbigniew Brzezinski, "U.S.-Soviet Relations," in Henry Owen, ed., *The Next Phase in Foreign Policy* (Washington, DC: The Brookings Institution, 1973), p. 118.

7. Brzezinski, *Power and Principle*, p. 148.

8. Ibid., p. 335.

9. Ibid., p. 333.

10. Zbigniew Brzezinski, *Game Plan: A Geostrategic Framework for the Conduct of the U.S.-Soviet Contest* (Boston: Atlantic Monthly Press, 1986), p. 8.

11. Ibid., pp. 8-15.

12. Ibid., pp. 11-15.

13. Ibid., pp. 30-45.

14. Ibid., pp. 100-2.

15. Ibid., pp. 110-11.

16. Ibid., pp. 117-18.

17. Ibid., p. 121.

18. Ibid.

19. Ibid., pp. 165-68.

20. Barry M. Blechman *with* Robert P. Berman, Martin Binkin, *and* Robert G. Weinland, "Toward a New Consensus on U.S. Defense Policy," in Henry Owen and Charles L. Schultze, eds., *Setting National Priorities: The Next Ten Years* (Washington, DC: The Brookings Institution, 1976), pp. 59-128, esp. 59.

21. Edwards, *Superweapon*, pp. 126-27.

22. Harold Brown, *Thinking About National Security, Defense, and Foreign Policy in a Dangerous World* (Boulder, CO: Westview Press, 1983), p. 16.

23. Ibid., p. 54.

24. Ibid., p. 67.

25. Ibid.

26. Ibid., pp. 56-57.

27. Ibid., pp. 59-60.

28. Ibid., p. 60.

29. Ibid.

30. Charles Tyroler II, ed., *Alerting America: The Papers of the Committee on the Present Danger* (New York: Pergamon-Brassey's, 1984), pp. ix-xi.

31. Paul H. Nitze, "Assuring Strategic Stability in an Era of Détente," *Foreign Affairs* (January 1976). Reprinted in Wolfram F. Hanrieder, ed., *Arms Control and Security: Current Issues*, 2d ed. (Boulder, CO: Westview Press, 1981), pp. 39-65, esp. 41.

32. Ibid., pp. 42-43.

33. Ibid.

34. Committee on the Present Danger, "What Is the Soviet Union Up To?" April 4, 1977. In Tyroler, *Alerting America*, p. 10.

35. Ibid., pp. 10-11.

36. Ibid., p. 11.

37. Ibid., p. 13.

38. Nitze, "Assuring Strategic Stability in an Era of Détente," p. 43.

39. Ibid., p. 53.

40. Carter, *Keeping Faith*, p. 223.

41. Nitze, "Assuring Strategic Stability in an Era of Détente," p. 56.

42. Ibid., p. 47.

43. Ibid., pp. 44-45.

44. Ibid., p. 57.

45. Brzezinski, *Power and Principle*, p. 159.

46. Strobe Talbott, *Endgame: The Inside Story of SALT II* (New York: Harper Torchbooks, 1980), pp. 46-59.

47. Ibid., p. 57.

48. Ibid., p. 61.

49. Ibid., p. 51.

50. Ibid., pp. 54-55.

51. Ibid.

52. Edwards, *Superweapon*, p. 116.

53. Brown, *Thinking About National Security*, pp. 81-82.

54. John M. Collins, *U.S.-Soviet Military Balance: Concepts and Capabilities, 1960-1980* (New York: McGraw-Hill, 1980), p. 139.

55. Brzezinski, *Power and Principle*, p. 457.

56. Herken, *Counsels of War*, p. 300.

57. Ibid., p. 301.

58. Leon V. Sigal, *Nuclear Forces in Europe: Enduring Dilemmas, Present Prospects* (Washington, DC: Brookings, 1984), p. 33.

59. Helmut Schmidt, "The 1977 Alastair Buchan Memorial Lecture," October 28, 1977, *Survival* 20 (January/February 1978):2-10. Reprinted in Wolfram F. Hanrieder, ed., *Helmut Schmidt: Perspectives on Politics* (Boulder, CO: Westview Press, 1982), p. 26.

60. See Sigal, *Nuclear Forces in Europe*, p. 39.

61. Ibid., p. 47.

62. Thomas B. Cochran, William M. Arkin, and Milton M. Hoenig, *Nuclear Weapons Databook*, vol. 1, *U.S. Nuclear Forces and Capabilities* (Cambridge, MA: Ballinger, 1984), pp. 179-80.

63. David N. Schwartz, *NATO's Nuclear Dilemmas* (Washington, DC: Brookings Institution, 1983), pp. 219-20.

64. Henry A. Kissinger, "NATO: The Next Thirty Years," *Survival* 21 (November-December 1979):265-66. Quoted by Schwartz, *NATO's Nuclear Dilemmas*, p. 234.

CHAPTER 7

1. Congressional Budget Office (CBO), *Modernizing U.S. Strategic Offensive Forces: The Administration's Program and Alternatives* (Washington, DC: U.S. Government Printing Office, May 1983), p. 24. Cited hereafter as CBO, *Modernizing U.S. Strategic Forces*.

2. Department of Defense, *Soviet Military Power* (Washington, DC: U.S. Government Printing Office, 2d ed. March 1983), p. 14.

3. *Report of the Secretary of Defense Caspar Weinberger to the Congress on the FY 1984 Budget, FY 1985 Authorization Request and FY 1984-88 Defense Programs*, February 1, 1983, Washington, DC, pp. 21, 25. Cited hereafter as *Defense Report 1984*. Subsequent reports will be cited similarly.

4. Ibid., p. 19.

5. ibid., p. 29.

6. Ibid., p. 34.

7. Ibid., pp. 52-53.

8. Ibid., p. 55.

9. *U.S. Defense Policy* 3d ed. (Washington, DC: Congressional Quarterly, 1983), pp. 88-89.

10. *Report of the President's Commission on Strategic Forces* (Washington, DC: April 1983). Cited hereafter as *Scowcroft Report.*

11. Strobe Talbott, *Deadly Gambits: The Reagan Administration and the Stalemate in Nuclear Arms Control* (New York: Knopf, 1984), pp. 304-5.

12. *Scowcroft Report*, p. 2.

13. Ibid., p. 6.

14. Ibid., p. 14.

15. CBO, *Modernizing U.S. Strategic Forces*, pp. 19-20, 23-24.

16. Ibid., p. 3.

17. Ibid., p. 46.

18. Richard F. Kaufman, "Causes of the Slowdown in Soviet Defense," *Soviet Economy*, 1, 1 (1985):9.

19. Ibid., p. 12.

20. *Defense Report 1984*, pp. 20-21.

21. *Defense Report 1985*, p. 20.

22. Paul Nitze, "Is SALT II a Fair Deal for the United States?" May 16, 1979. Reprinted in Charles Tyroler II, *Alerting America: The Papers of the Committee on the Present Danger* (Washington, DC: Pergamon-Brassey's International Defense Publishers, 1984), pp. 159-65.

23. Description of Perle's proposal from Talbott, *Deadly Gambits*, pp. 241-42.

24. Ibid., p. 235.

25. Ibid., p. 238.

26. Ibid., p. 240.

27. Ibid., p. 241-42.

28. *US Defense Policy*, p. 70.

29. Talbott, *Deadly Gambits*, pp. 241-42.

30. *Economic Report of the President*, February 1985 (Washington, DC: U.S. Government Printing Office, 1985), p. 322.

31. Office of the Assistant Secretary of Defense (Comptroller), *National Defense Budget Estimates for FY 1984*, March 1983, p. 62. Cited hereafter as *Defense Budget Estimates for FY 1984.*

32. Ibid., p. 83.

33. George Rathjens, "Reactions and Perspectives," in Ashton B. Carter and David N. Schwartz, eds., *Ballistic Missile Defense* (Washington, DC: Brookings Institution, 1984), p. 421.

34. Sidney D. Drell, Philip J. Farley, and David Holloway, "Preserving the ABM Treaty: A Critique of the Reagan Strategic Defense Initiative," *International Security* 9, 2 (Fall 1984):68.

35. Ibid., p. 71.

36. Ibid., pp. 74-75.

37. Ibid., pp. 75-76.

38. Ibid., pp. 77-78.

39. Ashton B. Carter, "BMD Applications: Performance and Limitations," in Carter and Schwartz, *Ballistic Missile Defense*, p. 120.

40. Colin S. Gray, "Deterrence, Arms Control, and the Defense Transition," *Orbis* 28, 2 (Summer 1984):229.

41. Ibid., pp. 231-32.

42. Ibid., p. 232.

43. McGeorge Bundy, George F. Kennan, Robert S. McNamara, and Gerard Smith, "The President's Choice: Star Wars or Arms Control," *Foreign Affairs* 63, 2 (Winter 1984/85):272.

44. Drell, Farley, and Holloway, "Preserving the ABM Treaty," pp. 53-63, 84-91.

CHAPTER 8

1. Adam M. Garfinkle, *The Politics of the Nuclear Freeze* (Philadelphia, PA: Foreign Policy Research Institute, 1984), pp. 91-92.

2. Randall Forsberg, "A Bilateral Nuclear-Weapon Freeze," *Scientific American* 247, 5 (November 1982):52-61. Page references from *Scientific American Offprints* (San Francisco, CA: W. H. Freeman).

3. Ibid., p. 2.

4. "The Challenge of Peace: God's Promise and Our Response," *Origins: NC Documentary Service* 13, 1 (May 19, 1983).

5. Ibid., p. 15.

6. Ibid., p. 17.

7. Albert Wohlstetter, "Bishops, Statesmen, and Other Strategists on the Bombing of Innocents," *Commentary*, June 1983, p. 17.

8. Ibid., pp. 18-19.

9. McGeorge Bundy, George F. Kennan, Robert S. McNamara, Gerard Smith, "Nuclear Weapons and the Atlantic Alliance," *Foreign Affairs* 60, 4 (Spring 1982):757.

10. Ibid., p. 761.

11. Ibid., p. 764.

12. Ibid., p. 765.

13. Karl Kaiser, Georg Leber, Alois Mertes, Franz-Josef Schulze, "Nuclear Weapons and the Preservation of Peace," *Foreign Affairs* (Fall 1982):1160.

14. Ibid., p. 1161.

15. Ibid., p. 1163.

16. Thomas C. Schelling, *The Strategy of Conflict* (Cambridge, MA: Harvard University Press, 1980), pp. 18-19, 38.

17. McGeorge Bundy, Robert S. McNamara, Cyrus Vance, E. R. Zumwalt, Jr. Letter to Senator Pete V. Domenici and Congressman James R. Jones, February 28, 1983, p. 3.

18. Ibid., p. 2.

19. McGeorge Bundy, Morton H. Halperin, William W. Kaufmann, George F. Kennan, Robert S. McNamara, Madalene O'Donnell, Leon V. Sigal, Gerard C. Smith, Richard H. Ullman, and Paul C. Warnke, "Back from the Brink," *The Atlantic Monthly* (August 1986):35.

20. Ibid., pp. 40-41.

21. U.S. Congress, Congressional Budget Office, *An Analysis of Administration Strategic Arms Reduction and Modernization Proposals*, March 1984, p. 6.

22. Alton Frye, "Strategic Build-down: A Context for Restraint," *Foreign Affairs* 2 (Winter 1983/84):294-95.

23. William W. Kaufmann, *The 1986 Defense Budget* (Washington, DC: Brookings Institution, 1985), p. 16.

24. Ibid., p. 17.
25. Thomas C. Schelling, "Confidence in Crisis," *International Security* 8, 4 (Spring 1984):55–66, esp. 58.
26. Ibid., p. 61.
27. Ibid., p. 60.
28. Ibid., p. 63.
29. Harold A. Feiveson and John Duffield, "Stopping the Sea-based Counterforce Threat," *International Security* 9, 1 (Summer 1984):187–202, esp. 189.
30. Ibid., p. 194.
31. Ibid., p. 191.
32. Ibid., pp. 194–96.
33. Ibid., p. 198.
34. The Harvard Nuclear Study Group, *Living with Nuclear Weapons* (New York: Bantam Books, 1983).
35. Ibid., p. 39.
36. Ibid., p. 138.
37. Ibid., p. 142.
38. Ibid., p. 140.
39. Ibid., p. 143.
40. Ibid., pp. 47–68.
41. Ibid., p. 168.
42. Ibid., p. 175.
43. Ibid., p. 170.

Acronyms

ABM	anti-ballistic missile
ACDA	Arms Control and Disarmament Agency
AEC	Atomic Energy Commission
AR	aggression risk
AWACS	airborne warning and control system
BMD	ballistic missile defense
CBO	Congressional Budget Office
CEA	Council of Economic Advisers
CEP	Circular Error Probable
COMINT	communications intelligence
ELINT	electronic intelligence
EMP	electromagnetic pulse
EMT	equivalent megatonnage
GLCM	ground-launched cruise missile
ICBM	intercontinental ballistic missile
IRBM	intermediate range ballistic missile
JCS	Joint Chiefs of Staff
JIS	Joint Intelligence Staff
JWPC	Joint War Plans Committee
LNO	limited nuclear option
MaRV	maneuvering reentry vehicle
MIRV	multiple independently targeted reentry vehicle
MPS	multiple protective shelter
NCA	National Command Authority
NMCS	National Military Command System
NSA	National Security Agency

NSC	National Security Council
PR	preemption risk
RV	reentry vehicle
SAC	Strategic Air Command
SAGE	semi-automatic ground environment
SALT	Strategic Arms Limitation Talks
SAM	surface-to-air missile
SCC	Special Coordinating Committee
SDI	Strategic Defense Initiative
SICBM	small intercontinental ballistic missile
SIOP	Single Integrated Operational Plan
SIPRI	Stockholm International Peace Research Institute
SLBM	sea-launched ballistic missile
SSBN	nuclear-powered ballistic-missile submarine
START	Strategic Arms Reduction Talks
TCP	Technical Capabilities Panel
TERCOM	terrain contour matching
TNW	tactical nuclear weapons
WSAG	Washington Special Action Group
WSEG	Weapons Systems Evaluation Group

Selected Bibliography

Ambrose, Stephen E. *Eisenhower*, vol. 1, *Soldier, General of the Army, President-elect, 1890–1952*. New York: Simon & Schuster, 1983.

————. *Eisenhower*, vol. 2, *The President*. New York: Simon & Schuster, 1984.

Blechman, Barry M., and Douglas M. Hart. "The Political Utility of Nuclear Weapons: The 1973 Middle East Crisis." *International Security* 7, 1 (Summer 1982):132–56.

Bracken, Paul. *The Command and Control of Nuclear Forces*. New Haven, CT: Yale University Press, 1983.

Brown, Harold. *Thinking About National Security, Defense, and Foreign Policy in a Dangerous World*. Boulder, CO: Westview Press, 1983.

Brown, Seyom. *The Faces of Power: Constancy and Change in United States Foreign Policy from Truman to Johnson*. New York: Columbia University Press, 1968.

Brzezinski, Zbigniew. *Game Plan: A Geostrategic Framework for the Conduct of the U.S.-Soviet Contest*. Boston: Atlantic Monthly Press, 1986.

————. *Power and Principle: Memoirs of the National Security Adviser, 1977–1981*. New York: Farrar, Straus, Giroux, 1983.

Bundy, McGeorge, George F. Kennan, Robert S. McNamara, and Gerard Smith. "Nuclear Weapons and the Atlantic Alliance." *Foreign Affairs* 60, 4 (Spring 1982).

Carter, Ashton, B., and David N. Schwartz, eds. *Ballistic Missile Defense*. Washington, DC: Brookings Institution, 1984.

"The Challenge of Peace: God's Promise and Our Response." *Origins: NC Documentary Service* 13, 1 (May 19, 1983) (The Bishops' Letter).

Cochran, Thomas B., William M. Arkin, and Milton M. Hoenig. *Nuclear Weapons Handbook*, vol. 1, *U.S. Nuclear Forces and Capabilities*. Cambridge, MA: Ballinger, 1984.

Collins, John M. *U.S.-Soviet Military Balance: Concepts and Capabilities, 1960–1980*. New York: McGraw-Hill, 1980.

Donovan, Robert J. *Conflict and Crisis: The Presidency of Harry S. Truman, 1945-48.* New York: W. W. Norton, 1977.

Drell, Sidney D., Philip J. Farley, and David Holloway. "Preserving the ABM Treaty: A Critique of the Reagan Strategic Defense Initiative." *International Security* 9, 2 (Fall 1984).

Edmonds, Robin. *Soviet Foreign Policy: The Brezhnev Years.* Oxford: Oxford University Press, 1983.

Edwards, John. *Superweapon: The Making of MX.* New York: W. W. Norton, 1982.

Enthoven, Alain C., and K. Wayne Smith. *How Much Is Enough? Shaping the Defense Program, 1961-69.* New York: Harper & Row, 1971.

Evangelista, Matthew A. "Stalin's Postwar Army Reappraised." *International Security* 7, 3 (Winter 1982/83):110-38.

Feiveson, Harold A., and John Duffield. "Stopping the Sea-based Counterforce Threat." *International Security* 9, 1 (Summer 1984):187-202.

Forsberg, Randall. "A Bilateral Nuclear-Weapon Freeze." *Scientific American* 247, 5 (November 1982):52-61.

Freedman, Lawrence. *The Evolution of Nuclear Strategy.* New York: St. Martin's Press, 1983.

———. *US Intelligence and the Soviet Strategic Threat.* London: Macmillan, 1977.

Gaddis, John Lewis. *The United States and the Origins of the Cold War, 1941-1947.* New York: Columbia University Press, 1972.

Garthoff, Raymond L. *Détente and Confrontation: American-Soviet Relations from Nixon to Reagan.* Washington, DC: Brookings Institution, 1985.

Gray, Colin S. "Deterrence, Arms Control, and the Defense Transition." *Orbis* 28, 2 (Summer 1984).

Grosser, Alfred. *The Western Alliance: European-American Relations Since 1945.* New York: Random House, Vintage ed., 1982.

Halperin, Morton H. *National Security Policy-Making: Analyses, Cases, and Proposals.* Lexington, MA: Lexington Books, 1975.

Harvard Nuclear Study Group. *Living with Nuclear Weapons.* New York: Bantam Books, 1983.

Herken, Gregg. *Counsels of War.* New York: Knopf, 1985.

Holland, Lauren H., and Robert A. Hoover. *The MX Decision: A New Direction in US Weapons Procurement Policy?* Boulder, CO: Westview Press, 1985.

Holloway, David. *The Soviet Union and the Arms Race.* New Haven, CT: Yale University Press, 1983.

Holzman, Franklyn D. "Is There a Soviet-U.S. Military Spending Gap?" *Challenge* 23, 4 (September/October 1980):3-9.

Huntington, Samuel P. *The Common Defense: Strategic Programs in National Politics.* New York: Columbia University Press, 1961.

Iklé, Fred Charles. "Can Nuclear Deterrence Last Out the Century?" *Foreign Affairs* 51, 2 (January 1973):267-85.

Kaiser, Karl, Georg Leber, Alois Mertes, and Franz-Josef Schulze. "Nuclear Weapons and the Preservation of Peace." *Foreign Affairs* (Fall 1982).

Kaplan, Fred. *The Wizards of Armageddon: Strategists of the Nuclear Age.* New York: Simon & Schuster, 1983.

Kaufman, Richard F. "Causes of the Slowdown in Soviet Defense." *Soviet Economy* 1, 1 (1985).

Kaufmann, William W. *The McNamara Strategy.* New York: Harper & Row, 1964.

_____ . *The 1986 Defense Budget.* Washington, DC: Brookings Institution, 1985.

_____ . "The Requirements of Deterrence." In William W. Kaufmann, ed. *Military Policy and National Security.* Princeton, NJ: Princeton University Press, 1956.

Kennan, George F. *Memoirs: 1925-1950.* Boston: Little, Brown, 1967.

_____ . *Memoirs: 1950-1963.* Boston: Little, Brown, 1972.

Kissinger, Henry A. *Nuclear Weapons and Foreign Policy.* New York: Harper and Brothers, 1957.

_____ , ed. *Problems of National Strategy.* New York: Praeger, 1965.

_____ . *White House Years.* Boston: Little, Brown, 1979.

_____ . *Years of Upheaval.* Boston: Little, Brown, 1982.

LaFeber, Walter. *America, Russia, and the Cold War, 1945-75,* 3d ed. New York: Wiley, 1976.

Laqueur, Walter. *Europe Since Hitler: The Rebirth of Europe,* rev. ed. New York: Penguin, 1983.

Lawrence, Richard D., and Jeffrey Record. *United States Force Structure in NATO: An Alternative.* Washington, DC: Brookings Institution, 1974.

McNamara, Robert S. *The Essence of Security: Reflections in Office.* New York: Harper & Row, 1968.

Nacht, Michael. *The Age of Vulnerability: Threats to the Nuclear Stalemate.* Washington, DC: The Brookings Institution, 1985.

Newhouse, John. *Cold Dawn: The Story of Salt.* New York: Holt, Rinehart and Winston, 1973.

Nitze, Paul H. "Assuring Strategic Stability in an Era of Détente." *Foreign Affairs* (January 1976). Reprinted in Wolfram F. Hanrieder, ed. *Arms Control and Security: Current Issues,* 2d ed. Boulder, CO: Westview Press, 1981, pp. 39-65.

Nixon, Richard. *The Real War.* New York: Warner, 1981.

Nogee, Joseph L., and Robert H. Donaldson. *Soviet Foreign Policy Since World War II.* New York: Pergamon, 1981.

Pranger, Robert J., and Roger P. Labrie, eds. *Nuclear Strategy and National Security: Points of View.* Washington, DC: American Enterprise Institute for Public Policy Research, 1977.

Rosenberg, David A. "The Origins of Overkill: Nuclear Weapons and American Strategy, 1945-1960." *International Security* 7, 4 (Spring 1983):3-71.

Rowen, Henry S. "The Evolution of Strategic Nuclear Doctrine." In Lawrence

Martin, ed. *Strategic Thought in the Nuclear Age.* Baltimore: Johns Hopkins University Press, 1979.

Schelling, Thomas C. *Arms and Influence.* New Haven, CT: Yale University Press, 1966.

———. "Confidence in Crisis." *International Security* 8, 4 (Spring 1984):55-66.

———. *The Strategy of Conflict.* Cambridge, MA: Harvard University Press, 1981.

Schilling, Warner R., Paul Y. Hammond, and Glenn H. Snyder. *Strategy, Politics, and Defense Budgets.* New York: Columbia University Press, 1968.

Schmidt, Helmut. *Defense or Retaliation: A German Contribution to the Consideration of NATO's Strategic Problem.* Edinburgh: Oliver and Boyd, 1962.

Schwartz, David N. *NATO's Nuclear Dilemmas.* Washington, DC: Brookings Institution, 1983.

Shulman, Marshall D. "Relations with the Soviet Union." In Kermit Gordon, ed. *Agenda for the Nation: Papers on Domestic and Foreign Policy Issues.* Washington, DC: Brookings Institution, 1968, pp. 373-406.

Sigal, Leon V. *Nuclear Forces in Europe: Enduring Dilemmas, Present Prospects.* Washington, DC: Brookings Institution, 1984.

Smith, Gerard. *Doubletalk: The Story of the First Strategic Arms Limitation Talks.* Garden City, NY: Doubleday, 1980.

Sorensen, Theodore C. *Kennedy.* New York: Harper & Row, Bantam ed., 1965.

Steinbrunner, John D., and Thomas M. Garwin. "Strategic Vulnerability: The Balance between Prudence and Paranoia." *International Security* 1, 1 (Summer 1976):138-70.

Talbott, Strobe. *Endgame: The Inside Story of SALT II.* New York: Harper Torchbooks, 1980.

———. *Deadly Gambits: The Reagan Administration and the Stalemate in Nuclear Arms Control.* New York: Knopf, 1984.

Tammen, Ronald L. *MIRV and the Arms Race: An Interpretation of Defense Strategy.* New York: Praeger, 1973.

Taylor, Maxwell D. *The Uncertain Trumpet.* New York: Harper & Row, 1960.

Tyroler, Charles II, ed. *Alerting America: The Papers of the Committee on the Present Danger.* New York: Pergamon-Brassey's, 1984.

U.S. Congress, Congressional Budget Office. *An Analysis of Administration Strategic Arms Reduction and Modernization Proposals.* March 1984.

———. *Modernizing U.S. Strategic Offensive Forces: The Administration's Program and Alternatives.* May 1983.

Ulam, Adam B. *The Rivals: America and Russia Since World War II.* New York: Penguin, 1971.

Van Cleave, William R., and Roger R. Barnett. "Strategic Adaptability." *Orbis* 18, 3 (Fall 1974):655-76.

Wohlstetter, Albert. "Bishops, Statesmen, and Other Strategists on the Bombing of Innocents." *Commentary* (June 1983).

_____ . "The Delicate Balance of Terror." *Foreign Affairs* 37 (January 1959): 209-34.

_____ . "Is There a Strategic Arms Race?" *Foreign Policy* no. 15 (Summer 1974):3-20.

_____ . "Rivals But No 'Race'." *Foreign Policy* no. 16 (Fall 1974):48-81.

Wolfe, Thomas W. *Soviet Power and Europe 1945-1970.* Baltimore, MD: Johns Hopkins University Press, 1970.

"X." "Sources of Soviet Conduct." *Foreign Affairs* (July 1947):566-82.

Index

About the Author

A Canadian by birth, David Schwartzman lives in New York City and is professor of economics in the Graduate Faculty of the New School for Social Research, where he has been chairman of the Department of Economics. He previously taught at McGill, Columbia, and New York universities. Between his early teaching stints, Schwartzman applied economics at the Dominion Bureau of Statistics in Canada. For several years Schwartzman was a member of the staff of the National Bureau of Economic Research. He has acted as a consultant to the Council on Wage and Price Stability, the Bureau of the Census, the Department of Justice, the Royal Commission on Farm Machinery of Canada, and in several antitrust cases.

Other books by the author are: *Decline of Service in Retail Trade*, *Oligopoly in the Farm Machinery Industry*, and *Innovation in the Pharmaceutical Industry*.